VW GTI, Golf, and Jetta, Mk III & IV
Find it. Fix it. Trick it.

D1036428

VW GTI, Golf, and Jetta, Mk III & IV
Find it. Fix it. Trick it.

Kevin Clemens

MOTORBOOKS

First published in 2006 by Motorbooks, an imprint of MBI Publishing Company, Galtier Plaza, Suite 200, 380 Jackson Street, St. Paul, MN 55101-3885 USA

The information in this book is true and complete to the best of our knowledge. All recommendations are made without any guarantee on the part of the author or Publisher, who also disclaim any liability incurred in connection with the use of this data or specific details.

We recognize, further, that some words, model names, and designations mentioned herein are the property of the trademark holder. We use them for identification purposes only. This is not an official publication.

MBI Publishing Company titles are also available at discounts in bulk quantity for industrial or sales-promotional use. For details write to Special Sales Manager at MBI Publishing Company, Galtier Plaza, Suite 200, 380 Jackson Street, St. Paul, MN 55101-3885 USA

Library of Congress Cataloging-in-Publication Data

Clemens, Kevin, 1957-
    VW GTI, Golf, and Jetta, Mk III & IV: Find it. Fix it. Trick it. / Kevin Clemens.
        p. cm.
    Includes index.
    ISBN-13: 978-0-7603-2595-7 (softbound)
    ISBN-10: 0-7603-2595-2 (softbound)
    1. GTI automobile—Maintenance and repair—Handbooks, manuals, etc. 2. Golf automobile—Maintenance and repair—Handbooks, manuals, etc. 3. Jetta automobile—Maintenance and repair—Handbooks, manuals, etc. I. Title.
    TL215.V6C545 2006
    629.28'72--dc22
                            2006016321

On the cover: *Fahrvergnügen* is German for "driving pleasure," which is exactly what you get with a VW. *Les Bidrawn*

On the cover inset: Nobody will ever mistake this engine for stock. *Les Bidrawn*

On the title pages: The nimble Golf quickly earned the reputation as a giant killer at the racetrack. *Volkswagen of America (VWOA)*

On the back cover: A third or fourth generation Golf or Jetta is the perfect canvas for your automotive expression. *Robert Hallstrom*

About the author
Kevin Clemens has been a part of the automotive industry for more than 25 years. Trained as an engineer, he has worked as a research scientist, designer of racing and sports car tires, and public relations counselor. He has been an editor and contributor for some of the industry's most influential automotive enthusiast magazines, such as *Automobile Magazine*, and is presently editor-at-large for *European Car* magazine. Clemens writes extensively about everything automotive, from racing vintage sports cars to the most sophisticated present-day technologies.

Editor: James Michels
Designer: Kou Lor

Printed in China

CONTENTS

PREFACE

Volkswagen's fortunes in the United States have had their ups and downs, but through it all Volkswagen enthusiasts have remained faithful to their beloved vehicles. One reason for this fanatic loyalty is the charisma the cars have as they come from the factory. Another is the room the Volkswagen engineers gave owners for modification and improvement to personalize their vehicles. Volkswagens are tough and robust. In many ways they are overengineered, but this has always proven to be a good thing to enthusiastic owners who wanted to take their cars onto a racetrack or hammer along a rally stage. The first and second generations of the Golf and Jetta were particularly adept at such activities, and even today, more than 15 years after the last ones were built, they can still be found leading the competition. Alas, until recently, the third and fourth generations of Golfs and Jettas have been ignored by those whose quest for performance turned toward Volkswagens. Fortunately, as these later cars have grown older, more and more of them have fallen into enthusiasts' hands, and they are finally beginning to receive the same loving attention as their illustrious predecessors. Volkswagen has helped this along with sensational powerplants like the narrow-angle VR6 and the turbocharged and intercooled 1.8T, and more recently with special performance models like the GTI 337 and the all-wheel drive R32. The purpose of this book is to push that enthusiasm further along—to promote the purchase, maintenance, and performance modification of Volkswagen's third and fourth generations of Golfs and Jettas. These are great cars that are just now being discovered by those who want to drive something different and distinctive. Their time has come.

Clewell

ACKNOWLEDGMENTS

In the process of creating this book, a great deal of assistance from a variety of people was necessary. All of them are fans of Volkswagens, and many of them have owned and loved the very cars that are written about here. Research assistance and encouragement was received from Volkswagen of America and, in Germany, from Volkswagen AG. Steve Keyes from VWOA was instrumental in setting up a visit to Volkswagen archives in Auburn Hills, and in Wolfsburg, Germany, archivist Dr. Ulrike Gutzmann provided her time and Volkswagen's resources in obtaining many of the photographs found in this book. Many of the maintenance and product photographs were taken at Schmelz Countryside Volkswagen in St. Paul, Minnesota, and the generous time and assistance of Jennifer Schmelz Wilke and Chris Wilke at this longtime Volkswagen dealership is gratefully acknowledged. Many of the modifications photographed for this book took place at SCI Performance in Minneapolis, Minnesota, under the watchful eye and practiced hand of owner Chad Erickson; his assistance throughout the project was vital. My colleagues at *European Car* magazine, Les Bidrawn and Robert Hallstrom, provided excellent photography for several sections of the book, as did local Twin Cities photographer and Volkswagen fanatic Kristopher Clewell. Lastly, without the enthusiastic support of Zack Miller and Jim Michels at Motorbooks, this book would have never become a reality.

—Kevin Clemens,
Lake Elmo, Minnesota

CHAPTER 1 | THE VOLKSWAGEN STORY

It seems that everyone has a Volkswagen story. Children of the 1950s, whose parents were among the first in the United States to buy a foreign car, remember the Beetle with its quirky engine in its trunk and its strangely rounded shape. They tell tales of amazing fuel economy and the complete lack of any heat in winter, despite the car's astonishing traction on snow and ice.

Volkswagen built more than 21 million Beetles, so everybody has a Volkswagen story to tell. *Volkswagen AG*

When those children grew up in the 1960s, the same Beetles became the symbol of the counterculture flower-power revolution and nearly ubiquitous on college campuses. The beloved Bug taught millions the meaning and importance of mobility.

When Volkswagen replaced the venerable rear-engined and air-cooled Beetle in the 1970s, the at-first skeptical VW fans eventually came to embrace the front-wheel-drive, water-cooled Volkswagen Golf/Rabbit as a new icon of practical transportation. Car enthusiasts, college students, and people who were simply cheap had a new kind of Volkswagen to love. The Golf/Rabbit and its siblings, the GTI, Cabriolet, and Jetta have turned out to be no less charismatic than the original Beetle, and new generations of VW owners have their own stories to tell of Volkswagen adventure.

Since the launch of that first generation of Golf and Rabbit, subsequent versions of the cars have become increasingly refined and sophisticated. This is a common form of automotive evolution, and it can be good or it can be bad. Too much refinement can rob a car of its soul, and too much sophistication can bankrupt its owner. Fortunately, the third and fourth generation of Golfs, Cabriolets, Jettas, and GTIs built between 1993 and 2004, have grown up to become real cars, perfectly attuned to driving in the modern world. And they remain affordable while still retaining that mischievous Volkswagen glint in their headlights.

AN AIR-COOLED WONDER

The story of the original Volkswagen Beetle has been told so often that it has become nearly mythical. Suffice it to say that in the 1930s Dr. Ferdinand Porsche designed a simple yet rugged "people's car." Adolf Hitler liked what he saw and ordered the car into production. Only a few cars were built before the factory began making war supplies, becoming a frequent target for Allied bombing raids.

After the end of the war, the Volkswagen was ridiculed for its crude design, but rose

The Golf has proven to be just as charismatic and fun loving as the original Beetle. *Volkswagen AG*

Ferdinand Porsche was the originator of the "Volkswagen" concept in the early 1930s. *Volkswagen AG*

WATER-COOLED GENESIS

Although efforts began in the early 1960s to develop a replacement for the Beetle, little work was done to design a conventional water-cooled engine. Ferdinand Porsche's original horizontally opposed flat four-cylinder air-cooled engine was made from lightweight aluminum and magnesium alloys. Most conventional water-cooled inline four-cylinder designs used cast-iron cylinder blocks and heads. Volkswagen's engineers and management just couldn't bring themselves to create what they considered a backward design.

By the end of the 1960s, the VW Beetle could no longer keep up with emissions and safety regulations, and it needed to be replaced. *Volkswagen AG*

from the ashes of its bombed-out factory to become the air-cooled Beetle, which would remain in production over seven decades with more than 21 million cars produced. While the original Beetle was already outdated when it went into production, it was a sound design that was manufactured from high-quality materials by a dedicated workforce.

Volkswagen was careful to make modifications and improvements only as needed throughout the Beetle's life, while keeping a close eye on costs. The result was that the lowly Beetle was profitable, not only for the Volkswagen Company, but also for Germany and its workers as they rebuilt their postwar economy. However, this cautious nature and careful evolution nearly killed the company when it came time to replace the aging Beetle in the early 1970s.

By the end of the 1960s, however, impending exhaust emissions legislation would eventually doom the air-cooled Volkswagen engine. It just wasn't possible to maintain low emission levels in an engine as prone to temperature fluctuations as one cooled by air. At the same time, rear-engine cars, whose handling characteristics at the limits were considered by the safety community to be unstable, were also under attack. As the summer of love came to an end, Volkswagen found itself in desperate need of a new car design that would meet the emissions, fuel economy, and safety challenges automakers would soon face.

Although there were a few water-cooled projects on

THE PEOPLE'S CAR

The name "Volkswagen" literally means "people's car," but when it was introduced in 1938, Adolf Hitler officially christened the car the KdF-Wagen. "KdF" came from the agency *Kraft durch Freude*, or "Strength through Joy," set up by the Nazis to promote worker morale. Fortunately it was Ferdinand Porsche's "Volkswagen" name that stuck, becoming a worldwide brand after the war.

The original Volkswagen Type 1 was homely, but would go on to capture the hearts of succeeding generations. *Volkswagen AG*

Volkswagen slapped a VW badge onto the water-cooled front-wheel drive NSU K70, but the car wasn't a success. *Volkswagen AG*

Volkswagen's research and development back burner, the company had recently purchased Audi (1966) and NSU (1969). Each of these companies had a water-cooled front-wheel-drive sedan that was ready to go into production. In the end, Audi was allowed to keep its 100LS model as its own, while NSU's new front-driver became the Volkswagen K70.

Compared with the Beetle, the K70 was a conventional four-door car with a front-mounted inline water-cooled four-cylinder engine. Its front-wheel drive was state of the art for the time. Despite building a new factory in Salzgitter, Germany, to produce the K70, its sales were dismal, and plans to bring the car to the U.S. market were canceled. However, the project did give Volkswagen engineers an opportunity to become familiar with front-wheel drive and water-cooled inline engines.

Meanwhile, Audi had been successful with its 100LS model, and in 1972 it introduced the Audi Fox (Audi 80 in Europe), styled by Giorgetto Giugiaro of Italy. This was a thoroughly modern vehicle with crisp, angular styling and an inline water-cooled four-cylinder engine that offered front-wheel drive. Volkswagen made some minor styling changes to the Audi and offered it as the Volkswagen Dasher (Passat in Europe) in 1973. The Dasher was a good car and for the first time brought buyers into Volkswagen's showrooms to buy something other than a Beetle. It would soon be joined by another Giugiaro-designed Volkswagen, one that would forever change the company.

ENTER THE GOLF

At the end of 1969, Giorgetto Giugiaro had been hired by Volkswagen to develop a replacement for the Beetle. By April of 1970, his concept had been submitted to and approved by Volkswagen's board. The new car would use Audi's water-cooled inline-four-cylinder engine, featuring a thin-wall cast-iron block and an aluminum-alloy cylinder head.

Giorgetto Giugiaro was hired to develop a new Volkswagen to replace the Beetle. This was his prototype from 1970 that would become the Golf. *Volkswagen AG*

The Volkswagen Golf debuted in 1974 in Europe and as the Rabbit in the United States in 1975. *Volkswagen AG*

Giugiaro's design for the new car was 8 inches shorter than the Beetle and a bit wider, yet because the engine was placed transverse in an all-new front-wheel drive chassis, it rode on a longer wheelbase. There was a lot more room inside the new car than there was inside an old Beetle. Giugiaro designed two- and four-door versions, both with a rear hatchback.

Front suspension used MacPherson struts, while the rear had a torsional beam axle with trailing arms and coil springs. The suspension was light and compact and capable of providing a good ride over rough roads. It was also full of potential for better handling in the future.

Volkswagen decided to call this new car the Golf in Europe when it was launched in 1974. The exact origin of the name has been lost; most Volkswagen executives today claim that the car was named for the German spelling of the Gulf Stream. Inexplicably, in the United States, the car carried the name Rabbit when it debuted in 1975.

EVOLUTION OF THE VOLKSWAGEN GOLF

Replacement for the Beetle started by Giugiaro

1970	Giugiaro concept for the Golf approved by management	1991	Third generation of Golf/Vento (Jetta) launched in Europe
1974	Golf launched in Europe	1993	Third generation of the Golf and Jetta launched in United States
1975	Rabbit launched in United States		
1976	GTI launched in Europe	1993	VR6 engine in Jetta GLX
1976	Golf diesel engine launched in Europe	1995	VR6 engine in Golf
1977	Rabbit diesel engine launched in the United States	1995	Golf III Cabriolet launched
1977	Gasoline fuel injection for the Rabbit	1997	1.9 TDI diesel engine in Golf/Jetta
1978	Rabbit produced in Westmoreland, Pennsylvania	1998	Fourth generation of the Golf launched in Europe
1979	Rabbit Cabriolet launched	1998	Fourth generation of Bora (Jetta) launched in Europe
1980	Rabbit Pickup launched in U.S. market		
1980	Jetta launched in United States	1999	Fourth generation of Golf/Jetta launched in United States
1983	Rabbit GTI launched in United States		
1983	Second generation of Golf launched in Europe	2001	1.8T engine in Golf/Jetta
1983	Second generation of Jetta launched in Europe	2001	Jetta Wagon launched in United States
1985	Second generation of the Golf launched in United States	2004	R32 Golf launched in United States
		2005	Fifth generation of the Golf launched in Europe
1986	Second generation of Jetta launched in United States	2005	Fifth generation of the Jetta launched in United States
1987	16-valve four-cylinder version of the Golf	2006	Fifth generation of Golf launched in United States
1987	Westmoreland, Pennsylvania, plant closes		

MAKING HISTORY

When the Golf/Rabbit was introduced in the mid-1970s, Volkswagen was desperate for a Beetle replacement. It was fortunate that the company finally had a success in its new water-cooled front-wheel drive car, both in sales and in what it represented in the automotive industry. Although others, like Austin with the Mini and Fiat with the 128, had paved the way with the concept, it was Giugiaro's VW design that caught on with the public.

So successful was the new VW that after a short time this size and type of automobile became known in Europe as the "Golf class." The Golf brought a whole new group of buyers into Volkswagen's showrooms. Its light weight and nimble handling made the cars a natural for enthusiasts, and it wasn't long before some of the company's backroom boys came up with a performance version. Introduced in Europe in 1976 and identified by three simple letters, the GTI blew apart the traditional concept of a sports car. Although the United States would have to wait until 1983 before experiencing the GTI, the car's reputation for fun and performance far preceded it.

The Jetta arrived in 1980 as a two- or four-door sedan. After a slow start, the Jetta would eventually outsell the Golf in the U.S. market. *Volkswagen AG*

During the 1970s and early 1980s, Volkswagen expanded the concept of the Golf. It produced a diesel engine for the car in 1977 and a cabriolet, with the help of coachbuilder Karmann, in 1979. A U.S. plant was opened in Westmoreland, Pennsylvania, in 1978, and an American-designed pickup truck was added to the mix in 1980.

Perhaps the most significant variant of the Golf/Rabbit came in 1980 with the introduction of the Jetta. This was a two-door or four-door version of the Rabbit, but with a full trunk replacing the hatchback. The two-box Rabbit became a three-box sedan, and a new niche of customers was found.

At first Jetta sales were slow, but ultimately the more up-market Jetta would grow to surpass the Golf in sales in many markets. When it came time to replace the original Golf/Rabbit in 1985, a new Jetta was an important part of the program. At this same time, Volkswagen took the opportunity to drop the U.S. market Rabbit name. From then on, the hatchbacks were to be known worldwide as Golfs.

Three little letters, G, T, and I, started a revolution in the performance car market. Europe got the GTI in 1976; the United States had to wait until 1983. *Volkswagen AG*

The Volkswagen Cabriolet was based upon the Golf/Rabbit platform and was built by Karmann in Germany. *Volkswagen AG*

The second generation of the Golf arrived in the United States in 1985. It was a bigger and softer car than the original. *Volkswagen AG*

HARD TIMES

Despite at one time nearly owning the hot-hatchback and "Golf class" market segments with the GTI and Golf, Volkswagen's fortunes took a downturn in the late 1980s. A worldwide recession, high costs, competition from Japanese car companies, and a long product cycle meant that many buyers were looking elsewhere for their small car needs. As sales remained sluggish in 1987, Volkswagen was forced to close its plant in Westmoreland, Pennsylvania.

The Golf and its Jetta sibling continued to improve, adding a 16-valve 134-horse-power engine for example, but sales continued to slide. In 1988 Volkswagen sold 169,000 cars in the United States. By 1990, this number had dropped to 136,000, and there was serious talk within Volkswagen's Board of Directors of leaving the U.S. market altogether. Something was needed to pull the company out of the doldrums, and all eyes turned to the upcoming launch of the third-generation Golf.

Even the addition of a 16-valve engine to the GTI in 1987 couldn't slow the drop in sales. *Volkswagen AG*

SAVING THE COMPANY

The launch of the third generation of Volkswagen's Golf and Jetta models was a disaster. To help keep prices in line with those of the Asian manufacturers, Volkswagen had decided to produce its cars in its Puebla, Mexico, plant. This plant had continued to produce versions of the original air-cooled Beetle for the Mexican market long after it had ended production in other parts of the world.

But assembling the decades-old Beetle was a vastly different proposition from producing modern automobiles for Volkswagen's increasingly upscale buyers, who expected European levels of engineering and quality. The cars built at first were so bad that the Volkswagen's U.S. managers took a brave stand and refused to accept them. Sales in 1992 had dropped to a dismal 49,553, as VW dealers had almost nothing to sell and potential buyers found other places to spend their money on a new car.

The new generation Golf III and Jetta III didn't exactly pull people into the showrooms either. They were bigger and heavier than their predecessors and were powered by a competent but somewhat mundane 115-horsepower 2.0-liter four-cylinder engine. The cars were certainly more refined than any previous Golfs and Jettas, but some of the edge that had made a car like the 16-valve GTI so fun to drive was missing.

A six-cylinder version of the Jetta, the GLX VR6 was launched in 1993 to considerable acclaim, but the uptake of the four-door performance car was slow. Beset with quality problems from the Mexico plant, better versions of the Golf and Jetta had to wait until more mainstream cars were properly built. Slowly, though, Volkswagen clawed its way back up the sales chart, and in 1997 the company's U.S. sales were up to 136,093.

FINALLY, SOME VARIETY

Between its launch in 1993 and its replacement in 1999,

The third generation of the Golf got off to a rocky start in 1993, when U.S. cars built in Mexico suffered from poor build quality. *Volkswagen AG*

ABOVE: The Jetta III was once again larger than the generation that preceded it. *Volkswagen AG*

RIGHT: Updating the Volkswagen Cabriolet to the third generation platform didn't occur until 1995. *Volkswagen AG*

the Golf III and Jetta III both ended up with a number of model variations, some of which were, and still are, quite appealing to the driving enthusiast. In Europe, the Jetta had a new name and was called the Vento. The base model Golf GL hatchback was available in two and four doors, while the base Jetta GL was a four-door sedan. Both of these cars were equipped with the 2.0-liter four-cylinder engine and could be ordered with automatic transmissions.

A GTI version of the Golf was available; it benefited from a slightly upgraded suspension and interior, but was powered by the same 115-horsepower engine as the base model. This left VW enthusiasts aghast at what had become of their beloved GTI. On the other hand, the Jetta GLX VR6 model, introduced in 1993, made good use of the VW Corrado sports car's narrow-angle six-cylinder engine, which produced a strong 172 horsepower. The GLX quickly developed a following and although didn't sell in large numbers was at least able to bring some excitement to the lineup. The Golf didn't receive the VR6 engine until 1995, but when it did, in the GTI, everyone welcomed the addition.

A year later, in 1996, both the Golf and Jetta were available with an all-new turbocharged direct-injection (TDI) 1.9-liter diesel engine. Following the direction of

many European manufacturers, Volkswagen introduced a new generation of diesel engines that gave exceptionally good fuel economy; they also were relatively quick, quiet, and free from the clouds of smoke most previous diesel engines had inflicted on their owners.

Meanwhile, Volkswagen took its time replacing the Cabriolet, continuing with the second generation version until 1995, when the third generation model, still built by Karmann, finally appeared.

Today, the third generation Volkswagen Golf and Jetta models, built from 1993 to 1999, are often considered little more than used cars. They represent a real bargain to the Volkswagen enthusiast who wants to make some straightforward modifications and have something special.

THE FOURTH GENERATION

With the company finally back on a firm footing, and the newly launched Volkswagen New Beetle (based upon the upcoming Golf's platform), the launch of the fourth generation of the Golf and Jetta in 1999 was much less traumatic for the company than the third generation had been.

The cars had grown larger again and picked up some more refinement. The Jetta had another new name in Europe and was now called the Bora. A Jetta Wagon joined the line-up in 2001, adding versatility, and the Cabriolet received a facelift for the 2002 model year, although it was still based upon the third generation's platform.

LEFT: The fourth generation of the Golf arrived in 1999 and was yet again larger and more refined than previous generations. *Volkswagen AG*

BELOW: Volkswagen added a station wagon to the Jetta line in 2001. *Volkswagen AG*

The Volkswagen R32 appeared in 2004 as the ultimate fourth-generation Golf. It has a 3.2-liter VR6 engine and all-wheel drive. *VWOA*

In Europe, the fourth generation of Golf was available with everything from a 1.4-liter four-cylinder up to a 2.3-liter VR5 five-cylinder engine. In the United States, the 2.0-liter base engine was revised for its role in the GL models, while the VR6 engine remained in several performance models. Revisions to the TDI diesel engine also resulted in better performance and emissions, although diesel engines were no longer welcome in pollution-conscious California.

One of Volkswagen's most significant new engines was launched in 2000. The 1.8T engine was a turbocharged four-cylinder that not only worked well in stock form, it also promised even more performance from some fairly modest upgrades. This engine rapidly became the darling of the European tuner crowd, who set about getting more and more performance from the 1.8-liter engine.

Since the introduction of the Rabbit, small performance cars have developed a significant following. Among the choices from Europe, Volkswagen Golfs and Jettas, especially those with the highly tunable 1.8T engine, have become the hot cars to own. In 2004, Volkswagen produced its own in-house hot rod, the all-wheel drive 3.2-liter VR6 version of the Golf, called the R32.

Although Volkswagen's fourth generation Golfs and Jettas aren't exactly in the "cheap car" range yet, the wide variety of performance and tuning parts and knowledge available make any of them an excellent "blank canvas" for someone who wants to not only own a VW, but make a VW their own.

Although the Rabbit gave hatchbacks mainstream acceptabiltiy in the U.S., the Jetta, with its more conventional sedan sytling, eventually became more popular. Both were nimble and quick. *VWOA*

CHAPTER 2

THE VOLKSWAGEN EXPERIENCE

The original air-cooled Volkswagen Beetle had proved to be the perfect starting point for a variety of different automotive adventures. Throughout the 1960s Beetles were raced on road courses, on drag strips, and in the deserts. The simple yet rugged Beetle engine was capable of producing significant horsepower if carefully modified, and a whole tuning industry grew up to get more from the humble Beetle.

But Volkswagen owners were interested in more than just performance. They customized and sculpted their cars into shapes never envisioned by Ferdinand Porsche when he penned the original rounded form in the 1930s. Bug-ins were organized in every part of the country, as owners wanted to get together and share their Beetle experiences. In the early 1970s, with the Beetle's replacement, the Golf, on the drawing boards, one had to wonder if it could ever reach the same cult status.

A NEW KIND OF VOLKSWAGEN

It didn't take long after the launch of the Rabbit/Golf before Volkswagen enthusiasts began to discover the potential of the new car. Europeans were the first to benefit from increased performance with the introduction of the GTI in 1976, but Americans weren't too far behind, getting the GTI in 1983.

The water-cooled inline four-cylinder engine in the Golf and Rabbit was light but robust and capable of significantly more performance than it developed in stock trim. It didn't suffer from as many limitations as the air-cooled Beetle engine, and it was a conventional design that could be easily worked on by any local machine shop.

The nimble Golf quickly earned the racetrack reputation as a giant killer. *VWOA*

But the front-wheel drive chassis of the Golf/Rabbit was its real strength. Nimble and predictable, it soon found its way onto the racetrack, where its cars quickly earned a reputation as giant killers in much the same way the Mini Cooper had during the 1960s. A variety of shock absorber, spring, and anti-roll bar packages were soon made available from European and American tuners. The "stress bar," a bolt-in reinforcement that helps prevent chassis flex under hard cornering was developed for the somewhat flexible first generation Golf; it has since become a staple of the high-performance tuning industry.

Since its engine, drivetrain, and chassis could be modified to produce a high-performance machine that would embarrass much higher-priced machinery, the Golf had reinvented the idea of the affordable sports car. By the time the second generation of Golf was introduced in 1985, the Volkswagen name was firmly established in the minds of automotive enthusiasts who were looking for cheap thrills.

It didn't take long for the performance of the original Golf to be appreciated. *Volkswagen AG*

"When the Volkswagen GTI first appeared in late 1982, it was not what it seemed. Its price was within the grasp of many young people of the day, and it became a favorite of boys and girls alike, the latter loving its ability to blow away annoying dorks in muscle cars."

—Car and Driver, *June 2000*

"The GTI is, in essence, the people's muscle car, a larger more powerful engine in an everyday body, Clark Kent's inner Superman."

—European Car, *July 2003*

Although the third generation's chassis was stiffer, its suspension was softer—to the detriment of crisp handling. *Volkswagen AG*

THE NEXT GENERATION

Although Volkswagen's corporate financial fortunes were waning at the end of the 1980s, the company was hard at work on the third generation of the Golf and its sister, the increasingly popular four-door Jetta sedan. Known internally as the A3, the cars were introduced amidst a crisis in quality control within the company and especially at the company's Puebla, Mexico, plant, but they managed to slowly fight their way into the market. Although this cost Volkswagen huge amounts of market share, enthusiasts soon recognized the potential of the third-generation Golf and Jetta and got to work improving them.

The chassis structure was good. It was stiffer and stronger than the previous cars had been and would form an excellent starting point for tuners who would make the cars lower and stiffer to help with cornering. However, the chassis needed help, as Volkswagen had chosen soggy spring and shock absorber rates to provide good ride comfort at the expense of the Golf's traditionally crisp handling. This could be fixed by switching to stiffer springs, shocks, and anti-roll bars.

The engine was another matter. Initially, both the Golf and the Jetta came with a 2.0-liter inline four-cylinder with a crossflow head having two valves per cylinder. Among Volkswagen fans this engine became known as the "two-point-slow." There was nothing inherently wrong with the engine, and its 115-horsepower was actually more than the previous generation 1.8-liter eight-valve engine had produced, but the Golf had grown heavier and other cars, notably those from

The third generation Golf looked wider and more refined. It was. *Volkswagen AG*

WOB-FZ 93

The 2.0-liter engine with only 115 horsepower was a disappointment in both the third and fourth generations of Golfs and Jettas. *Volkswagen AG*

" . . . every generation has remained true to the Golf formula, which combines classless hatchback style with quality, technology, safety, and value."

—Motor Trend, *July 2003*

Japan, had overtaken it in raw performance. The 2.0 was a disappointment, but one that Volkswagen would set about righting throughout the third generation and into the fourth generation (A4) of the Golf and Jetta when it arrived in 1999.

ROBUST AND STRONG: AN EXCELLENT STARTING POINT

One reason for the immense popularity of the Volkswagen Golf among performance enthusiasts is its inherent strength. From its birth in the mid-1970s through today, Volkswagens have responded well to tuning for greater horsepower and performance. The robust nature of the light but strong thin-wall cast-iron engine block has proven to be an excellent foundation for everything from sporty street cars to full-out racing machines. As with any high-performance engine, proper assembly techniques and a near-fanatical devotion to detail will result in a Volkswagen powertrain that is both powerful and reliable.

Because Volkswagen fans have been modifying these cars for so long, a huge tuning industry has grown up to supply performance parts for nearly every Volkswagen model. This is a real advantage, as the aftermarket companies have done all of the engineering and borne the costs of research and development. Prices for Volkswagen performance parts are reasonable, especially when compared to other cars with equal performance. Many times the standard Volkswagen part will suffice, when you would have needed a special uprated part if you were working on an engine from another manufacturer.

Volkswagens have always been strong cars, and the fourth generation Golf benefited from advanced computer models to help manage energy distribution in a collision. *Volkswagen AG*

THE ENGINES (1993–2005)

The 2.0-Liter Four Cylinder
First Generation 2.0 (1993–1999)

The A3 (third generation) of the Golf and Jetta were launched in the United States in 1993 with a new 2.0-liter inline four-cylinder engine with a crossflow cylinder head. The Volkswagen codename for this engine was ABA. It used a two-piece intake manifold with long runners for improved low-end torque for better around-town driving.

Volkswagen's eight-valve 2.0-liter inline four was the base engine in the third generation cars. *Author*

CROSSFLOW CYLINDER HEAD

A crossflow head has the intake manifold on the opposite side of the engine from the exhaust manifold, so intake gasses flow across the combustion chamber. A crossflow engine has more efficient airflow, and it reduces the transfer of heat from the exhaust manifold to the intake charge to further improve performance.

The ABA engine used the Motronic engine management system from Bosch, controlling both ignition and fuel injection. This system can be modified using different aftermarket engine management chips to coax more performance from the engine.

The ABA engine could be summed up:

Type:	In-line four-cylinder
Block:	Cast iron
Displacement:	1,984 cc
Bore diameter:	82.5 mm (3.25 inches)
Stroke:	92.8 mm (3.65 inches)
Cylinder head:	Aluminum
Valves per cylinder:	2
Compression Ratio:	10.0:1
Engine Management:	Bosch Motronic
Horsepower:	115 hp @ 5,400 rpm
Torque:	122 lb-ft @ 3,200 rpm

Three transmissions were used with the ABA engine. The 020 five-speed was the only manual transmission, while the 096 four-speed automatic was used in most third generation four-cylinder cars. However, after 1995 some four-cylinder cars came with the 01M four-speed automatic.

SECOND GENERATION 2.0 (1999–2005)
When the A4 fourth generation Golf and Jetta was launched in 1999, it came with a revised version of the 2.0-liter four-cylinder engine. Depending upon when it was built, this was designated as the AEG, AVH, or AZG engine.

The new engine was 18 millimeters shorter than before, with shorter connecting rods to allow a more sloping hood. A new "pendulum" style engine mount provided better isolation of noise and vibration. The intermediate shaft that ran the oil pump and distributor in the ABA engine was eliminated, with the oil pump being moved to the front of the engine block, where it was chain-driven by the crankshaft. The water pump was also built into the front of the block and is driven off of the

Electronic engine management requires computerized scan tools to aid in vehicle repair, but also allows relatively easy performance upgrades. *Author*

ENGINE MANAGEMENT CHIPS

Volkswagen Golf and Jetta models use sophisticated computer-controlled engine management systems (EMS) to coordinate ignition and fuel injection. The primary reason for this is to control exhaust emissions and ensure good fuel economy. But Volkswagen's concern was to produce good performance in every conceivable driving condition. Tuners, on the other hand, may be looking to increase performance in one specific area (acceleration, for example) while they are willing to sacrifice performance in others (such as fuel economy). They can do this by "burning" new computer chips that replace the stock version in the engine management system to change the spark- and fuel-delivery parameters. Chips are easy to change, but not every chip manufacturer gets the horsepower and performance results that they claim. By the time the fourth generation cars appeared, it was no longer necessary to change physical components in the engine management system; the car's computer could be reprogrammed using a remote computer that interfaces with the second-generation on-board diagnostics (OBD-II) port under the car's dashboard.

camshaft drive belt. The distributorless ignition system fires two spark plugs simultaneously, but as only one of the cylinders is in the compression stroke, only one spark has any effect. The horsepower rating of the engine remained the same.

Because of all of these changes, few parts interchange between the third and fourth generation 2.0-liter engines. Transmissions used with this generation of 2.0-liter included the 02J five-speed manual and the 01M four-speed automatic.

The AEG, AVH and AZG engine could be summed up:

Type:	In-line four-cylinder
Block:	Cast iron
Displacement:	1,984 cc
Bore diameter:	82.5 mm (3.25 inches)
Stroke:	92.8 mm (3.65 inches)
Cylinder head:	Aluminum
Valves-per-cylinder:	2
Compression Ratio:	10.0:1
Engine Management:	Bosch Motronic
Horsepower:	115 hp @ 5,200 rpm
Torque:	122 lb-ft @ 2,600 rpm

THE 2.8-LITER VR6

Engine design has always been an area for innovation for Volkswagen. The original air-cooled Beetle's horizontally opposed four-cylinder engine used aluminum-magnesium alloys and air-cooling at a time when cast-iron engines and upright radiators were much more common. So in the same spirit of innovation, the VR6 engine had its six cylinders arrayed into two rows of three, offset at a narrow 15-degree angle. It used an efficient combustion chamber design based on VW's four-cylinder engine from the 1980s and produced 172 horsepower at 5,400 rpm and 173 lb-ft of torque at 4,200 rpm.

This compact design, initially designated internally as AAA, was the brainchild of Ulrich Seiffert, VW's chief of research and development. It allowed the use of a single cylinder head, reducing cost and simplify manufacturing. Originally designed for Volkswagen's Corrado sports coupe, the VR6 was also used in the large Passat sedan before finding its way into the Jetta in 1994 and then the Golf in 1995. The engine had no distributor, and it used Bosch's Motronic engine management system.

The 2.8-liter VR6 was available in the A3 Golf and Jetta with a 02A five-speed manual transmission or either the 096 or 01M four-speed automatic transmissions. In the fourth generation of the Golf and Jetta, the 2.8-liter VR6 was known as the AFP engine and was available with the 02M six-speed manual transmission, or with the 01M four-speed automatic. With a manual transmission, EPA mileage figures were 19 miles per gallon city and 26 miles per gallon highway. *Ward's International* named it as one of its "10 Best Engines" and *Popular Mechanics* gave it a "Design and Engineering" award.

In 2002, the VR6 engine was boosted to 200 horsepower, thanks to a new 24-valve cylinder head, and was available with a six-speed manual or a 09A five-speed automatic transmission. This engine was designated as BDF.

WHY A VR6?

The Volkswagen VR6 engine has a narrow 15-degree angle between its two banks of three cylinders. This compares to a more usual 60-degree or 90-degree angle for V-6 engines. The narrow angle resulted in a compact engine that fit in the space of a Volkswagen inline four-cylinder engine and also required only one cylinder head to cover both banks of cylinders. The name VR6 is derived from the Vee cylinder configuration and the German word *Reihenmotor*, meaning inline. In other words, the VR6 is an inline V-6.

Electronic engine management requires computerized scan tools to aid in vehicle repair, but also allows relatively easy performance upgrades. *Author*

The 2.8-liter VR6 engine (AAA, AFP) could be summed up:

Type:	15-degree V-6
Block:	Cast iron
Displacement:	2,792 cc
Bore diameter:	81 mm (3.19 inches)
Stroke:	90.3 mm (3.56 inches)
Cylinder head:	Aluminum
Valves per cylinder:	2 (4 valves per cylinder in 2002)
Compression Ratio:	10.0:1
Engine Management:	Bosch Motronic®
Horsepower:	172 hp @ 5,400 rpm (through 2002)
Torque:	173 lb-ft @ 4,200 rpm (through 2002)

1.9 TDI DIESEL

In 1997 a new diesel engine, designated either ALH or AHU made its debut in the Jetta TDI. Although Volkswagen diesels had been available in Golf and Jetta models before, this 1.9-liter turbocharged direct-injection (TDI) diesel four-cylinder engine was highly advanced and clean burning. It produced 90 horsepower and delivered 40 miles per gallon in the city and 49 miles per gallon on the highway, when driving through the 02A five-speed manual transmission. *European Car* magazine called it "the hassle-free diesel," noting that " . . . the TDI may be the first diesel on these shores that can actually be considered fun to drive."

In 2004, a new version of the diesel engine was introduced. The new TDI PD ("*pumpe düse*" or pump injector)

A turbocharged direct injection (TDI) diesel engine added to the Golf and Jetta's versatile appeal. *Volkswagen AG*

used a new kind of diesel fuel injector that injected diesel fuel at extremely high pressure to reduce engine knocking and noise, especially at idle and improve exhaust emissions. This engine, designated BEW, produced 100 horsepower and 177 lb-ft of torque.

The ALH and AHU engine could be summed up:

Type:	In-line four-cylinder
Block:	Cast iron
Displacement:	1,896 cc
Bore diameter:	79.5 mm (3.19 inches)
Stroke:	95.5 mm (3.40 inches)
Cylinder head:	Aluminum
Valves-per-cylinder:	2
Compression Ratio:	19.5:1
Engine Management:	electronic
Horsepower:	90 hp @ 4,000 rpm
Torque:	149 lb-ft @ 1,900 rpm

The BEW engine was similar and could be summed up:

Type:	In-line four-cylinder
Block:	Cast iron
Displacement:	1,896 cc
Bore diameter:	79.5 mm (3.19 inches)
Stroke:	95.5 mm (3.40 inches)
Cylinder head:	Aluminum
Valves-per-cylinder:	2
Compression Ratio:	19.0:1
Engine Management:	Electronic
Horsepower:	100 hp @ 4,000 rpm
Torque:	177 lb-ft @ 1,900-2,400 rpm

1.8T

In 2001, Volkswagen introduced the 1.8T engine to the Golf GTI and GLS and the Jetta GLS models. This 1,781-cc engine was derived from the Audi TT model and initially produced 150 horsepower at 5,700 rpm and 155 lb-ft of torque at 1,750 rpm. The Volkswagen 1.8T used an innovative five-valve per cylinder head (three intake, two exhaust valves), double overhead camshafts, and a turbocharger and intercooler to produce an engine with good power output and excellent flexibility.

A flat torque curve gave 155 lb-ft all the way from 1,750 rpm to 4,600 rpm and helped the Golf GLS 1.8T accelerate from zero to 60 miles per hour in 7.3 seconds in *Car and Driver* testing. *Motor Trend* saw 7.6 seconds for zero to 60 miles per hour. The 1.8T in the Golf would also return EPA estimates of 24 miles per gallon city and 31 miles per gallon highway when equipped with a manual transmission.

While the 1.8T engine in stock form was good enough, it also proved to be adaptable to tuning by aftermarket suppliers. Because its turbocharger boost levels were computer controlled, tuners were able to develop software upgrades that would increase the boost level and thus horsepower. Within limits, the computer could be programmed to produce as much horsepower as desired at any rpm, modifying the ignition and fuel maps to work with the extra air supplied by the

The 1.8T turbocharged gasoline engine opened a new chapter in Volkswagen enthusiasm. *Volkswagen AG*

turbocharger. Just by changing programming, up to 40 more horsepower could be seen, and a whole new generation of VW aftermarket tuners grew up around the 1.8T engine.

In 2002, the 1.8T was upgraded to 180 horsepower and a six-speed manual transmission replaced the five-speed. *Car and Driver* reported zero to 60-mile per hour times in the 6.5-second range.

The AWD, AWW and AWP engine could be summed up:

Type:	In-line four-cylinder
Block:	Cast iron
Displacement:	1,781 cc
Bore diameter:	82.5 mm (3.25 inches)
Stroke:	92.8 mm (3.65 inches)
Cylinder head:	Aluminum
Valves-per-cylinder:	5
Compression Ratio:	10.0:1
Engine Management:	Bosch Motronic
Horsepower:	150 hp @ 5,700 rpm
Torque:	155 lb-ft @ 1,750 rpm

R32

With the fifth generation of the Golf just around the corner, it was a surprise when in 2004 VW introduced the most potent version of the Golf ever. Dubbed the R32, this 3.2-liter 24-valve VR6 fourth generation Golf produced 240 horsepower, driving through a six-speed manual transmission to all four wheels using VW's "4MOTION" system. The R32 was fast. *Motor Trend* saw 5.9 seconds in its zero to 60-mile per hour acceleration runs and 14.2 seconds at 97.6 miles per hour in its quarter-mile acceleration runs.

The 3.2-liter R32 VR6 engine produced 240-horsepower and helped bring Volkswagen back into the performance game. *VWOA*

The R32 VR6 engine (BJS) could be summed up:

Type:	15-degree V-6
Block:	Cast iron
Displacement:	2,792 cc
Bore diameter:	84 mm (3.31 inches)
Stroke:	95.9 mm (3.78 inches)
Cylinder head:	Aluminum
Valves-per-cylinder:	4
Compression Ratio:	11.3:1
Engine Management:	Bosch Motronic
Horsepower:	240 hp @ 6,250 rpm
Torque:	236 lb-ft @ 2,800 rpm

ENGINES FOR OTHER MARKETS

Outside of the U.S. market, the Volkswagen Golf was available with a larger variety of engine sizes and types. Between 1991 and 2004, inline four-cylinders included 1.4-, 1.6-, 1.8- and 2.0-liter variations with several versions of the 1.9-liter diesel four-cylinder engine also available. The 2.8-liter and 3.2-liter (R32) VR6 engines were used in other markets, and a special 2.3-liter VR5 engine (a VR6 minus one cylinder) was also part of the European lineup. For the third generation Golf CL sold in Canada, a 90- horsepower 1.8-liter engine (designated ACC) was included, and the Golf GL, Jetta GL, and Jetta GLS models in Canada could be ordered with a 1.9-liter turbocharged ECOdiesel engine (AAZ) that produced 75 horsepower.

DRIVING SENSATIONS

Appendix A of this book contains a test-drive checklist that you can use when you are buying a specific Volkswagen Golf or Jetta. In that list will be a variety of checks and examinations that you or your mechanic will want to make to ensure that you know everything that might later become a problem with your purchase. But beyond these specific test-drive checks, what's it like to drive a Volkswagen? In other words, why do so many Volkswagen enthusiasts prefer the driving characteristics of a Golf or a Jetta over the wide range of other vehicles that are available to them in the car market?

STEERING AND HANDLING

If you come to the Volkswagen Golf or Jetta from a large car or a sport utility vehicle, you're in for a treat. Unlike the numb, lifeless steering that many ordinary vehicles possess, the Golf's rack-and-pinion setup provides plenty of feedback. This means that a good driver can sense what is going on with the two front tires from sensations that are transmitted through the steering system. If the steering suddenly gets light, and the roads are wet or even icy, the driver knows that the grip level of the front tires is being compromised by the road conditions, and that it's time to reduce speed and drive more carefully.

Both the Golf and the Jetta are front-wheel-drive vehicles (the R32 has all-wheel drive), a setup that is not always

Driving a Volkswagen gives an experience unlike that found in other cars. *Clewell*

Performance and handling is a big part of every drive in a Volkswagen. *Hallstrom*

considered optimum for high-performance handling. This is because the front wheels must not only steer the car but they also must put power down as the car accelerates away from a corner. If your car has lots of horsepower, it's easy to overpower the front wheels, reducing the amount of cornering that they can manage. This is known as understeer. Fortunately, the cure for power-on understeer is to gently reduce the amount of power with the throttle until the front tires regain grip. Rapidly reducing the power by abruptly lifting your foot from the throttle is the wrong thing to do, as it can unsettle the car and the rear tires can breakaway into what's called lift-throttle oversteer.

Despite all of the "common" wisdom out there about front-wheel drive vehicles, they can actually be made to perform exceptionally well on the street and on a racetrack. Many of the current championship racing series in the United States and around the world feature front-wheel-drive coupes and sedans competing directly with rear-wheel- and all-wheel-drive vehicles. In truth, the die was cast in the mid-1970s when Volkswagen introduced the front-drive GTI, with its uprated suspension and small and nimble configuration.

Another thing many people will notice about driving a Volkswagen is the firmness of its suspension. Even the Golf III GL, which was criticized by Volkswagen fans for its soft and supple ride, will still feel pretty firm to those coming from bigger, more conventional vehicles. This firm ride helps Golfs and Jettas maintain their poise on twisty roads, which can be safely negotiated at much higher speeds than is possible in most SUVs and family sedans.

Although few Volkswagen vehicles destined for the United States come from Germany anymore, there is still a heritage of performance and unlimited Autobahn speed limits that underlie every Volkswagen's design brief. Cars that are designed for safe travel at high speeds are going to feel more connected and controlled, even at lower everyday speeds. Every aspect of a Volkswagen Golf and Jetta, from the choice of wheels and tires to the firm supportive seats, helps the driver react to ever-changing conditions on the road.

Automotive electronics have become a major contributor to vehicle safety, and Volkswagen's fourth generation Golf and Jetta models have their share of electronic devices to help the

Supportive seats are a big part of the handling package. *Volkswagen AG*

driver. Antislip regulation (ASR), a form of traction control, was standard on all 1.8T- and some VR6-equipped models. This system helps send power to the driving wheel with the most grip, helping the car move away when starting out on a slippery surface. Electronic Differential Lock (EDL), also a part of the 1.8T package, further reduces wheel spin on loose surfaces or icy roads.

A wide range of models was also available with Electronic Stability Program (ESP) as an option. This driver's aid senses when the car is not following the path intended by the driver's input with the steering wheel and automatically applies individual brakes to adjust the vehicle's path to the desired one. The system is remarkably effective for normal motorists, but can be limiting when driving hard on an autocross or a racetrack. For these situations it is possible to manually override the ESP system.

ENGINE AND DRIVETRAIN

If the chassis, suspension, and interior of a Volkswagen Golf and Jetta are European in feel and execution, so too does the engine reflect its German heritage. Although the eight-valve 2.0-liter four-cylinder engine with its long stroke for greater torque was specifically designed for U.S. drivers, the power characteristics are still recognizable to any fan of performance driving.

Volkswagen engines are not large displacement V-8s. They require some involvement on the part of the driver, but they reward such involvement with plenty of performance. This is especially true for the VR6 engine and, of course, for the turbocharged and intercooled 1.8T engine, but can even be felt in the innovative 1.9 TDI diesel powerplant. While the 2.0-liter four-cylinder engine feels merely adequate, the VR6 engine feels strong through all of the gears—a real thoroughbred. Its power delivery is smooth and its narrow-angle banks of cylinders make a sound that is much like the pleasing growl of a straight six. The 1.8T engine, on the other hand, is notable for its torque, which has a broad peak that ranges from 1,750 through 4,600 rpm. The rush of acceleration is impressive.

All of this performance only comes when the Volkswagen engines are maintained in proper tune, with regular oil changes and consumable items like spark plugs, hoses, and belts changed at regular service intervals. As robust as these Volkswagen engines are, when you begin your search for a car to purchase, you'll find plenty that have been mistreated and never serviced. A car whose owner has kept good records is always a plus.

Although Volkswagen offers an electronically controlled automatic transmission on the Golf and Jetta models, choosing this option over the five-speed or six-speed manual transmission mutes much of the car's responsiveness and takes away some of the fun of driving. True, some of the later five-speed automatics are available with Tiptronic manual shifting, but the experience just never is quite the same as shifting a good manual transmission. Volkswagen's clutch action is light, and its shifter is just a bit notchy, making for an enjoyable driving experience. A slipping clutch or worn-out synchronizers in the transmission, on the other hand, will kill all of that joy, so make sure you drive any car you are considering at a high enough speed to use all of the gears.

SUSPENSION AND BRAKES

As has already been mentioned, the suspension of a Golf or Jetta is a bit stiffer than that found in most cars. By the same token, either of these cars can be taken onto a racetrack or autocross course in stock form without embarrassment. Body roll is held in check with front and rear anti-roll (sway) bars and the superior chassis stiffness of the third and fourth generation cars allows the suspension to do the work when cornering hard. When the limits are reached, they are usually signaled to the driver by the gentle loss of traction at the front of the vehicle (understeer).

From the outside, the indication that the limits have been reached are usually preceded by the inside rear wheel lifting clearly off the pavement, an event which is only barely noticeable inside the vehicle. This three-wheel cornering attitude is nothing to worry about and has been a characteristic of Volkswagen Golf performance driving since the beginning. If wear and tear on the suspension of the car you are considering doesn't measure up to this high standard, you may want to pass it up and look for one that does.

Volkswagen's brakes are also up to the task of high performance driving. All but the earliest base models use four-wheel disc brakes and anti-lock is also standard. In almost every driving condition, anti-lock brakes improve not only stopping distance but also driver control in an emergency. Brakes are relatively easy to maintain and any shaking, vibration, or pulsing in the brake pedal during a hard stop will take away from the driving enjoyment.

INTERIOR AND EXTERIOR

The compact size, particularly of the Golf but also of the Jetta, gives the cars a level of agility that is much appreciated in crowded parking lots and narrow driveways. The modest exterior dimensions of the Golf belie the roomy interior (at

Volkswagen improved its brakes in later models, sometimes accenting the calipers with color. *Author*

Ergonomically designed controls make the cabin a good place for a driver. *Volkswagen AG*

least for the front seat occupants) and the hatch provides access to ample trunk space. In the case of the Jetta, the trunk is positively huge and configured in a way to manage large quantities of luggage.

Volkswagen puts plenty of emphasis in its seats and driver ergonomics, making a Volkswagen one of the easier cars to find all the controls and switches by feel when you drive away on a rainy night. The seats themselves, especially in the performance-oriented models, seem firm at first, but provide plenty of support when driving long distances and when carving through favorite back roads, two favorite pastimes of Golf and Jetta enthusiasts.

CHAPTER 3 | **WHAT MODEL TO BUY**

During the period from 1993 through 2005, Volkswagen built a broad product range based upon the Golf and Jetta platform. The Golf was available as a two-door and four-door hatchback as well as a two-door convertible. The Jetta was available as a four-door sedan and as a wagon. As we have already learned, the third generation of the Golf and Jetta extended in the U.S. market from 1993 through 1999, while the fourth generation went from 1999 through 2005, and a variety of engines were available over that period.

THE THIRD GENERATION
TELLING THEM APART

GOLF GL 1993–1999
Two-Door and Four-Door Hatchback
Although the third generation Golf was launched in Europe in 1991, it wasn't until 1993 that the Golf III GL base model was introduced in the United States. Golf IIIs bound for the United States were built in Volkswagen's Puebla, Mexico, plant. The Golf III GL came with a 2.0-liter 115-horsepower four-cylinder engine and was available with a five-speed manual or four-speed automatic transmission.

Volkswagen had shifted the emphasis on the Golf III away from performance and more toward safety and environmental concerns. In Europe, the Golf III could be returned to the factory for recycling of its materials after it had lived its useful life. Body rigidity and strength was improved over the previous generation of Golf, improving crash-worthiness. Features like four-wheel disc brakes with anti-lock (ABS) and front occupant air bags (all but the earliest production cars)

emphasized the safety aspects, while 24 miles per gallon city and 32 miles per gallon highway emphasized economy. The object was to compete in the low-price segment against Japanese models like the Honda Civic and Toyota Corolla, although the Golf III GL never came close to the sales success of those models.

The Golf III GL changed little during its production life, positioned as the entry level Volkswagen. Today, this model is viewed as little more than a used car and can be purchased cheaply. As such, it can make a good and economical choice for an enthusiast looking for a starting point for a highly modified third-generation Golf.

GOLF CABRIOLET 1995–2001
Two-Door Convertible
There had never been a cabriolet based upon the second generation of the Golf. The original Golf/Rabbit body had remained in production at the Karmann factory in Osnabrück, Germany. A new Cabriolet, based upon the Golf III was announced for the 1994 model year, but in fact the first cars weren't delivered until late 1994 as 1995 models.

Karmann did a significant amount of engineering, increasing the strength of the new Golf III Cabriolet by 20 percent over the previous generation. The floor, bulkhead, and dash were all reinforced and the rollover bar served as supports for the side window glass and anchored the shoulder belts. The Cabrio's list of standard features included a height-adjustable steering column, sport seats with cloth trim, power windows and mirrors with defog, cup-holders, cruise control, and a premium eight-speaker stereo sound system with an optional CD changer. The convertible top, as with

The Golf III GL was available as a two- or four-door hatchback. *Volkswagen AG*

The Golf-based Cabriolet provided open-air motoring in a well-equipped package. *Volkswagen AG*

the previous model, consisted of six layers and had a heated glass rear window. Safety features included dual front air bags, ABS disc brakes, and many of the crush structures that had also improved crash protection on the regular Golf III. The powertrain of the Golf III Cabriolet was the same as that of the Golf III GL; the 115-horsepower four-cylinder straining a bit more under the 250-pound weight increase of the open-topped car.

In 1997, a Highline model was added with standard leather upholstery, alloy wheels, body-color side moldings, and fog lamps. In 1998, the GLS model also included an electrically operated top and optional side-impact air bags. Aside from the joys of top-down motoring, the Cabriolet's lower body rigidity and greater weight don't make it a great candidate for performance tuning. Cabrios, however, are popular for customized interiors and exteriors.

GTI 1993–1999
Two-Door Hatchback
The three letters "GTI" had nearly mythical significance to Volkswagen fanatics, so when the third generation Golf III GTI appeared in the United States in 1993, much was expected. Instead, the GTI was little more than a trim package that included air conditioning (CFC-free), sport seats, a power glass sunroof, an upgraded sound system, a height adjustable

> *"But like the generation that first embraced it, the GTI matured over the years, losing a bit of its callow cool and performance focus as it grew in weight and size."*
>
> —Car and Driver, *June 2000*

steering wheel, alloy wheels, halogen headlights, and the requisite GTI badges. The engine was the same lowly 2.0-liter, 115-horsepower four-cylinder from the Golf III GL model; in the eyes of enthusiasts, Volkswagen had sunk to a new low.

The company wisely didn't offer a GTI in 1994 as it re-evaluated its options for the flagship of the Golf lineup. The exciting Jetta GLX VR6 was introduced in 1994 to the U.S. market to great acclaim, especially in the press, so Volkswagen did the obvious thing for 1995 and introduced the Golf III GTI VR6.

> *"The 2.0L crossflow 8V GTI set a low-water mark for Volkswagen, as it was significantly less powerful and heavier than a MKII GTI 16V."*
>
> —European Car, *July 2003*

The three most important letters in Volkswagen's alphabet. *Volkswagen AG*

Fitting the VR6 engine into Golfs and Jettas made perfect sense and created potent performance cars. *Volkswagen AG*

This was the GTI for which enthusiasts had been waiting. With 172 horsepower and 173 lb-ft of torque it would sprint from zero to 60 miles per hour in around seven seconds and was electronically limited to a top speed of 130 miles per hour. Equipped with a close-ratio O2A/O2J five-speed gearbox with cable actuation (a four-speed automatic was optional), stiffer front and rear shock absorbers (gas shocks at the rear), electronic traction control, anti-lock brakes with four-wheel discs, and 15-inch alloy wheels with performance tires, the GTI VR6 was a hot car right out of the box. Volkswagen made a great deal about the GTI VR6's new "Plus" front suspension that was used to combat excessive torque steer under hard acceleration, and to help maintain control in the event of a blowout of a front tire.

Although some Volkswagen purists don't consider anything but a four-cylinder car to be a "true" GTI, the VR6's slightly more aggressive front end, revised grille, body-colored bumpers and moldings, front fog lights, roof-mounted "stinger" antenna, and discrete "VR6" badges helped let the world know that this GTI was something special.

In 1996, the GTI VR6 was further enhanced with even stiffer shock absorbers and a 10-millimeter lower ride height at the front. A leather seat option supplemented the already excellent and supportive standard sport seats, making the interior an even better place for a driver to sit.

The VR6 badge is one hint that something special is under the hood. *Author*

Less enticing was Volkswagen's decision to place the GTI name on a 2.0-liter four-cylinder version of the Golf III, equipped with smaller front brakes, 14-inch alloy wheels, midlevel performance tires, and a GTI badge in place of the one that said VR6. It was a pretty nice car, capable of accelerating from zero to 60 miles per hour in about 9 seconds, but it just wasn't the same as the full-house VR6-engined version. The 2.0-liter GTI received a leather option in 1998, and other interior upgrades included red accents throughout the cabin.

In 1997, Volkswagen offered a "Driver's Edition" of the GTI VR6. Catching on to the rising sport-compact car craze, it included new seven-spoke alloy wheels, red-painted brake calipers, and twin tail pipes with a bright finish. The exterior was available in new colors that included Yellow and Jazz Blue, along with Red, Black, and White. The inside had special sport cloth upholstery with a choice of red, blue, or yellow trim, while red accents in the cabin were included on the leather shift knob, handbrake handle, and steering wheel.

If you want a third generation Golf III, there is no doubt that the one to buy is a GTI VR6. Powerful and fun to drive, this is a car that, even in stock trim, won't be embarrassed by many other cars on the road or on a racetrack. The 1996 and later versions, with their stiffer shocks and lowered ride height had some advantages, but upgrades to the standard suspension are easy to make, so using a 1995 car as a starting point won't make much difference.

Although prices continue to drop, many GTI VR6 owners know what they have and want to keep them, so the cars are becoming scarce on the used car market. The four-cylinder GTI, although a nice enough car, will ultimately be a disappointment to anyone who has driven a VR6-engine version. On the other hand, the third-generation GTI can make a good candidate for an engine swap, using a later turbocharged 1.8T engine from a fourth generation car. Still, the growl from the narrow-angle VR6 engine is worth the hunt and the price of admission.

JETTA GL 1993–1999
Four-Door Sedan
As with the Golf III, the Jetta III was launched in Europe in 1991, this time with the name Vento. It was introduced to the United States in 1993 and built in Volkswagen's quality-troubled Puebla, Mexico, plant. Powered by the same 115-horsepower four-cylinder engine as the Golf III, the Jetta also shared the Golf's basic platform, stretched 14 inches to accommodate its commodious trunk that boasted 15 cubic feet of luggage space.

The Jetta III was quieter and more refined than the previous generation of Jetta and quickly began outselling the Golf III. Despite being the base version of the Jetta III, The GL could be ordered with anti-lock brakes, automatic transmission, air-conditioning (CFC-free), cruise control, and a power sunroof. From the outside, the GL can be identified by its black sideview mirrors; they are body colored on all other Jetta III models.

In 1996, power rack and pinion steering was standard on the Jetta III GL, and a Bose audio system was optional. As

The GL was the base version of the Golf and Jetta. *Author*

with the base Golf III GL, the base Jetta is just a used car in most people's eyes, but can make a fine starting point for an ambitious Volkswagen tuner looking for the convenience of a four-door sedan.

JETTA GLS/GLX VR6 1994–1999
Four-Door Sedan
As far back as the early 1980s, Volkswagen had offered GLS versions of the Jetta. Similar in content to the GTI version of the Golf, this had even included the use of the GTI's 16-valve engine late in the life of the second generation of the cars.

In 1994, Volkswagen offered three versions of the Jetta for the U.S. market: the base GL, the upmarket GLS, and the flagship GLX VR6. The Jetta GLS had a split folding rear seat, a CD changer, and power windows. The GLX VR6 added the superb 172-horsepower VR6 engine, traction control, anti-lock brakes, the new "Plus" front suspension, leather seats, fog lamps, a rear spoiler, a rear "stinger" radio antenna, and 15-inch BBS alloy wheels with performance tires. This was a real performance sedan and a worthy and lower-priced competitor to the BMW 3-series and the Audi A4.

In 1996, the GLS gained power rack-and-pinion steering, while on the GLX new seven-spoke alloy wheels replaced the BBS wheels from the earlier car. In 1997, a Jetta III GT version was introduced, with all that the Jetta GLX VR6 offered, except for the VR6 engine. The GT was powered by the ordinary 2.0-liter four-cylinder engine from the base GL model.

Much the same as the VR6 engine defined the Golf III GTI's performance potential, the GLX VR6 gave the same sort of performance in a four-door sedan. It was fast and fun to drive and, with more of them built than Golf III GTI VR6s, is considerably more accessible on the market. The Jetta III GLX VR6 is something of a Q-ship—it can be a very subtle way to go very fast.

A GLS badge indicated a car that was slightly higher up in the Volkswagen food chain. *Author*

JETTA TDI 1998–1999
Four-Door Sedan
Volkswagen had introduced diesel engines to the Golf/Rabbit in the late 1970s, and had offered the oil burners in the second generation of the Golf and the Jetta. The third generation Golf III GL, Jetta III GL, and Jetta GLS were offered in Canada with a turbocharged 1.9-liter four-cylinder ECOdiesel engine.

In 1998, the Jetta III TDI was offered in the United States. It had an all-new and sophisticated turbocharged direct-injection diesel engine with a complex engine management system that allowed it to produce exceptionally low exhaust emissions. With 90 horsepower and 149 lb-ft of torque, the Jetta III TDI was quick and fun to drive while still delivering 40 miles per gallon city and 49 miles per gallon highway. The Jetta III TDI led the way in the concept of a diesel engine with enough performance to be fun as well as frugal.

The TDI diesel engine found a happy home in both Golfs and Jettas. *Author*

GOLF TREK, K2, JAZZ JETTA TREK, J2 AND JAZZ 1996–1999
Four-Door Hatchbacks and Sedans
Volkswagen's marketing and advertising in the mid-1990s focused upon active Generation X-ers, children of the Baby Boomers who were just coming into an age where they would become car buyers. In 1996, the limited edition Jetta III Trek was introduced to the U.S. market. In addition to added fog lights, rear spoiler, and special seats, it came with a custom-built Trek 21-speed mountain bike and roof rack bike carrier. Special sticker "badges" proclaimed "Trek" to all the world.

A marketing effort with Trek and K2 resulted in another set of rear badges for Golfs and Jettas. *Author*

The marketing effort was successful, and in 1997 it was expanded to include the Golf III. In addition, a K2 version of the Jetta III and Golf III was available, equipped with either K2 El Camino skis or a K2 Juju snowboard and a suitable roof rack and badging stickers.

Sports marketing had worked so well that Volkswagen's marketing group decided to branch out, offering in 1997 a Jazz version of both the Golf and the Jetta that featured a six-disc CD changer, alloy wheels, and a Jazz decal on the trunk along with special colors. In every way these limited editions were creations of Volkswagen's marketing department and had no special enhancements when it came to performance.

TREK'S MOUNTAIN BIKE

The Trek mountain bike included with Volkswagen Trek models was built around a 7005 aluminum-alloy frame with a full chromoly fork that was designed for durability and low weight. Gear changing was through SRAM Grip Shift ESP 500 twist shifters and an ESP 5.0 rear derailleur. Brakes were Shimano Altus, and the seat and handgrips displayed the Volkswagen logo. The Volkswagen Trek bikes, all of which were purple, came in five frame sizes.

MODELS IN EUROPE

The Golf III started production in July 1991 for the European market. A variety of different models were available:

1991
Golf CL   1.4 liter
Golf CL, GL 1.8 liter
Golf GL, GT 1.8 liter
Golf GTI   2.0 liter
Golf VR6   2.8-liter VR6
Golf CL   1.9-liter diesel
Golf CL, GL, GTD   1.9-liter diesel
1993
Golf GL, GTD   1.9-liter TDI diesel
Golf Cabriolet   2.0 liter

These models continued until 1997, when the fourth generation of the Golf was introduced in Europe. The third generation of Jetta, called Vento in Europe, was never very popular. In the United States, this three-box sedan was considered chic and accounted for 60 percent of Volkswagen's sales, and the Golf hatchback was viewed as an economy car. In Europe, however, the hatchback was considered sporty, while the sedan was a car suitable only for an old man. The Vento was available with a full range of four-cylinder gasoline and diesel engines, but it remained a slow seller in Europe.

STRENGTHS AND WEAKNESSES OF THE THIRD GENERATION GOLF AND JETTA

Because the Golf and Jetta share so many of their chassis and mechanical components, the areas of strength and weakness of the two cars are similar. The first and foremost concern of either car will be rust. While mechanical components are easy to repair or replace, the structural soundness of any vehicle can be severely compromised by the ravages of corrosion.

Rusting near the license plate on the Golf hatch is also common. *Author*

Although Volkswagen had made steady progress in corrosion protection after a disastrous start with the rust-prone original Rabbit, the third generation cars still had a few problem areas. The hatchback door of the Golf III is a particularly troublesome area. Rust can form around the lower edge of the bonded-in rear window, and bubbling can occur near the license-plate recess. Likewise, the top edge of the rear hatch, where the wiring enters and exits near the hinges, collects water and dirt that may cause corrosion to form. This corrosion can also result in damage to the wiring that will prevent the license plate and taillights from operating properly. Cars driven in harsh winter climates may also suffer from the

The rear hatch of third generation Golf models is particularly prone to rusting. *Author*

The undercarriage of third generation cars usually battles corrosion pretty well, unless an accident or rock damage gives rust a place to start. *Author*

usual corrosion of the exhaust system and of the suspension arms and components.

While not always a safety issue, if you are going to be later modifying the car, you'll find a rust-free undercarriage much easier to work on than one that is heavily crusted with rust. Other than the tailgate, unless the car has been involved in an accident that has compromised its undercoating protection; the Golf III and Jetta III are above average in their corrosion resistance.

By now, any of the third generation cars you will be looking at will be more than a few years old, and in that time you shouldn't be surprised to find certain parts are worn or even worn out. Foremost among these are the car's shock absorbers. The third generation Golf and Jetta were widely criticized for being underdamped when they were new, and the passage of time will not have improved matters. The good news is that there are a variety of spring and shock absorber packages available on the aftermarket that will not only return the cars to their original state, but will also be able to vastly improve their soggy handling.

The other parts of the suspension and driveline will suffer the usual "used car" maladies of worn bushings (especially those that locate the rear axle), worn CV-joints, a slipping clutch, noisy wheel bearings, warped or worn brake rotors, and rusted or seized brake calipers. The handbrake cable can seize on these cars due to corrosion, preventing the handbrake from working. None of these problems are particularly serious in themselves, but taken together they can represent a significant expense in parts and labor if they need to be corrected.

The electrical system of the third generation cars falls into that gray area of a time when automotive electronics was just beginning to take off. Unfortunately for many used car buyers,

the health of the system can really only be assessed through the use of a computerized scan tool, either by a Volkswagen dealer or a well-trained independent mechanic.

Items like the anti-lock brake system, the air bags, and the engine management computer can all set trouble codes and illuminate warning lights on the dash. These must be analyzed with a scan tool before the appropriate repair actions can be taken. The instruments in the dash also occasionally suffer from faults, often traceable to a failed voltage stabilizer at the rear of the instrument panel. The motor assembly of the electric sunroof can cause problems, and if it does, the sunroof is usually replaced as an entire unit, typically from parts obtained at a salvage yard. The snazzy "stinger" antenna on the rear of the roof of performance models can also fail, drastically reducing radio reception.

The really good news is that Volkswagen engines are strong and can easily pass 150,000-miles without any major rebuilds. The timing belt on the four-cylinder cars is the primary maintenance item and must be religiously changed every 60,000-miles to prevent catastrophic engine failure. Other items like the water pump, power steering pump, alternator, and the air conditioning compressor can also suffer from wear as they would on any car. Nevertheless, the engine internals of any of the Volkswagen engines considered here are plenty robust for long mileage and strong enough to withstand significant tuning. A rattle on acceleration can often be traced to a loose heat shield on the exhaust system, and the exhaust mounting brackets can break, allowing the whole system to move about.

If there is an Achilles' heel in the mix, it's the 020 five-speed manual transmission, which is known to have relatively weak synchronizers (especially second gear); also it can jam

Overall, Volkswagen's third generation Golfs and Jettas were plenty robust and reliable. *Clewell*

into gear if the gears are shifted too brutally. The primary problem was Volkswagen's use of rivets to hold the ring gear in the differential to its carrier. If a rivet comes out, it can wreck the inside of the transmission as it floats around between the gears. The solution is to replace all of the rivets with hardened bolts.

In addition, the reverse gear is not synchronized, so shifting into reverse while the car is rolling forward can cause damage that will result in the car being stuck in reverse. Performance-savvy Volkswagen enthusiasts know to baby their transmissions a bit, especially when driving hard, to ensure a long life. Clutches of Volkswagens have a reputation for being nearly bulletproof and long wearing, even if a car has been modified for more performance.

The fourth generation Golf maintained a resemblance to the original first generation Golf. *Volkswagen AG*

THE FOURTH GENERATION
TELLING THEM APART

GOLF GL 1999–2005
Two-Door and Four-Door Hatchback

Production of the fourth generation of the Golf began in the Wolfsburg, Germany, plant in August of 1997. Gone was the Roman numeral designation from the third generation Golf III, and it would be another two years before the new Golf and Jetta models would come to the United States, by

The fourth generation Jetta was called the Bora in Europe. *Author*

way of Volkswagen's plant in Mexico. In Europe, the Jetta received yet another new name when it started production in July of 1998; it was now called the Bora. The chassis of the fourth generation Golf and Jetta were closely aligned with that of the Audi A3, which was never imported to the United States, as well as the New Beetle, which Volkswagen had introduced to much fanfare in the United States in 1998.

The new Golf was just over 5 inches longer and 1.18 inches wider than the previous car, and its wheelbase was longer by just over 1.5 inches. MacPherson struts were still used at the front, and the rear suspension retained its torsion beam rear axle. The coil springs and shock absorbers were now separated, with the rear coil springs mounted further forward on the trailing arms to provide less intrusion into the luggage space. Power steering was standard across the board and the front suspension was set with significant caster to help with directional stability.

The interior of the fourth generation Golf had become significantly more luxurious, even in the base GL trim. Standard items included a height-adjustable driver's seat, side air bags for the front seats, an adjustable steering column, power steering, four-wheel disc brakes with antilock, and fold-down rear seats with headrests.

The 115 horsepower 2.0-liter four-cylinder engine in the Golf GL model was similar to 2.0-liter engine of the third generation, but had numerous detail changes. Volkswagen had gone to "distributorless" direct ignition, so the now-redundant intermediate shaft inside the engine was eliminated. This required moving the oil pump to the front of the engine, where it was driven from the crankshaft by a chain. The cylinder block was lowered for better packaging, resulting in a need for shorter connecting rods. The new 2.0-liter four-cylinder engine weighed less, was more rigid, and was quieter than its predecessor, although it still was only rated at a disappointing 115 horsepower. Transmission choices were a five-speed manual or optional four-speed automatic transmission.

"The fourth generation Golf, introduced in 1999, wears expensive, finely tailored duds for a car of its price, but remains prone to some slovenly habits."

—Car and Driver, *February 2002*

Although the fourth generation Golf GL offered some of the vestiges of the European car experience, it was bigger and heavier than its predecessors and was moving further and further from the idea of a sporty playmate. The problem was that other companies, notably those from Japan, were more than willing to step into the void left by Volkswagen's rise up the market. Buying a used fourth generation Golf GL today isn't difficult, as they are nothing special. Tuning parts are available to make them handle and perform better, but in most cases you'd be better off starting higher up on the Volkswagen food chain.

The interior and seats were significantly improved in the fourth generation cars. *Volkswagen AG*

ONE TO BUY | **2004 GOLF GL 2.0 4-DOOR**

This 2004 Golf GL, with only 8,609 miles on the odometer, was like new. *Author*

Color: Silver
Interior: Beige
Transmission: Automatic
Mileage: 8,609 miles
Asking Price: $16,850

An exceptionally clean four-door Golf on a Dodge dealer's used car lot. With so few miles, the Golf was like brand new and even had wisps of its original new car smell. The exterior of the car was unblemished, and it started and ran as well as it did the day it left the factory. The tires were like new and the car was still under factory warranty. If you were looking for reliable basic transportation, this four-door GL would have been an excellent choice.

The much-loved Cabriolet was killed off by the New Beetle Convertible at the end of 2003. *Volkswagen AG*

GOLF CABRIOLET GL 2002–2003
Two-Door Convertible

Rather than engineer a whole new convertible from the fourth generation of Golf, Volkswagen did as it had in the past and ordered Karmann to continue building the Golf III Cabriolet. It received a significant facelift however, with a new front fascia and body panels that made it visually similar to the fourth generation of the Golf, although with an interior recognizable from the third generation cars.

Using the 115-horsepower engine from the Golf GL, the Golf Cabriolet continued in production without the expense of engineering a new version on the latest fourth generation platform. The launch of the New Beetle Convertible killed the Golf Cabriolet at the end of 2003.

GOLF TDI 1999–2005
Two-Door and Four-Door Hatchback

A 1.9-liter turbocharged direct-injection (TDI) diesel engine was available in the fourth generation of Golf GL and GLS. It produced 90 horsepower, returned EPA fuel economy figures of 42 miles per gallon in the city and 49 miles per gallon on the highway with a five-speed manual transmission. Enhancements to the previous generation included an integrated turbocharger with variable-vane geometry to increase torque and improve fuel economy. For commuters who need excellent fuel economy but want a bit of fun, the Golf TDI remains a good choice, although at a price of slightly more engine noise than is experienced with the gasoline engine cars. The TDI diesel engine was not available in California or New York after 2000, due to those states' stringent exhaust emission regulations.

"What little pain the Jetta TDI inflicts on drivability strikes us as worth the gain in fuel economy."

—Car and Driver, *March 2004*

DR. DIESEL, I PRESUME?

Gasoline engines use an electric spark arcing through a spark plug to ignite an air/fuel mixture that has been compressed by the upward motion of the piston in the cylinder. A diesel engine does away with the spark plug and instead compresses air to an extremely high pressure (which causes its temperature to rise) and then injects a small amount of fuel into the combustion chamber. This fuel spontaneously ignites, forcing the piston downward and producing power. The compression ratio in a gasoline engine is usually about 10:1; in a diesel engine, the air must be compressed much more (19:1 and higher) to produce ignition when the diesel fuel is injected. This high compression results in extremely high torque outputs from diesel engines.

Adding a VR6 badge to the hatch gave the GTI real authority. *Author*

A revised version of the diesel engine, the TDI PD, was introduced in 2004 in the United States. It used special pump injectors that inject diesel fuel at extremely high pressure into the combustion chamber to reduce noise at idle and improve exhaust emissions. The PD technology increased performance, with 100 horsepower and 177 lb-ft of torque available.

GOLF GTI VR6 1999–2003
Two-Door Hatchback
The VR6 engine had been a hit in the third generation Golfs and Jettas, so it was natural for it to also appear in the fourth generation cars. Now producing 174 horsepower (2 higher than before) and 181 lb-ft of torque (up 8 lb-ft), the 2.8-liter narrow-angle six-cylinder engine did not disappoint with a zero to 60 mile per hour time of 7.7 seconds and the same eagerness to perform it exhibited in the earlier car. The performance increase resulted primarily from a new variable-length intake manifold that automatically tuned the intake tract length for optimum horsepower and low-end torque. In 2000, the VR6 version of the GTI was designated as GTI GLX while the "base" version with the newly introduced 1.8T engine was designated GTI GLS.

In 2003, Volkswagen surprised everyone with the introduction of a 24-valve VR6 engine for the GTI VR6. With four-valves-per-cylinder, this engine produced 200 horsepower at 6,200 rpm and 195 lb-ft of torque at 3,200 rpm. A six-speed manual transmission helped the latest iteration of the VR6 deliver zero to 60 mile per hour times of around 7.5 seconds, a top speed of 146 miles per hour with respectable fuel economy of 21 miles per gallon city and 31 highway. A "Technology Package," exclusive to the GTI VR6, included Climatronic electronic climate control, automatic rain-sensing wipers, and a self-dimming rearview mirror. The 200-horsepower car came with five-spoke 17-inch alloy wheels with 225/45HR-17 all-season performance tires.

The GTI had grown up and become respectable. No longer was it the entry level to performance. The fourth generation cars were larger, quieter, more comfortable, and safer than any GTI had been before, and in the process of becoming refined, they had lost their hooligan nature.

"My fondness for the GTI is ingrained in my psyche, right next to Mom, Dad, and my first 'real' girlfriend. I cannot imagine a world without one."

—European Car, July 2003

The GTI remained Volkswagen's definition of a performance car. *Author*

ONE TO BUY | 2003 GTI VR6

A 2003 GTI VR6 in Mineral Gray with Graphite Leather interior. *Author*

Color: Mineral Gray
Interior: Graphite Leather
Transmission: Six-speed manual
Mileage: 62,866 miles
Asking Price: $13,797

This was a particularly attractive car with its light gray exterior and dark leather interior. It was in the used car section of a major domestic dealership and had been advertised on the Internet. The outside of the car was dirty, but showed no blemishes. The car's high-performance tires were about half-worn, and with the mileage on the car it is safe to assume that they are the car's second set. The mileage is high for a three-year-old car, although the interior showed no signs of excess wear. Driving the car was a treat as it was powerful and quick, and its VR6 engine was very willing. A growling sound from the right front wheel suggested a CV joint or a worn wheel bearing would need to be attended to soon after purchasing the car.

THE EVOLUTION OF THE GTI VR6

	1995–1998	1999–2002	2003
Displacement	2,792 cc	2,792 cc	2,792 cc
Valves/cylinder	2	2	4
Compression ratio	10.0:1	10.0:1	10.5:1
Horsepower	172@5,800 rpm	174@5,800 rpm	200@6,200 rpm
Torque(ft-lbs)	177@4,200 rpm	181@3,200 rpm	195@3,200 rpm

GOLF 1.8T 2001–2005

Two-Door and Four-Door Hatchback

In 2001, Volkswagen introduced the 1.8T engine to the Golf GLS and GTI GLS models. This 1,781-cc engine was derived from the sporty Audi TT, where it produced 180 horsepower. In the GTI, the 1.8T engine was dialed back initially to 150 horsepower at 5,700 rpm and 155 lb-ft of torque at 1,750 rpm. The 1.8T used five valves per cylinder with double overhead camshafts and a turbocharger and intercooler. The 1.8T got off to a slow start, as few could see the advantage of the turbocharged engine over Volkswagen's delightful VR6 powerplant.

That changed in 2002 when Volkswagen upgraded the 1.8T to 180 horsepower and added a six-speed manual transmission to the mix. In reality, aftermarket tuners had already discovered ways to liberate up to 40 more horsepower from the turbocharged engine, primarily through reprogramming the engine management system to produce more turbocharger boost. With 180 horsepower and up, the GTI 1.8T could begin to compete with all but the hottest Honda Civics that were the mainstay of the burgeoning sport-compact car craze.

In the middle of 2002 a special edition of the Golf, called the VW GTI 337 was introduced. Only 1,500 cars were made available to U.S. buyers, and the car had significant upgrades that appealed to enthusiast. These included:

- 180-horsepower 1.8T turbocharged engine
- Six-speed transmission
- Lowered sport suspension
- 18-inch BBS RC wheels
- Brake system from Audi's TT
- Red brake calipers
- Michelin Pilot Sport 225/40-ZR18 tires
- Recaro racing bucket seats
- Monsoon CD/Cassette 8-speaker sound system
- Front air dam
- Rear deck hatch spoiler
- Leather-trimmed steering wheel and shifter with red stitching
- Special edition golf ball shift knob
- Only available in Silver

The addition of the 1.8T turbocharged engine in 2001 gave the Golf a whole new and more sophisticated demeanor. *Author*

With its sport suspension, the ride of the GTI 337 was very firm, but the tradeoff was superb handling. The notchy six-speed transmission with its cable shifter was a joy, and the car would sprint from zero to 60 miles per hour in 6.2 seconds. The name 337, by the way came from Volkswagen's original EA337 engineering project name for the Golf. The GTI 337 was a clearly aimed at the no-nonsense performance driving enthusiast and it has become highly sought after among Volkswagen fans.

In the middle of the following year, 2003, the 20th Anniversary GTI was laun-ched for the U.S. market. This time 4,000 cars were available, with sport suspension, a six-speed manual transmission, 18-inch wheels and tires, and special trim items. Volkswagen had learned from the Trek and K2 third generation cars that special versions of their vehicles would attract buyers, and the GTI was quickly becoming popular again.

"With the new 1.8T option, no longer will you have to make the excuse that you bought a Golf because it's practical and safe. Just let the sound of a whirring turbo and screeching rubber serve as your rationale. "

—Motor Trend, *June 2000*

The 20th Anniversary (in the United States) GTI of 2003 was a strikingly attractive special edition of the GTI. *VWOA*

This special 20th Anniversary Edition badge reminded owners that their cars were descended from the Rabbit. *VWOA*

ONE TO BUY

The rare GTI 337 was named in honor of the original Golf's internal project code name. *eBay photo*

2002 GOLF GTI 337

Color: Silver
Interior: Gray and red 337 Recaro interior
Transmission: Six-speed manual
Mileage: 14,975
eBay Buy it Now Price: $16,500

This eBay-listed GTI 337 appears to be quite a good opportunity. The 337 models were a rare special edition, and this car (reportedly owned by a 55-year old nonsmoker who didn't drive it much) looks from its photographs to be in exceptional condition. A few upgrades have been made, including a K&N air filter, clear side marker lights, and different center caps for the 18-inch BBS wheels. The original parts also come with the car. Although one should always be cautious buying a car sight unseen over the Internet, the low miles and inclusion of a Carfax Report in the listing should give the prospective buyer confidence in the purchase of this rare special edition GTI.

The R32 was Volkswagen's answer to the all-wheel drive Subaru WRX STi and was the most potent version of the Golf produced to date. *VWOA*

The R32's interior was designed for serious performance fun. *VWOA*

R32 2004–2005

Two-Door Hatchback

In 2004, Volkswagen introduced the most potent version of the Golf ever seen. Dubbed the R32, this 3.2-liter 24-valve VR6-powered fourth generation Golf produced 240 horsepower, driving through a six-speed manual transmission to all four wheels (using VW's 4MOTION all-wheel drive system). Interest in sport compact cars was reaching new heights, thanks in large part to all-wheel drive cars like the Subaru WRX STi and Mitsubishi Evo. Volkswagen's offerings were falling behind these rally-based performance machines, and something needed to be done.

The R32 was fast. *Motor Trend* measured 5.9 seconds in its zero-to-60-mile per hour tests and 14.2 seconds at 97.6 miles per hour in its quarter-mile acceleration runs. With 18-inch wheels and tires, a sport suspension almost an inch lower than the standard GTI suspension, dual exhaust pipes, stiff front and rear anti-roll (sway) bars and an interior that combined luxury with performance, the R32 owner had no problem justifying its $29,100 price tag. The adaptation of the 4MOTION all-wheel drive resulted in the use of a true multilink independent rear suspension in place of the GTI's torsion-beam axle. Four-piston brake calipers and 13.1-inch ventilated front discs provided stopping power.

Twin exhausts from the 3.2-liter VR6 engine added to the performance image. *VWOA*

Although the Volkswagen R32 couldn't quite match the acceleration of the rally-bred Subaru and Mitsubishi offerings, it was the quickest production machine that Volkswagen had ever produced. *European Car* magazine, which gave the R32 its 2004 "Grand Prix" award, said, "The R32 reinforces why we love cars: driving something alive and fun." They also added, "The R32 is to the Golf what the GT 350 is to the Mustang."

"The R32 gets you 90 percent of the performance and 125 percent of the interior content at the same price as those pesky-pesky turbocars. It's the polished, adult approach to an edgy, adolescent high-performance craving."

—Motor Trend, *June 2004*

JETTA GL 1999–2004
Four-Door Sedan

Despite the popularity of the GTI versions of the Golf, Volks-wagen's big seller by far in North America was the Jetta. The new Jetta, as with previous models, shared much with its Golf sibling (60 percent of the parts were shared) and occupant safety was a priority. The frame was reinforced and impact beams spread deformation energy over the vehicle structure. Like the new Golf, in addition to front impact air bags, side impact air bags were provided for the front seat passengers. The side air bags were integrated into the front seats to provide proper positioning for occupants of a variety of sizes.

The fourth generation Jetta's wheelbase grew by 1.5 inches, and its overall length was 1 inch shorter. The Jetta GL's base 115-horsepower 2.0-liter engine wasn't as powerful as the cars from Honda and Toyota with which the Jetta competed, but

"Those who like typical VW driving dynamics will love the new Jetta, and those who don't won't get it and probably never will."

—Motor Trend, *April 1999*

Volkswagen's sedan still offered a European driving feel that the others couldn't quite duplicate.

The base Jetta GL was well equipped even in standard trim with a telescopic/tilt steering wheel, premium stereo cassette, air conditioning, dual side air bags, anti-lock brakes, rear headrests, 15-inch alloy wheels, remote locking, pollen air filter, trunk power outlet, child seat attachment, rear reading lights, and trunk netting and tie downs. This was a refined and comfortable European sedan (that was still made in Mexico) that provided Volkswagen with a broad range of upscale customers who were looking for stylish, yet affordable transportation.

JETTA GLS 1999–2004
Four-Door Sedan

The Jetta GLS was available in base trim with a 115-horsepower 2.0-liter four-cylinder engine and optionally with a 174-horsepower VR6 engine. A GLS TDI version was also available with Volkswagen's 1.9-liter TDI diesel engine. Throughout its

"Considering Jetta's 'operational' competitors, Honda Civic and Toyota Corolla, and its 'strategic' competitors, Acura Integra and BMW 3 Series, it is rather obvious which competitors have been eclipsed and which should be afraid."

—Motor Trend, *April 1999*

ONE TO BUY | 2000 JETTA GLS 2.0

This 2000 Jetta GLS 2.0 was really just an average used car. *Author*

Color: Teal
Interior: Gray cloth
Transmission: Five-speed manual
Mileage: 80,739 miles
Asking Price: $8,797

If you were looking for an average used Jetta, this car would fit the bill. It was clean with just a few parking lot dings on the outside. This Jetta had a new set of tires. Under the hood it was nearly spotless, but the interior showed wear on the driver's seat and on the driver's door trim. The car drove well, although the clutch release was right at the very top of the pedal travel. There is no clutch adjustment on this car, so likely it will need a new clutch cable sometime soon. The mileage was high for the year, but the car ran and drove well.

Another used Jetta with a slightly scruffy exterior. *Author*

The leather interior of this high-mileage car was showing some wear. *Author*

Color: Teal
Interior: Gray leather
Transmission: Automatic
Mileage: 80,786 miles
Asking Price: $9,995

The most common color for Jetta GL 2.0 models seems to be the green-blue hue of teal. Fortunately, the Jetta looks good in this color. This car was at an independent used car lot and was parked next to a BMW and an Audi. The car had a cracked grille, which the salesman said would be repaired. It also had significant scuffs on the outer edges of the bumpers. Inside the interior was leather and the driver's seat was worn and slightly discolored. The car started and drove well, with the automatic transmission shifting properly. Although there was nothing specifically wrong with this car, it hadn't been loved by its previous owner. With so many better cars on the market, it wasn't an inviting a prospect to own.

life, the GLS was always a slightly nicer and better equipped version of the base GL model, usually with alloy wheels, a sunroof, better sound system offerings, and better interior trim materials.

JETTA TDI 1999–2004
Four-Door Sedan
As with the Golf, a 1.9-liter turbocharged direct-injection (TDI) diesel engine was available in the fourth generation of the Jetta GL and GLS. It produced 90 horsepower, returned EPA fuel economy figures of 42 miles per gallon in the city and 49 on the highway with a five-speed manual transmission. Unfortunately, also as with the Golf, the TDI diesel engine was not available in California or New York after 2000, again due to exhaust emission regulations.

Volkswagen's updated diesel engine, the TDI PD, was introduced to the U.S. market Jetta in 2004. It uses special pump injectors that inject diesel fuel at extremely high pressure into the combustion chamber to reduce noise at idle and improve exhaust emissions. The PD technology increased performance, as 100 horsepower and 177 lb-ft of torque were available.

Once again, the TDI badge denotes the frugal high fuel economy of a diesel engine. *Author*

CHAPTER 3 | WHAT MODEL TO BUY

JETTA WAGON 2001–2004

Four-Door Wagon

In 2001, Volkswagen added a station wagon to the Jetta line. At first, considering the hatchback Golf's easy cargo space accessibility, this would have seemed unnecessary. The Jetta Wagon, however, had enough space to carry four adults and a large amount of luggage, something the Golf had trouble doing. Available with gasoline and diesel engines, the Jetta Wagon was never a huge seller, but was popular among its practical minded owners.

The Jetta Wagon appeared in 2001 and was available with every engine option, from a frugal TDI diesel through a potent 2.8-liter VR6. *Author*

A TDI diesel makes a Jetta Wagon into an excellent choice for long commutes. *Carol Blotter*

2003 JETTA TDI WAGON

John Deikis
Psychologist
Chelsea, Michigan

John Deikis is a real car guy. He's owned Porsches, VWs, and Saabs, and he competes in vintage races, driving an old MG. Every day, he commutes 160 miles round-trip to his job as a psychologist in Battle Creek. That's over 40,000 miles per year, and when John wanted to replace his aging Honda Accord, he carefully considered a diesel-powered Volkswagen. "It took a few months to find one, but really it took me that long to convince myself that I wanted one. I'd thought about a Honda Insight. I'd had a diesel Rabbit years ago, and wanted to see what the latest diesels were like, but was concerned about all of the problems with the TDI that have been reported on the nationwide VW enthusiast's web site (www.TDIClub.com)."

Deikis finally settled on a silver 2003 Jetta TDI Wagon with 43,000 miles on the clock. "I wanted the space. My son's Golf can handle lots of cargo, and I figured the Wagon could take even more. It has four doors, but is still small enough to make a good commuter car." John was looking for reliability too, and on that front the Jetta TDI has had only a so-so record. His Jetta has been in the shop several times for things like a fault in the wiring loom for the diesel glow plugs and a broken sunroof. More seriously, the driver seat started smoldering when the seat heater shorted, a problem that apparently happens with some frequency. The repair included new upholstery and heaters, although the side bolsters no longer have heater elements. After some negotiation, Volkswagen even paid to replace a pair of John's pants that were singed.

On the plus side, Deikis reports getting 45 miles per gallon of B20 Biodiesel fuel at a more or less constant 80 miles per hour on his long commutes. "The seats are comfortable, the fit and finish are good, it's quiet at high speed and, although it's not a sports car, it handles and corners well with surprisingly good ride comfort." John's commuter car currently has around 123,000 miles on it, but his plans are ambitious. "I hope to drive it well over a half-million miles over the next few years."

JETTA GLX 1999–2003

Four-Door Sedan

The fourth generation of the Jetta continued with a GLX model, featuring the 2.8-liter VR6 engine. This was a particularly nice car with the smooth and refined power from the six-cylinder engine well matched to a sporty yet comfortable interior.

In 2000, the GLX received an 8-speaker Monsoon sound system as standard equipment (it was optional on other Jetta models) and in 2001, a Sport Luxury option group included a sport suspension with 17-inch performance tires. Leather upholstery was available. In 2002 a six-speed manual transmission helped reinforce the performance sedan image; a five-speed automatic was also available. In the middle of 2002 the 2.8-liter engine was uprated with four valves per cylinder and now produced 200 horsepower.

The GLX with its VR6 engine continued until the end of 2003, when it was replaced by the Jetta GLI. Interestingly, the very first 2004 GLI models came with the 2.8-liter VR6 engine, until February of 2004, when it was replaced with the 1.8-liter turbocharged four-cylinder engine in all Jetta GLI models.

Left: Adding the VR6 engine to a Jetta made it into a GLX and a real high-performance sport sedan. *Author*

Below: The 2004 Jetta GLI came with a 180-horsepower 1.8T engine, 18-inch BBS alloy-wheels, and a lowered sport suspension. *VWOA*

The Jetta GLI interior included Recaro seats and a special steering wheel. *VWOA*

JETTA GLI 2004

Four-Door Sedan

In February 2004, the year before launching the new fifth generation of the Jetta, Volkswagen provided a Jetta GLI with a 180-horsepower 1.8T turbocharged engine, six-speed manual transmission, 18-inch BBS alloy wheels and performance tires, a power sunroof, Monsoon sound system, lowered sports suspension, rear spoiler, side skirts, red GLI badges front and rear, and darkened headlights and taillights. Inside were special GLI Recaro sport seats and a special steering wheel and interior trim package. It was a nice way to send off the last of the fourth generation Jettas.

STRENGTHS AND WEAKNESSES OF THE FOURTH GENERATION

The fourth generation cars have a real advantage over previous models when it comes to rust and corrosion protection. Laser welding, weld bonding, and fully galvanized sheet metal helped meet this goal. In addition to double-side-galvanized steel, the new Golf underwent a zinc-phosphate coating, cathodic dip coating, application of a water-diluted filler, application of a water-based color coat and a two-coat clear coat. Volkswagen offered a 12-year warranty against body perforation to back up its confidence in its corrosion protection.

One area that can cause a minor corrosion problem is the washer jet on the rear hatch of Golf models. The hose that feeds this jet can sometimes pull loose, so that a leak will develop, dripping windshield-washing fluid into the hatch and eventually causing corrosion. The fix is simple: pull the interior trim panel back (carefully) and push the hose back onto the nozzle.

The interiors of all of the cars were quite durable, although rattles from the door speakers can be annoying. The heated front seats, a nice feature in northern climates, can short out, causing the seat itself to catch on fire. The sunroof is also prone to squeaks and problems, and the fix is usually a replacement of the whole roof and track system. There were also occasional problems with window regulators that allowed the door window to fall into the door.

The 2.0-liter inline four-cylinder and VR6 engines were largely carried over from the third generation and had few problems. The ignition coil pack problem from the third generation VR6 engine cars followed on into the fourth generation and can cause the engine to run roughly.

The TDI diesel engine, however, proved to be trouble-prone, due in part to its emissions control systems. The engine was equipped with a crankcase ventilation system (CCV) that pulled oily fumes from the crankcase and introduced them to the intake system, where they could burn up in the combustion chamber. It also had an exhaust gas recirculation (EGR) system that introduced burned exhaust gasses back into the intake to help reduce exhaust emissions. When

The fourth generation cars, like this 2003 Jetta Wolfsburg Edition, used double-sided galvanized steel to all but eliminate the rust problems typical of previous generation cars. *VWOA*

the oil fumes mixed with the carbon particles from the EGR, a sticky black tarlike substance formed in the intake. This buildup would eventually impede airflow, causing a decrease in engine performance. The repair was to disassemble the intake system and clean out the tar buildup, but the solution was to fit an aftermarket oil vapor separator that could reduce the amount of oil reaching the intake.

Other diesel problems may result from the quality of the fuel used. Frequenting stations with high amounts of fuel turnover can help reduce the amount of water with which the fuel filter must deal. Diesel engines also suffered from short-lived mass airflow sensors in the engine management system, and the part was expensive to replace. In addition, the connectors in the wire harness for the diesel glow plugs can get dirty, causing the check engine light to illuminate and making the engine hard to start.

Although Volkswagen's manual transmissions are a pleasure to use, they don't stand up to abuse very well. Enthusiastic drivers need to baby them just a bit to prevent future failures. The clutch return spring in early cars (1999) can fall out of position and the clutch pedal may not return fully. Although they were an improvement over the previous generation's transmissions, they still used rivets to hold the ring gear in the differential to its carrier, and if a rivet comes out it can wreak havoc. The solution is to replace all of the rivets with hardened bolts. In addition, the reverse gear is not synchronized, so shifting into reverse while the car is rolling forward can cause damage that will result in the car being stuck in reverse.

The suspension also was built on established principles and is reliable, aside from a recall in 2000–2001 for a front-suspension control arm that could gradually loosen and separate from its bracket under normal driving.

Some owners of some models, especially Jettas, have noted that the plastic tray under the engine is very prone to damage in areas of the country where it snows. The low ground clearance of the cars is part of the problem and some

owners fit longer springs to raise the car and make it more capable in winter driving. An aluminum under tray for the front is also available on the aftermarket, and is actually cheaper than the plastic replacement part from Volkswagen.

Buying a used fourth-generation Golf or Jetta should not be an ordeal. The cars benefited from Volkswagen's experience with the three previous generations. Corrosion protection had reached a high level, and mechanically the cars were well developed and used proven components. Aside from rejecting specific vehicles that have been wrecked or abused or that have abnormally high mileage, the biggest choice facing a prospective buyer is to decide on a fuel-sipping economy car, a luxury sedan, a sporty convertible, or a sport-compact demon.

Buying a fourth generation car should not be an ordeal, as there are plenty of them on the market. *Volkswagen AG*

CHAPTER 4 | **BONDING**

You've finally done it. After doing all of the research, driving a bunch of cars, going over the Buyer's Checklist in Appendix A, haggling with the owner or dealer, you've finally made your choice and bought a Volkswagen Golf or Jetta. If your car came with a full set of service records, and they show that everything is up to date, then off you go to enjoy your new toy. More likely, the records are spotty or even nonexistent, and you really don't know the last time the tires were rotated or the air filter was changed.

Don't despair! There are many projects that you can do in your own garage or driveway that will make your Volkswagen feel like new. Most of these projects are inexpensive, requiring just a few ordinary tools and will not only result in improved reliability and performance, but doing them will create a bond between you and your Volkswagen. Before you get started, though, there are some basic things about safety you'll want to review, and some suggestions about tools and how to use them that you'll find helpful.

SAFETY

Garage safety is an important topic. If you injure yourself and need to heal, it'll be just that much longer before you can go out and play with your Golf or Jetta. Most of garage safety is common sense, but some of it is proper technique. All of it is your first priority when you are working on your car.

Work space

The first thing you need to do is create a safe working environment. If you have an indoor garage, you are ahead of the game, but a lot of the projects we have in mind you can do outdoors on a sunny day. The first thing your workspace needs is plenty of light. This can come from plug-in drop lights, good overhead lighting or even portable flood lights. A fluorescent light gives off very little heat and can light up the entire area under the hood. Make sure the cords for your lights don't create a tripping hazard and that you keep your hands and any liquids away from extremely hot glass light bulbs.

Not everybody has all the space they want, but make sure that you have enough space to work around your car on both sides, at front and at rear. If this means moving the lawnmower outside for a day or two, then do so. There is almost nothing worse than tripping over a yard tool and having it fall into and dent your pride and joy.

If it is cold outside, and you have the garage door shut, make sure you open it before starting the engine. Carbon monoxide gas is an invisible killer, and running an engine in a closed garage will be lethal in a very short period of time.

Fire hazards

It goes without saying that you should never smoke while working on your car.

Gasoline is almost unbelievably flammable, and any time you are working on the fuel system there is a chance that a stray spark could cause a fire. Keep at least one good-sized fire extinguisher handy. It's a good idea to make sure the extinguisher is near the exit so you won't be trapped if you are running to get it and the unthinkable should happen.

Beyond gasoline, a variety of other automotive chemicals and lubricants are flammable, and be careful whenever and wherever you use them. Keep open flames away from the battery, as flammable hydrogen gas can build up near the battery when it is charging and cause an explosion. Remember that a stack of oily rags can also build up heat and spontaneously combust under certain conditions, so make sure you dispose of rags properly. Don't leave them lying around your garage.

Eye Protection

In many ways, your eyes are the most vulnerable part of your body. Any time you work under the car, dirt or road debris can fall into your eyes. Not only is this painful, it can leave you temporarily blind and you may further injure yourself as you try to seek help. Solvents sprayed from aerosol cans can splash back and hit your eyes and bolts can break and sent shards of metal into your face.

Fortunately, the solution is easy: wear OSHA-approved eye protection whenever you are working in the garage.

Jewelry and Loose Clothing

You should always remove watches, rings, and other jewelry when you work on your car. Such metallic materials will conduct electricity and could produce a short circuit with the car's electrical system and a painful burn to your skin.

Loose clothing can get caught in a running engine or in power tools and cause an injury. So can hair. If you have long hair, put it under a hat to keep it safely out of the way.

Protect Your Skin

Many of the solvents used in automotive work can cause cancer, and you should try to limit your exposure to them. Rubber gloves that are designed to be resistant to such chemicals allow you to work freely without worrying about long-term effects. For ordinary mechanical repairs, a pair of heavy-duty mechanics gloves will protect your hands from cuts, scratches, and bumps, while still giving the flexibility needed to attach fasteners and work safely.

It takes some time to get used to working with gloves on, but the payoff is fewer injuries and cleaner hands. Gloves can also help prevent burns when you touch a hot exhaust system or when you're changing brake pads. Be careful about wearing absorbent gloves when you are draining a hot cooling system, as the liquid coolant will quickly go through the glove and cook your hand inside.

When you finish working, there are a variety of waterless hand cleaners available that cut through oil and grease. After using the waterless stuff, wash your hands with soap and water and then consider using a moisturizer on your skin to help replace all of the natural skin oils that you have just removed.

Working Under the Car

A variety of maintenance projects will require you to raise the car and sometimes remove the wheels. You should:

- Always use an appropriate floor jack to lift the car.
- Never work under a car that is supported only by a jack.
- Always use at least two jack stands to support the car.
- Never use cinder blocks, bricks, or other objects to support the vehicle.
- Always make sure you are lifting the vehicle in a safe way that won't damage the underside of the vehicle. (There are two jacking points on each side of the car, marked by indentations in the lower panel, just behind the front wheel and just ahead of the rear wheel.)
- Never start the vehicle and engage a gear when one drive wheel is touching the floor. (One way to ensure safety is to disconnect the battery when the car is in the air.)
- Always block the wheels on the opposite side or end that you are lifting. (If you are raising the right front, block the left rear.)
- Never jack up the car on an uneven or loose surface that can shift and cause the car to fall.

Special Considerations

There are several systems in modern cars that can be dangerous for the home mechanic:

Air conditioning—The A/C system operates at extremely high pressures and contains dangerous gasses. Aside from changing the drive belt, the air conditioning should be worked on by those who have the necessary tools

VOLKSWAGEN DEALER

Jennifer Schmelz Wilke is the director of parts and service and the third generation to work at her family's Volkswagen dealership. *Author*

Jennifer Schmelz Wilke
Director of Parts and Service
Schmelz Countryside Volkswagen
St. Paul, Minnesota

A surprising number of Volkswagen dealers have been in business for decades. Such is the case for Schmelz Countryside Volkswagen in St. Paul, Minnesota. Jennifer Schmelz Wilke is the third generation of her family to work at the Volkswagen dealership. Her grandfather started the business in 1960 and quickly grew it into one of the leading Volkswagen sales and service centers in the Midwest.

Her experience with Volkswagen customers has left Jennifer with some strong impressions. "Volkswagen owners tend to be better educated, and as such they understand the need to take care of their cars," explains Jennifer. The dealership's sprawling service bay is a busy place, and fully half of the cars in for service are third or fourth generation Golfs and Jettas. "VW owners are very proud of their cars and loyal to the brand. They understand quality, and they understand that service is a process that will keep their car going," she adds.

Most of the cars in the service area are in for routine maintenance, and Schmelz Countryside is very clear that they only follow what Volkswagen recommends when it comes to service. "We show the customer what Volkswagen recommends at each mileage and don't try to sell them extras that they don't need," Jennifer said. "These are very reliable and durable cars, if you maintain them as the factory intended."

The dealership won't do any modifications to customers' cars, but will refer them to several local Volkswagen specialists for performance upgrades to suspensions or exhaust systems. Just selling Volkswagens as they came from the manufacturer and maintaining them by the book in the service department has been the secret to more than 40 years of success for Schmelz Countryside Volkswagen.

and experience to do so safely. Some unscrupulous mechanics have begun using low-cost propane or butane to replace R134 when they work on A/C systems. Although these hydrocarbons will work, they are extremely flammable and any leak could cause an explosion. What's more, the use of such materials voids your car's warranty. Make sure your A/C technician is properly trained and knows how to work on Volkswagen's system.

Air bags and seatbelt tensioners—Air bags inflate when an explosive charge rapidly produces a huge volume of gas that inflates the bag. These explosive devices are extremely dangerous and only factory trained service technicians should test, disassemble, or service these units. Remember, late-model Volkswagens can have several air bags and care must be taken when working on the dashboard or seats. In addition, some later Volkswagen models have pyrotechnic seatbelt tensioners that use a small explosive charge to pull the front seatbelts tight in the event of a collision. Improper handling of these devices can be extremely dangerous, and only trained service technicians should work on them.

A SHOP MANUAL

Although we're showing you the basics of Volkswagen maintenance, you'll really need a shop manual for your specific vehicle to get the job done right. The Volkswagen factory shop manual is an excellent reference and can be obtained from any Volkswagen dealership.

An equally good alternative is one of the Bentley manuals from Bentley Publishers (www.BentleyPublishers.com) of Cambridge, Massachusetts. One volume covers the third generation of Volkswagen Jetta, Golf, GTI, and Cabriolet (Bentley Stock Number: VG99, ISBN: 0-8376-0366-8) while the fourth generation cars are covered by the Volkswagen Jetta, Golf GTI Service Manual (Bentley Stock Number: VG05, ISBN: 0-8376-1251-9).

THE RIGHT TOOLS

While you won't need a full mechanic's tool chest to work on your Volkswagen, you will need a set of wrenches and sockets, screwdrivers, pliers, a hammer, and a few other hand tools. It makes no sense to buy cheap tools. They won't last as long as high-quality tools; they can round off the heads of bolts, making them difficult to remove; and they can be dangerous if they distort or break when you are using them with real force. Buy the good stuff and it will last a lifetime.

All of the nuts, bolts, and fasteners in your Volkswagen are metric; that means that you'll need metric wrenches and sockets to work on your car. Don't try to use SAE-sized wrenches that are "close," as eventually you'll end up rounding off or damaging the bolt.

Maybe the most important tool you can own is a torque wrench. Nearly every bolt and nut found on your Volkswagen has a proper torque specification, which will ensure that it will remain tight without being over tightened. You don't have to use the torque wrench on every bolt (although you could), but certainly it should be used on critical fasteners. To work on your Golf or Jetta your tool collection should include:

- Metric combination wrenches—8- to 19-millimeter
- Metric socket set—8- to 19-millimeter
- Spark plug socket
- Assorted metric Allen wrenches (including a 17-millimeter for the transmission oil drain)
- A few assorted Torx-drive sockets
- Socket ratchet drive
- Ratchet extensions (3-inch and 6-inch)
- Torque wrench
- Two slotted screwdrivers (big and small)
- Two Phillips screwdrivers (big and small)
- Needle-nose pliers
- Slip-joint pliers
- Adjustable Crescent wrench
- Ball-peen hammer
- Pry-bar
- Flashlight
- Fluorescent drop light
- Floor jack
- Jack stands
- Wheel chocks
- Utility knife
- Rubber gloves
- Mechanic's gloves
- Waterless hand cleaner

SCAN TOOLS

All of the Volkswagen models covered in this book use electronic engine management systems to control fuel delivery and ignition. They also use an On-Board Diagnostic (OBD) system that is integrated into the engine management system.

All cars sold in the United States since the late 1980s have OBD, per government regulation. In 1996, all cars sold in the United States began to use the second generation of OBD, called OBD-II. All fourth-generation Golfs and Jettas are OBD-II compliant. Third-generation models are a mixed bag; there's a sticker under the hood that will tell you whether or not the car is OBD-II compliant. If you plan to buy a scan tool for your third or fourth generation Golf or Jetta, make sure you get one designed to work with the OBD system on your car.

The OBD system monitors emissions-related components, the automatic transmission, the anti-lock braking system, and the air bag system. An irregularity or fault in any of these systems will store a trouble code in the OBD system memory and illuminate the "check engine" light on the dashboard.

Checking the OBD memory for fault codes and resetting the memory takes a special factory scan tool (VAG 1551/1552) or the aftermarket equivalent. Unfortunately for the home mechanic, doing something as simple as changing the car's battery can sometimes trigger a fault code that illuminates the check engine light. Although aftermarket scan tools can be used to examine the codes, in most cases such work should be carried out by a trained service technician with access to the proper tools and most recent factory updates.

ENVIRONMENTAL CONCERNS

Many of the lubricants, materials, and chemicals used in modern automobiles pose risks to the environment if they are not handled and disposed of properly. Automotive antifreeze coolant, for example, has a sweet odor and flavor that is particularly attractive to cats and dogs, yet it is fatally poisonous if ingested in even small amounts. Used motor oil is a hazardous waste material and may contain heavy metals from worn engine bearings.

Always make sure you've thought of how you will dispose of fluids before you drain them, and ensure that your drain pan is more than big enough to hold all of the liquids. Never pour automotive fluids onto the ground, down a drain, or into a ditch, stream, or pond.

Don't mix different kinds of liquids together in the same waste containers. Many quick oil change businesses and auto parts stores will accept used motor oil for recycling as long as it has not been mixed with other chemicals. Consult local authorities as to the proper way to dispose of automotive wastes in your area.

MAINTENANCE SCHEDULES

Volkswagen has a specific recommended maintenance schedule for your vehicle. Following it will help assure that your vehicle will be reliable and maintain its high level of performance.

In this chapter we will discuss several maintenance procedures that go beyond Volkswagen's requirements. Such extra vigilance is not harmful and may help maintain your car at its peak of operational performance.

10 MAINTENANCE PROJECTS YOU CAN DO

1 DUST AND POLLEN FILTER CHANGE

 DIFFICULTY: Easy

 MODELS: All Mk IV models (1999-2005)

COST: $

 PARTS: Pollen filter

 TOOLS: none

Some late Mark III models and all Mark IV Golf and Jetta models (1999–2005) have a dust and pollen filter as a part of the heating and ventilation system. This filter is a boon to asthma sufferers, as it can remove pollen from the air coming into the car's ventilation system. Access to the filter is through a trim panel located under the hood on the passenger side of the vehicle.

How often do I change the filter?

Volkswagen recommends that the dust and pollen filter be replaced every 20,000 miles. Obviously if you have been driving through especially dusty environments, you might want to replace it more often.

DUST AND POLLEN FILTER CHANGE PROCEDURE

1. Open the hood.

2. Remove the rubber gasket surrounding the cover on the passenger side of the vehicle under the windshield.

The dust and pollen filter is under the cowl on the passenger side of the vehicle. The first step is removing the plastic cover, held on with three bolts. *Author*

The pollen filter element in its plastic frame can be pulled out of its recess. This can be a difficult process. *Author*

3. Press the tabs on either side of the filter frame and pull it with the filter out of its holder.

Above: Remove the filter element from its plastic frame and replace it with a new element. *Author*

4. Pull the filter out of the frame and replace it with a new filter element.

   HINT: make sure the filter is pointing in the right direction in the frame

5. Orient the frame back into its holder and carefully press it back into place.

Slide the filter element and frame back into position. It may be easier if you pull upward slightly on the plastic molding above the filter opening. *Author*

Make sure you have the filter properly seated or you will get leaks into the passenger foot well when it rains. *Author*

6. Refit the cover, making sure the rubber gasket is in place.

   HINT: The cover has a lip that makes it difficult to get into place. Some mechanics cut this lip off to make installation easier, but the lip is important. It keeps water from entering, and if you have a leak in the passenger footwell, it could be that someone has cracked or improperly installed the cover.

   If you find your cover is missing the lip or is cracked, replace it. They're not too expensive, and, given the location of various expensive electronic components, a faulty cover can cause problems far more severe than just wet feet.

Reinstall the outer cover; do not overtighten the three retaining screws. *Author*

2 HEADLIGHT, BRAKE LIGHT, AND INDICATOR BULB REPLACEMENT

DIFFICULTY: Easy

MODELS: All

COST: $–$$

PARTS: Replacement light bulb

TOOLS: Hand tools

After opening the door, the bulb holder can be accessed. *Author*

Over the third and fourth generation of the Golf and Jetta, Volkswagen has used a variety of different types of headlights and taillights. Although there are some differences between them, the overall bulb-changing procedure is quite similar from model to model.

Headlights

The headlights bulbs are enclosed in headlight housings that include the reflector and the headlight lens. Single or dual bulbs may be used, depending upon the models. The bulbs are changed working from the back side of the headlight. The bulb holder is removed by releasing a spring clip and withdrawing the bulb socket and wiring.

It is important to never touch the glass of the replacement bulb with bare skin. This will leave traces of skin oils on the glass which will cause the bulb to burn out prematurely. Clean gloves or a tissue should be used to handle the bulbs.

Volkswagen uses halogen headlight bulbs. A variety of replacement bulbs are available. Some of these provide silver or blue lighting, similar to the High Intensity Discharge (HID) headlights available on high-end luxury and performance cars. Uprated bulbs cost around $40–$50.

HID light bulbs are also available that fit in the original housings, but most lighting manufacturers do not recommend

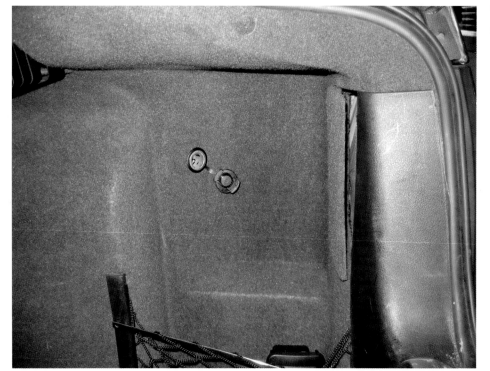

The taillight bulbs are accessed through a trap door in the trunk. *Author*

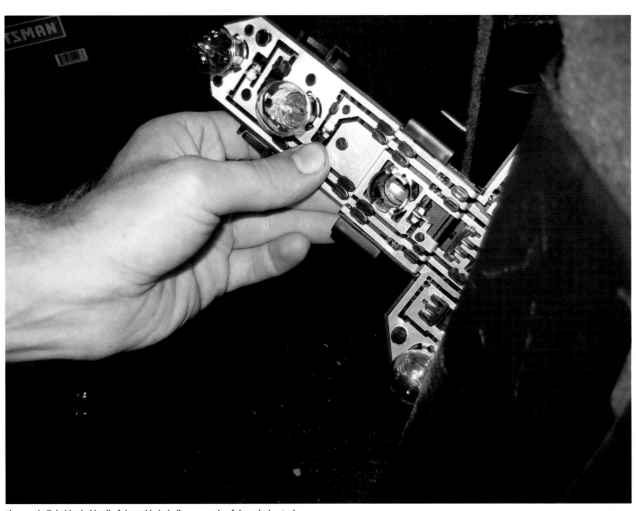

The rear bulb holder holds all of the tail light bulbs on its side of the vehicle. *Author*

The headlights and the front bulbs are accessed through a panel under the hood at each side of the car. *Author*

You may need to use a screwdriver to pry down the clip that holds the access panel. *Author*

using them, as their extra light output will overwhelm the optics of the headlight, producing glare for oncoming drivers. Complete replacement HID headlight units are available for Volkswagen models, costing more than $400.

Brake Light and Indicators

In general, bulbs for taillights, and brake lights can be replaced without removing the entire lighting unit from the vehicle. Access from behind is usually accomplished by releasing retainer clips and pulling the bulb holder out of its housing, at which point the bulbs are easy to access.

For taillights and brake lights, the access is through the trunk, after first removing an access panel in the trunk liner. At the front, some models have the turn-signal and parking light bulbs integral with the headlight housing unit in bulb holders that are held in place with spring clips.

The panel can then be removed. *Author*

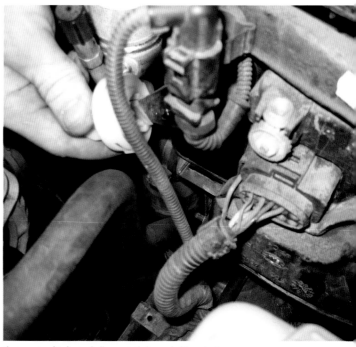

The turn signal indicator bulbs are in their own holders. *Author*

Above: Remove the turn signal bulbs from their holders and replace. *Author*

Left: Make sure that the panel returns to its original position against the gasket that prevents water from entering the lighting unit. *Author*

3 OIL CHANGE

 DIFFICULTY: Easy

 MODELS: All

 COST: $$

 PARTS: Oil, oil filter, drain plug seal

 TOOLS: Wrenches, torque wrench, oil filter wrench or big pliers, basin to catch oil

With the arrival of quick oil change shops on almost every street corner, few people change their own oil any more. Yet changing oil puts you in touch with the inner workings of your Volkswagen and gives you a chance to inspect other things that might otherwise go neglected.

Why change oil?

Automobile engines rely on a constant supply of pressurized oil to prevent engine parts from rubbing together and wearing. Motor oil forms an extremely thin film between metal parts, and this film can be disturbed when oil becomes dirty with contamination or begins to break down over time.

Oil can get dirty from airborne particles that make it past the engine's air filter when the vehicle is driven in dusty environments. Oil contamination can also result as a byproduct of the combustion process, which mixes small particles of soot and water vapor into the oil.

The purpose of the oil filter is to strain these particles of dirt and soot out of the engine oil. Changing the filter at the same time that the oil is changed removes this dirt from the engine completely.

Kinds of Oil

Traditional motor oils are refined from crude petroleum stocks that are pumped from the ground. During the refining process, heavy grades of oils and paraffin waxes are distilled out, leaving motor oil.

Motor oil comes in different viscosities, which is a measure of how thick the oil is at different temperatures. You can think of it as how easily the motor oil pours. In the old days, motor oils came in single viscosities, but today's multigrade oils have been engineered to provide low viscosity (easy pouring) at start-up when the engine is cold and high viscosity after the engine has warmed to provide maximum protection.

Additives such as detergents and dispersal agents are added to motor oil to help keep the inside of the engine clean and help the oil filter trap dirt. For this reason, the oil filter should always be replaced when changing oil.

Synthetic motor oils have recently become popular. These are engineered fluids that are not refined from petro-

leum crude, but rather constructed into chains of carbon atoms to have precisely the characteristics that the oil manufacturer specifies. Generally speaking, synthetic oils are more resistant to high-temperature breakdown and can provide a margin of safety beyond ordinary petroleum-based oils. What's more, they flow more easily in cold temperatures. If you live in a cold climate, synthetic oils are an excellent choice for winter driving.

TRACK DAYS AND HIGH PERFORMANCE DRIVING

High speeds and high-performance driving put extra stress on the engine's lubrication system. Make sure you have fresh oil in your engine and that it is topped to the proper level. This is an excellent time to take advantage of the superior protection afforded by synthetic oils. Some manufacturers make high-performance synthetic motor oils for racing (usually 15W-50 viscosity) that are a great choice for cars that see use on a racetrack. Make sure you warm the engine up completely before driving hard on the track. High pressure caused by cold oil has been known to blow the oil filter completely off of the engine. You might want to bring a spare oil filter to the track with you, just in case this unlikely event happens.

How often do I change oil?

Volkswagen has specific oil change intervals established for each of its engine families.

All 1993–1996 models:
- Change oil and filter at 7,500 miles
- Change oil and filter at 15,000 miles
- Change oil and filter every 7,500 miles thereafter

All 1997–2005 models:
- 2.0-liter Inline-4: Change oil and filter at 5,000 miles, 10,000 miles, 20,000 miles, and every 10,000 miles thereafter
- 2.8-liter VR6: Change oil and filter at 5,000 miles, 10,000 miles, 20,000 miles, and every 10,000 miles thereafter
- 1.8T turbocharged Inline-4: Change oil and filter every 5,000 miles
- 1.9 TDI turbocharged diesel Inline-4: Change oil and filter at 5,000 miles, 10,000 miles, 20,000 miles, and every 10,000 miles thereafter

Note: If you feel uncomfortable with a 5,000-mile or 10,000-mile oil change interval, you can use without any concerns the tried-and-true 3,000-mile interval that many auto maintenance experts recommend.

Which oil do I use for my VW?

Gasoline engines—Most four- and six-cylinder Volkswagen gasoline engines left the factory filled with 5W-40 motor oil. This is a good choice, as it provides good flow at cold temperatures (the "5" designation) and high viscosity at high temperatures (the "40" designation). Other acceptable oils include 10W-40 and 15W-50.

Volkswagen says the oil can be either petroleum-based or synthetic, although the extra high-temperature protection and easier cold flow provided by synthetic oil makes it particularly attractive for use in the 1.8T turbocharged inline four-cylinder engine.

Diesel engines—The 1.9 TDI and 1.9 TDI PD turbocharged diesel engines require a special type of engine oil formulated specifically for diesel engines. These diesel oils carry an American Petroleum Institute (API) rating of CF4 or CG4. Volkswagen recommends that only synthetic motor oil be used in its diesel engines.

The drain plug is located on the back edge of the oil pan. Some models use a 17-millimeter hex-head bolt for a drain plug, while others require an 8-millimeter Allen wrench. Make sure you have the engine oil drain plug and not the transmission oil and final drive drain, which is part of the transmission housing. *Author*

ENGINE OIL CAPACITY, WITH FILTER

1.8-liter inline four:	4.2 quarts (4.0 liters)
2.0-liter inline four ('93–'99):	4.2 quarts (4.0 liters)
2.0-liter inline four ('99–'05):	4.4 quarts (4.2 liters)
2.8-liter VR6 ('97–'99):	5.3 quarts (5.0 liters)
2.8-liter VR6 ('99–'05):	6.1 quarts (5.8 liters)
1.8T turbo inline four:	4.6 quarts (4.4 liters)
1.9 TDI and TDI PD diesel inline four:	4.8 quarts (4.5 liters)

OIL CHANGE PROCEDURE (2.0-LITER AND 1.8T ENGINES)

1. Warm the car's engine up to normal operating temperature. Warm oil flows easier and will also pick up any stray dirt in the engine

2. Lift the front of the car and place it on jack stands. Jack stands should be placed on hard level surfaces, and the car's parking brake should be applied

3. Remove lower belly pan from beneath front of engine. On some models, the cover is held on with T25 Torx bolts.

4. Remove drain plug and allow the oil to drain into pan.

    HINT: Spray the area around the drain plug with brake cleaner and wipe with rag to clean away dirt before removing drain plug.

    CAUTION: Engine oil will be hot—don't get burned when it comes rushing out of the oil drain.

    Some Volkswagen models use a 17-millimeter hex-head bolt for the engine oil drain plug, while others use an 8-millimeter Allen head bolt. Use the proper wrench, depending upon which your car has.

PROTECTING THE ENVIRONMENT

Used engine oil is hazardous to the environment and must be disposed of properly. Many quick-change oil locations and auto parts stores will accept used oil for recycling. In most communities, a used oil filter can be disposed of in the trash; just make sure the oil has been drained then wrap the filter in a plastic bag to keep remaining oil from dribbling out.

After safely raising the front of the vehicle, some models will require removal of the lower belly pan to access the oil filter. This cover may be held on with T25 Torx bolts. *Author*

Be careful when the hot oil drains from the oil pan. Make sure your drain pan will hold all of the oil. *Author*

5. Replace drain plug washer seal with a new one and reinstall oil drain. Always use a new washer seal.

HINT: Some early Mk III models had a "permanent" steel washer on the oil drain. This should be pried off and replaced with a new oil-drain washer during every oil change

Be careful when threading the oil drain bolt. Tighten it all the way by hand before putting a wrench on it and tightening it to 22 lb-ft (30 N-m) on four-cylinder engines and 37 ft-lb (50 N-m) on V-6 engines. If you don't have a torque wrench, use a wrench to just make it tight; don't over tighten it, or you could strip the treads.

6. Move the drain pan under oil filter at front of the engine. You'll need it there to catch oil that runs out of the filter when you remove it.

7. Remove the oil filter. The oil filter is in an awkward spot. Working from beneath the car, you may be able to get a filter wrench on it, or like the mechanics in most VW shops, you can grab it with a giant pair of pliers and twist. Don't worry about damaging the outside of the filter, as it will be discarded anyway.

CAUTION: Oil dribbling down from the filter will be very hot!

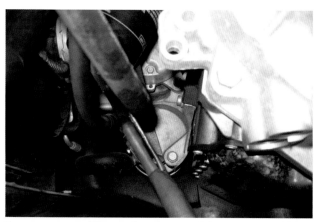

You can use a proper oil filter wrench or a large pair of pliers to unscrew the old oil filter from the engine block. This is a messy job, and watch out for hot oil spilling out of the filter. *Author*

Below: The oil filter is best reached from underneath the car. *Author*

Before installing the new oil filter, take some engine oil and smear it around the rubber O-ring that is attached to the new filter. This will make the filter seat easier and also make it easier to remove next time. Tighten the oil filter by hand (do not use a wrench) and make it snug. *Author*

8. Replace oil filter. Before installing the new filter, take a bit of engine oil and smear it around the rubber sealing ring at the end of the filter. This will improve sealing and make it easy to remove the oil filter next time.

    HINT: Not all oil filters are created equal. It makes sense to use a high-quality filter to ensure proper operation. Volkswagen's factory part from the dealership is a good choice.

    HINT: Use a clean rag and wipe the sealing surface on the engine before mounting the oil filter. Sometimes, the rubber sealing ring from the old filter detaches itself and stays on the engine, and by wiping the sealing surface you can also check that this hasn't happened

    Tighten the oil filter by hand only! Do not use a wrench, but use firm pressure to make sure the filter is very snug

9. Reinstall lower belly pan. Although you might be tempted to leave the pan off so that you can check for leaks, it will be difficult to get on when the car is sitting on the ground.

10. Remove car from jack stands. It's important the car sits level when you fill it with oil and check the dip stick.

11. Fill engine with oil of proper viscosity. Usually, with the filter change, the dipstick will show full with about a quart less than the specified amount of oil. Don't add more at this point; you'll top it off later.

Above: Fill the engine with the proper amount of engine oil of the proper grade. Because of the filter change, it will probably take about a quart less to reach the full mark on the dipstick. Start the engine and let it idle for a couple of minutes, before shutting off and topping the oil to the full level on the dipstick. *Author*

Left: When putting the front belly plan back into place, make sure all of the tabs and slots line up properly. This step will make it hard to see if there are any leaks, but is much easier to do while the front of the car is still raised. *Author*

12. Run engine and check for leaks.

CAUTION: Specifically for turbocharged engines (but a good idea for any engine), as long as the oil pressure light on the dash flashes, the engine must be run only at idle. Do not use the accelerator to increase engine speed, as oil needs to find its way throughout the engine. Touching the accelerator pedal during this critical time could damage the turbocharger.

If the light doesn't go off in 20 seconds, shut off the engine and look under the hood for a leak.

13. Shut off engine, wait a few minutes and check dipstick for oil level

Check the engine oil level two to three minutes after shutting off the engine. Top off with oil to reach the "full" mark on the dipstick. You should check the oil level a day or so after changing the oil to make sure that the engine isn't leaking.

SPECIAL CONSIDERATIONS FOR VR6 OIL FILTERS

Volkswagen's VR6 engine uses a replaceable filter element instead of a disposable oil filter. The oil drain for this filter is located at the bottom of the filter unit.

1. Remove oil drain Allen bolt from the bottom of the filter sealing cap. Use a basin to catch the oil draining from the filter

2. Remove the oil filter cap (lower part of filter housing) using a 36-millimeter socket.

This is the later type of VR6 oil filter and cap. The all-paper filter element fits over the plastic guard. Make sure you put it on the correct way. It can be forced on incorrectly and may cause engine damage. *Author*

VR6 engines use a replaceable oil filter element that fits in this filter unit. It must be drained first before the oil filter cap and filter element are removed. The new filter element comes with a replacement O-ring and sealing washer for the oil drain plug. This is the early type that has a metal base on the filter element that snaps into a holder in the oil filter cap. *Author*

3. Withdraw the old oil filter and place new filter into housing. Make sure the old rubber O-ring is removed. Make sure that the filter is reinstalled in the correct direction. If you have to force it, it's not right. People have destroyed their VR6 engines by putting the VR6 oil filter in the wrong way around!

4. Lubricate new rubber O-ring with engine oil and place between cap and housing.

5. Tighten the filter cap to 18 lb-ft (25 N-m) using a 36-millimeter socket.

6. Lubricate new oil drain rubber O-ring with engine oil and install in along with the oil drain bolt 7 lb-ft (10 N-m).

SPECIAL CONSIDERATIONS FOR 1.9 TDI DIESEL OIL FILTER

Volkswagen's 1.9 TDI engine uses a replaceable oil filter element that is accessed from the top of the engine compartment.

1. Remove upper engine cover (three bolts under round plastic covers).

2. Remove oil filter sealing cap and O-ring gasket.

3. Pull oil filter up and out.

   CAUTION: Engine oil will be hot, and the saturated oil filter will drip

4. Install new filter.

5. Replace oil filter sealing cap with new rubber O-ring gasket. Use engine oil to lubricate the rubber O-ring before assembly.

6. Install upper engine cover.

HOW THE DEALERSHIP DOES IT

If you take your Volkswagen to a dealer for an oil change, they may use a suction extraction system to pull oil out of the engine through the dipstick tube. Aside from being quicker (time is money at a dealer service shop), the advantage of this system is less wear and tear on the oil drain plug, which could be cross-threaded and not seal properly. Not all Volkswagen dealers use suction extraction systems.

Diesel engines also use a replaceable filter element. In this case, the filter unit is not drained before changing. The black oil filter cap atop the silver cylinder in the photo is removed after removing the engine cover and the filter element is pulled straight out. The new filter comes with a replacement O-ring for the cap. *Author*

4 ENGINE AIR FILTER CHANGE

 DIFFICULTY: Easy

 MODELS: All models

 COST: $

 PARTS: Air filter element

 TOOLS: A few screw drivers and some rags

The air filter is located in a housing under the hood. (This is a Mk III Jetta with a 2.0-liter engine.) *Author*

All of the air that moves through your Volkswagen's engine passes through the engine air filter. This filter traps dirt and dust and helps keep your engine from wearing prematurely.

The filter is made from a porous paper that allows only slight restriction to airflow, but traps larger particles, preventing them from entering the engine. This dirt and dust builds up in the filter, eventually clogging it and reducing the engine's performance. That's why it's important to change the engine air filter regularly.

How often should I change the air filter?

Volkswagen recommends changing the engine air filter every 40,000 miles. Obviously, if you drive in extremely dirty or dusty environments, you should consider changing the filter more frequently.

HIGH-PERFORMANCE ENGINE AIR FILTERS

Several aftermarket companies make "high-performance" engine air cleaners for Volkswagens. These companies claim that their products provide better airflow to the engine, and thus produce more power and better fuel economy. Some of these "performance" air filters require modification to the air intake, while others drop directly into the stock location. Despite the claims of such companies, it is difficult to quantify performance gains from switching engine air filters.

ENGINE AIR FILTER CHANGE PROCEDURE

Each engine type has its own slight differences, but the following general procedure applies:

1. Remove the two vacuum hoses on the engine side of the air filter cover.

2. Disconnect the electrical connector from the mass airflow sensor (MAF).

Carefully remove the vacuum lines that run to the filter housing. Unclip the top of the housing and remove it. *Author*

3. Loosen the hose clamp on the intake hose and disconnect hose.

4. Loosen air cleaner housing screws (or flip two housing clips, depending upon model) and remove air filter cover.

5. Remove old engine air filter element.

6. Clean the inside of the air filter housing with a clean rag. Some vehicles have a "snow screen" wire mesh across the air intake inside the air filter housing. If it's there, wipe it off and make sure that it isn't clogged with leaves or other debris.

7. Install new engine air filter element.

Above: Remove the upper part of the housing from the engine air intake hose. *Author*

Below: Remove the paper element from the lower air intake housing. *Author*

8. Replace air filter cover and tighten retaining screws or flip retaining clips.

   CAUTION: At the bottom of the air filter housing on the outside are vacuum lines. If you don't pay attention, these lines can move out of position and rub against the alternator pulley. This will eventually wear a hole into the line, causing a vacuum leak and the "check engine" light to come on.

Above: The old filter may be in a plastic holder. If so, remove the old filter from the holder and put a new filter into the holder. Replace the filter and holder into the lower housing unit. *Author*

Below: Replace the upper air filter housing and reattach the air intake hose from the engine. *Author*

8. Reconnect intake hose and tighten clamp.

9. Reconnect electrical connector for mass airflow sensor.

10. Reconnect vacuum hoses on the engine side of the air filter cover. The brown hose goes on the brown connector, the black hose goes on the black connector.

Above: Tighten the clips and be sure to reattach the vacuum lines—black on black and brown on brown. *Author*

Left: If you are careless when removing the air filter housing, a vacuum line that runs under the air filter assembly can move out of position and rub against an engine pulley. This can lead to the pulley wearing a hole in the vacuum line, causing the engine to run poorly. Inspect everything after completing this job to make sure no hoses are rubbing on any pulleys. *Author*

5 TIRE ROTATION

 DIFFICULTY: Easy

 MODELS: All models

 COST: Nil

 PARTS: None

TOOLS: Floor jack, jack stand, tire lug wrench, torque wrench, small hook, tire pressure gauge, never-seize compound, spray wax

Most people ignore their tires. It's not unusual to find cars with tires that are badly worn and that are 5 psi or more underinflated.

This can be dangerous for several reasons. Tires with worn tread don't provide as much traction on wet roads and can be susceptible to dangerous hydroplaning on flooded roads. Abnormally worn tires can produce vibrations, which can accelerate wear of the vehicle's suspension components. Underinflated tires run hotter that normal, which can cause rapid wear and even sudden failure. Tires that are not properly inflated can also result in handling instabilities that may compromise a Volkswagen's ability to avoid an accident.

It's not hard to prevent all of these problems simply by rotating your tires on the schedule that Volkswagen recommends and checking the tire's air pressure once a week.

How often should I rotate my tires?

Volkswagen recommends rotating your tires every 10,000 miles. If you stick with this schedule it's not unusual to get 40,000 miles or more from the tires that originally came on your Volkswagen.

When you go to buy new tires, your tire dealer will often throw in free tire rotation as part of the package, and you should take advantage of this at whatever interval the tire dealer recommends. Rotating tires more often than Volkswagen's recommendation won't hurt anything.

WINTER TIRES

Volkswagen's front-wheel drive puts significant weight over the driving wheels, and if winter conditions aren't too severe, most people who live in cities and suburban environments get through the winter with all-season tires. If your Volkswagen has high-performance summer tires, or if you live in a place with significant winter, you might need to consider fitting winter tires.

This can be more easily done if you buy a spare set of wheels for your winter tires, and several mail order companies will ship a mounted and balanced winter tire package to you, wheels and all. Make sure that if you do get new wheels, that you also get a new set of special wheel bolts, if required.

Unlike the old days, when your dad would put a pair of snow tires on the back of the old rear-wheel-drive station wagon, front-wheel-drive Volkswagens really need winter tires on both the front and rear wheels. In fact, tire manufacturers say if you only have two winter tires, or if you have two newer winter tires, they should go on the rear of a front-wheel drive vehicle to avoid a handling imbalance that could result in the rear skidding before the front (oversteer) when going around a corner. There are a variety of high-technology winter tires available, and finding tires in the proper size for your Volkswagen won't be a problem.

TIRE ROTATION PROCEDURE

1. Using a small screwdriver or wire with a hook in it, remove the caps (if so equipped) covering the vehicle's wheel bolts.

Some VW models have small plastic caps on the heads of their wheel bolts. These must be removed before accessing the bolts themselves. *Author*

2. Using a lug wrench, loosen the wheel bolts on one side of the car

3. Raise one whole side of the vehicle using the floor jack and then support it on jack stands. Make sure the vehicle is in gear and that the parking brake is set. Block the wheels on the opposite side of the vehicle to ensure it cannot roll away. Lift the vehicle only under the proper lifting points under the car.

4. Remove the wheel bolts and remove both wheels from one side of the car. Sometimes the wheel will stick to the hub. You may need to hammer with a rubber mallet on the inside of the tire to get the wheel to loosen from the hub. This can be prevented in the future using the spray wax hint below

   HINT: Some GTI models have a special center trim piece. You should not need to remove it to rotate the tires, but should you ever need to remove this center trim, a special tool is provided in the vehicle tool kit

5. Inspect the tread area and sidewalls of both tires carefully. Volkswagen recommends rotating the front tires to the rear and the rear to the front, unless abnormal wear is present. Abnormal wear might include cupping of the outside shoulders or uneven wear of the blocks. This might indicate a suspension alignment problem and should be checked by a mechanic. If abnormal wear is present, the tires should be cross-rotated. In this case, the right front should swap with the left rear, and the left front should swap with the right rear. This will require jacking up the other side of the vehicle—do it safely, using jack stands.

New tires generally have between 8/32 and 10/32 inch of tread depth. If a tire is worn below 2/32 inch (1.6 millimeter) of remaining tread depth, it should be replaced. One way to quickly measure acceptable tread depth is put a U.S. one-cent penny into the groove, head first. If the tread comes to at least the top of Lincoln's head, there is more than 2/32 inch remaining. Tires have tread wear indicators, or wear bars, located around the tire. When the tops of these wear bars begin to wear, it's time for new tires.

If you have an air impact wrench, you don't have to loosen the wheels before lifting and supporting the car. If you are working without air tools, make sure you loosen the front and rear wheel bolts before raising the car. *Author*

When you are putting the wheels back onto the car, thread each of the wheel bolts carefully by hand to ensure that none of them is cross-threaded. *Author*

8. Lower the car off of the jack stands.

9. Tighten the wheel bolts. The wheel bolts should be tightened in a diagonal pattern. Imagine the five bolts are arrayed around a clock face. Starting with a bolt at the top of the wheel (in the 12 o'clock position): Tighten 12, then 7, then 2, then 10, then 4. If you don't have a torque wrench, make the bolts tight. If you do have a torque wrench, the torque value for all wheel bolts is 89 lb-ft (120 N-m).

10. Check the air pressures and adjust to the recommended levels, which can be found on a placard inside the vehicle door jams, glove box lid or trunk lid.

11. Repeat the procedure on the other side of the vehicle.

12. Replace the plastic covers onto the wheel bolts (if so equipped).

6. Put the rear tire on the front and the front tire on the rear.

NOTE: Because Volkswagen uses wheel bolts instead of studs and lug nuts, it is sometimes difficult to hold the wheel in place while starting the first bolt. You can try sitting next to the wheel and putting your foot under the tire to lever it up into position

HINT: If you smear a bit of anti-seize compound (available at auto parts stores) onto the wheel bolts, it will make them easier to take off next time.

HINT: Spraying some wax onto the back side of the wheel flange (where it meets with the hub) will make it easier to take the wheel off next time. Just be sure you don't get any spray wax onto the brake rotors or brake pads.

7. Tighten the wheel bolts with the wrench (make them just snug at this point).

Above: Check the tires' inflation pressures and adjust the front and rear tires to the proper level. Tire pressures are listed on a sticker found on the driver's doorjamb or in the glove box. *Author*

Left: Tighten the wheel bolts with a torque wrench to the proper level. The technician here is using a "torque stick," a special tool that ensures the proper level of torque when used with an air impact wrench. *Author*

6 TRANSMISSION FLUID CHECK/CHANGE

DIFFICULTY: Moderate

MODELS: All

COST: $

PARTS: Gear oil, automatic transmission fluid

TOOLS: Basic wrenches, 17-millimeter Allen wrench socket

If Volkswagen Golfs and Jettas have an Achilles' heel, it's probably their manual transmissions. If they are abused too much by their drivers, the synchronizers will wear quickly, causing the transmissions to be hard to shift.

One way to prolong the life of the manual transmission in your Golf or Jetta is to change gear oil in the transmission and final drive unit. These share the same oil supply in the manual transmission, while the automatic transmission has a separate transmission and final drive unit, each of which must be separately checked.

Note that Volkswagen does not have a recommended oil change interval for changing transmission and final drive oil. If you don't know the service history of your car and it has more than 60,000 miles on it, you might consider changing the gear oil.

TRANSMISSIONS USED WITH ENGINES

Mark III Golf and Jetta
020 five-speed manual used in all cars with
    four-cylinder engines except TDI
02A five-speed manual transmission used with
    six-cylinder VR6 and TDI
096 four-speed automatic transmission used with
    four-cylinder or VR6 engines from 1993–1995
01M four-speed automatic transmission used with
    four-cylinder or VR6 from 1995 on

Mark IV Golf and Jetta
02J five-speed manual transmission used on all
    four-cylinder and VR6 engines
02M six-speed manual transmission used on
    four-cylinder and VR6 engines
02Y six-speed manual transmission used with
    4Motion system in R32
01M four-speed automatic transmission used on
    four-cylinder and VR6 engines
09A five-speed automatic transmission used on
    four-cylinder and VR6 engines

Automatic Transmissions

Automatic transmissions are difficult to service and are best left for experienced service technicians.

The early Volkswagen four-speed automatic transmissions (coded 096) used a normal dipstick to check the automatic transmission fluid level. Fluids such as Dexron II or III ATF may be used in the 096 transmission.

Later four-speed automatic transmissions (coded 01M) do not have a dipstick and checking that the transmission has the proper amount of fluid involves interfacing a Volkswagen Scan Tool (VAG 1531) to the vehicle to check the temperature of the fluid while running. This is work that is best performed by an experienced service technician.

In the later five-speed automatic transmission (coded 09A), the transmission and final drive share lubrication (Volkswagen Synthetic ATF).

PROCEDURE FOR CHECKING FINAL DRIVE OIL LEVEL ON AUTOMATIC TRANSMISSION CARS

1. Park the car on a level spot.

2. Open hood.

3. Remove the wiring harness from the speedometer drive unit. This is located on the far left-hand side of the top of the transmission.

4. Unbolt the speedometer gear drive and pull it out of the transmission (on some cars this is held in place with a Torx T40 bolt).

5. Clean the bottom of the speedometer gear driveshaft and reinstall it.

6. Remove the speedometer gear drive again. The bottom of the speedometer gear drive is also a dipstick used to gauge the amount of oil in the final drive. The difference between the minimum level (the bottom of the shaft) and the maximum level (the top of the first step in the shaft) is about 3.4 fluid ounces, or about 0.1-liters.

7. Add small amounts of the proper gear oil or synthetic automatic transmission fluid (ATF) through the hole from the speedometer gear drive and recheck until the proper level has been reached.

8. Reinstall the speedometer gear drive and reattach the wiring.

Gear Oil for Automatic Transmissions

Transmission	Gear Oil	Amount
096 transmission	SAE 75W/90 synthetic gear oil	0.75-liter
01M transmission	VW synthetic ATF	0.75-liter
09A transmission	VW synthetic ATF	7.0-liters (total)

Manual Transmissions

Volkswagen used a variety of different specifications for gear oil in the different years of Golf and Jetta models. Checking the proper level of gear oil is similar for each of the different models.

Gear Oil for Manual Transmissions

Transmission	Gear Oil	Amount
O20, 02A five speed	VW G50 synthetic oil SAE 75W90	1.9 liters
02J five speed	VW G50 synthetic oil SAE 75W90	2.0 liters
02M six speed	VW G51 synthetic oil SAE 75W90	2.3 liters
02Y six speed	VW G50 synthetic oil SAE 75W90	2.6 liters

PROCEDURE FOR CHECKING/CHANGING GEAR OIL IN MANUAL TRANSMISSIONS

1. Park car on a level surface.

2. Open hood.

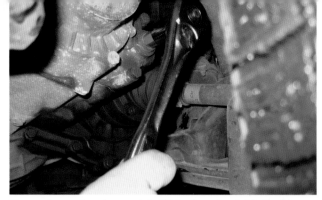

Wipe any dirt away from the transmission fill plug (located on the left side of the transmission housing). Using a 17-millimeter Allen wrench socket, carefully remove this plug. *Author*

3. Wipe any dirt away from the transmission fill plug (located on the left side of the transmission housing). Using a 17-millimeter Allen wrench socket, carefully remove this plug. There are two reasons to do this. First, it allows you to check the fluid level (it should be right at the lower edge of the fill plug hole). Second, if you drain the oil first, then can't get the fill plug loose, you won't have any oil in your transmission and won't be able to drive it to a repair shop.

Jack up the front of the car, place it on jack stands, and remove the splash guard panel from under the front of the car. *Author*

4. Position a pan under the transmission drain plug (located on the bottom of the transmission) and remove the plug with a 17-millimeter Allen wrench socket.

5. Allow the oil to drain. If the engine and transmission is warm, the oil will drain more quickly.

Above: Position a pan under the transmission drain plug (located on the bottom of the transmission) and remove the plug with a 17-millimeter Allen wrench socket. *Author*

Below: Allow the transmission gear oil to drain. *Author*

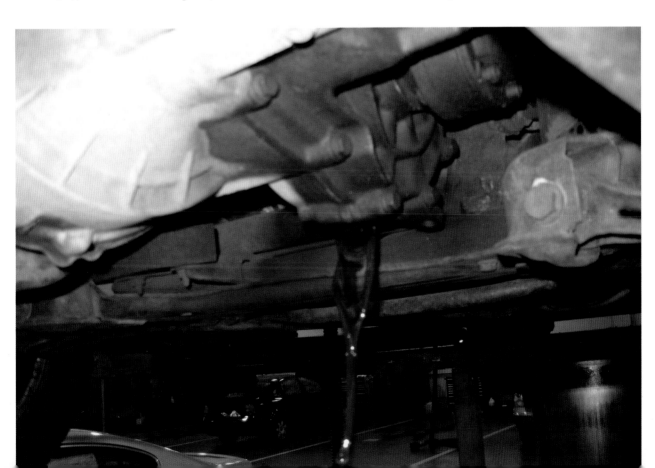

Replace the drain plug. CAUTION: This is a steel plug going into an aluminum housing—do not over tighten! Through the fill hole, carefully add 75W90 synthetic gear oil to the transmission. When oil begins to drain out of the fill hole, replace the fill plug and tighten carefully. Do not over tighten this plug! Because the fifth gear is in the way of proper filling on some transmissions, Volkswagen mechanics will add some additional oil (about a pint) through the speedometer gear drive at the top of the transmission. Unbolt the speedometer gear drive and pull it out of the transmission. (On some cars this is held in place with a Torx T40 bolt.) *Author*

6. Replace the oil drain plug.

CAUTION: This is a steel plug going into an aluminum housing—do not over tighten!

7. Through the fill hole, carefully add 75W90 synthetic gear oil to the transmission.

8. When oil begins to drain out of the fill hole, replace the fill plug and tighten carefully. Do not over tighten this plug!

9. Because the fifth gear is in the way of proper filling on some transmissions, Volkswagen mechanics will add some additional oil (about a pint) through the speedometer

gear drive at the top of the transmission (see section above about checking final drive on automatic transmission equipped cars).

Some Notes on the R32 Six-Speed Transmission

The 02Y six-speed manual transmission used on the R32 Golf uses a variety of electronic systems to help control the 4MOTION all-wheel drive system that was developed by Haldex. The Haldex clutch has its own oil and filter system and servicing this system requires the use of Volkswagen Vehicle Diagnostic Testing and Information System VAS 5051. Servicing of this system is best left to trained Volkswagen service technicians.

Clean the bottom of the speedometer gear drive shaft and reinstall it. Remove the speedometer gear drive again. The bottom of the speedometer gear drive is also a dipstick used to gauge the amount of oil in the final drive. *Author*

7 | FUEL FILTER DRAINING/REPLACEMENT

 DIFFICULTY: Easy

 MODELS: Filter replacement-all, filter draining-diesel engines

 COST: $

 PARTS: New duel filter, hose clamps

 TOOLS: Hand tools

Gasoline Fuel Filter

Volkswagen states that the fuel filter used with gasoline engines is designed to last the lifetime of the car and does not need to be replaced. This is fine as long as you know the history of the car you have purchased, and know that it has never been subjected to dirty or contaminated fuel.

The fuel filter is located under the floor of the vehicle, under the right rear door between the fuel pump in the fuel tank and the fuel injection system under the hood. If it becomes clogged, it will not allow the proper fuel pressure to reach the fuel injectors, causing the engine to run poorly.

Changing the fuel filter is straightforward, and there is no reason not to do this after purchasing a used Volkswagen Golf or Jetta.

Diesel Fuel Filter

The fuel filter fitted to diesel Golfs and Jettas is located in the engine compartment and is designed to trap water that may be in the diesel fuel. A water drain fitting at the bottom of the filter is used to drain approximately 100 cc (1.7 oz.) of water and fuel from the bottom of the filter to prevent it from contaminating the rest of the engine.

This should be done every 10,000 miles, and the filter should be replaced every 20,000 miles, per Volkswagen's maintenance schedule.

PROCEDURE FOR REPLACING GASOLINE FUEL FILTER
1. Lift car with jack and support safely with jack stands.

2. Using a 17-millimeter socket, remove attaching bolt that holds fuel filter to vehicle.

CAUTION: The fuel in the filter is under high pressure and will spray when the hoses are removed. Make sure there are no nearby possible sources of ignition and that you have a container to catch the spraying fuel.

CAUTION: The fuel in the filter is under high pressure and will spray when the hoses are removed. Make sure there are no nearby possible sources of ignition and that you have a container to catch the spraying fuel. Carefully cut the spring clips that hold the hoses onto the filter. *Author*

3. Carefully cut the spring clips that hold the hoses onto the filter. Pull the hoses off of the filter.

Above: Pull the hoses off of the filter. *Author*

Left: Lift car with jack and support safely with jack stands. Using a 17-millimeter socket, remove attaching bolt that holds fuel filter to vehicle. *Author*

75

Pull the filter out of its housing (where applicable) and replace it with a new one. *Author*

4. Pull the filter out of its housing (where applicable) and replace it with a new one.

5. Slide new hose clamps of the proper size over the ends of the fuel line and slip the lines onto the new filter. Tighten the clamps.

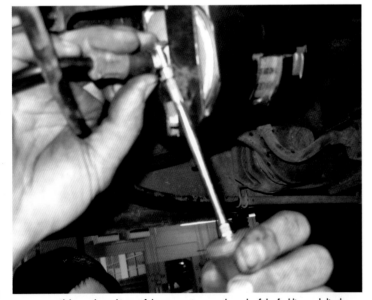

Slide new hose clamps of the proper size over the ends of the fuel line and slip the lines onto the new filter. Tighten the clamps. Reposition the fuel filter and reattach it to the vehicle. Remove the jack stands and return the car to the ground. Start the engine. It will start once and die. Start the car again and let it run as the fuel filter fills. With the engine idling, check under the car to make sure that there are no fuel leaks. *Author*

6. Reposition the fuel filter and reattach it to the vehicle.

7. Jack up the car, remove the jack stands and return the car to the ground.

8. Start the engine. It will start once and die. Start the car again and let it run as the fuel filter fills. With the engine idling, check under to car to make sure that there are no fuel leaks.

PROCEDURE FOR REPLACING DIESEL FUEL FILTER

1. Label and disconnect fuel filter inlet and outlet lines on fuel filter on passenger (right) side strut tower under the hood.

2. Remove the control valve clip and remove control valve.

3. Remove inlet and outlet lines.

4. Unbolt filter bracket and remove the filter from the bracket.

5. Install a new filter into the bracket.

6. Fill the new filter with diesel fuel prior to remounting bracket into vehicle.

7. Remount bracket and reattach fuel lines. Use new fuel line hose clamps if needed.

8. Reattach control valve and clip using a new O-ring.

9. Start the engine (it may take a few tries) and check for leaks.

8 CHECKING AND CHANGING BRAKE FLUID/BLEEDING BRAKE SYSTEM

DIFFICULTY: Moderate

MODELS: All (1993–2005)

COST: $

PARTS: Brake fluid

TOOLS: 11-millimeter wrench (front), 7-millimeter wrench (rear), DOT 4 Super brake fluid, pressure or vacum brake bleeding system or small diameter plastic hose, rags

Clean the area around the cap of the brake fluid reservoir. Top off the reservoir with fresh DOT 4 Super brake fluid. *Author*

Brake fluid absorbs moisture from the air. This moisture can cause corrosion within the brake system, and it also reduces the brake fluid's boiling point. This reduction in boiling point can reduce the brake system's performance, especially when using the brakes hard, as during a long descent or in competition.

How often should I change the brake fluid?

Volkswagen recommends flushing out the old brake fluid and replacing it with fresh fluid every two years, regardless of the mileage the vehicle covers during that time period.

In addition, the level of the brake fluid in the plastic reservoir under the hood should be checked regularly to ensure it is at its proper level.

CHECKING BRAKE FLUID PROCEDURE

1. Open hood.

2. The brake fluid reservoir is on the left (driver's) side of the car, under the air cleaner hose (Mk IV) and against the firewall.

3. The reservoir is translucent so that the brake fluid level can be gauged at a glance. The fluid should be near the "max" level, but should never be higher than that level. The brake fluid level will drop over time as the brake pads wear .

If you need to add brake fluid:

1. Use a rag to carefully clean dirt away from the top of the reservoir.

2. Unscrew the cap to the reservoir.

3. Fill only using DOT 4 Super Brake Fluid from a new, unopened bottle of brake fluid.

4. Do not overfill.

5. Carefully reinstall the cap onto the reservoir.

6. Clean up any spilled brake fluid promptly. Brake fluid will remove paint from your vehicle if it is not wiped up quickly.

7. Store brake fluid for short periods of time in an airtight container.

TYPES OF BRAKE FLUID

Brake fluid is available in several different grades, with different specifications:

Boiling Point Degrees Fahrenheit

	DOT 3	DOT4	DOT4 Super	DOT5
Dry Boiling Point	401	446	500	500
Wet Boiling Point	284	311	329	356

DOT3 brake fluid is the bargain basement stuff you find in grocery stores and discount auto parts stores. DOT4 Super is a high-performance brake fluid that conforms to standard MVSS116 DOT4. DOT5 brake fluid is a silicon-based fluid that doesn't absorb water and doesn't attack paint. DOT5 fluid should not be mixed with other types of brake fluid. It is heavier in viscosity, which can sometimes cause tiny bubbles of air to become trapped during the bleeding process, resulting in a spongy feeling in the brake pedal. The higher viscosity can also affect the performance of the anti-lock braking system in some cars. Volkswagen does not recommend using DOT5 silicon fluid and only recommends the use of DOT4 Super brake fluid. It is the one you should use.

ORDER IN WHICH TO BLEED BRAKES FOR EACH BRAKING SYSTEM

Golf/Jetta/GTI
Mk III 1993–1998   right rear/left rear/right front/left front
Teves 04 ABS/EDL
Teves 20 GI ABS/EDL

Golf/Jetta/GTI
Mk IV 1999–2001   right rear/left rear/right front/left front
ITT Mark 20 IE

Golf/Jetta/GTI
Mk IV 2002–2005   left front/right front/left rear/right rear
ITT Mark 60 IE

BRAKE FLUID CHANGING/BRAKE SYSTEM BLEEDING PROCEDURE

1. Open hood.

2. Clean the area around the cap of the brake fluid reservoir.

3. Top off the reservoir with fresh DOT 4 Super brake fluid.

4. If you have a pressure bleeding system, follow the directions for the system, bleeding each wheel location in the order recommended below.

5. To bleed the brake system manually, move to the first wheel (see chart below) and carefully loosen the brake bleed nipple with a wrench. Tighten the nipple and then attach a plastic hose over the brake bleed nipple.

6. Put the other end of the plastic hose in a jar that is partially filled with fresh brake fluid so that the end is submerged.

7. Have a helper pump the brake pedal several times, and then press down and hold it.

8. Open the bleed nipple so that fluid travels from the brake system through the plastic hose and into the jar. Close the nipple and let the helper release the pedal.

9. Repeat as necessary, checking to make sure the level of brake fluid in the reservoir never falls below the "min" marking. If bleeding the brakes, repeat until no air bubbles are seen coming out of the bleed nipple. If changing brake fluid, repeat until clean, new brake fluid is seen coming out of the bleed nipple. Replenish brake fluid in the reservoir as necessary.

10. Tighten the brake bleed nipple (do not over tighten) and remove the plastic hose.

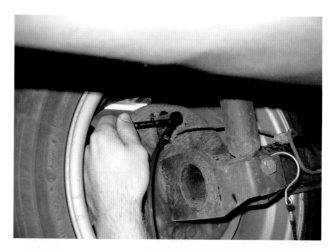

To bleed the brake system manually, move to the first wheel (see chart in the text) and carefully loosen the brake bleed nipple with a wrench. Tighten the nipple and then attach a plastic hose over the brake bleed nipple. *Author*

Above and top: Put the other end of the plastic hose in a jar that is partially filled with fresh brake fluid, so that the end is submerged. Have a helper pump the brake pedal several times and then press down and hold it. Open the bleed nipple so that fluid travels from the brake system through the plastic hose and into the jar. Close the nipple and let the helper release the pedal. Repeat several times, checking to make sure the level of brake fluid in the reservoir never falls below the "min" marking. *Author*

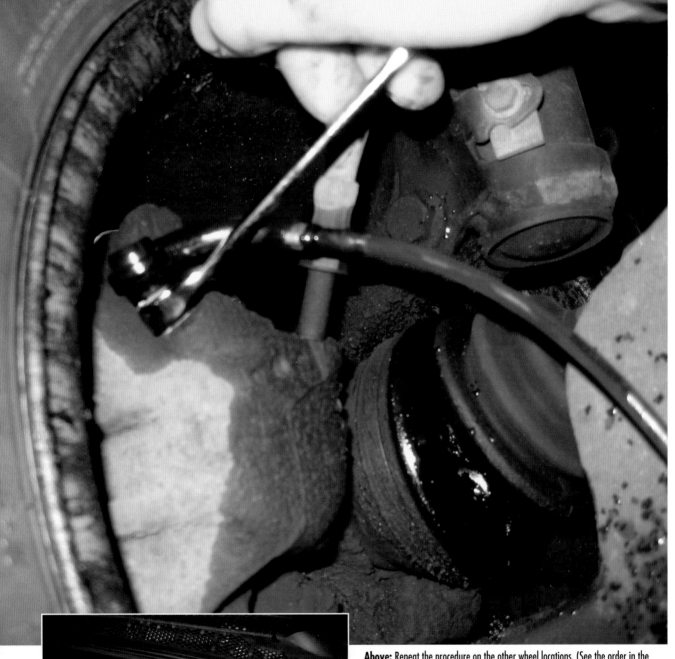

Above: Repeat the procedure on the other wheel locations. (See the order in the text.) *Author*

Left: Make sure the fluid level in the reservoir always stays above the "min" level. *Author*

11. Repeat the procedure on the other wheel locations (see the order chart on p. 78). Make sure the fluid level in the reservoir always stays above the "min" level.

12. If the reservoir has been completely emptied and air has entered the system from the reservoir, the system must be bled using Volkswagen Scan Tool VAG 1551/1552 to purge the air that will be trapped in the anti-lock braking valve body. See your Volkswagen service technician.

9 COOLANT CHECKING AND REPLACEMENT

DIFFICULTY: Moderate

MODELS: All models

COST: Low

PARTS: proper coolant (see text)

TOOLS: Hand tools

Volkswagen engines use cast-iron engine blocks and aluminum cylinder heads. In addition, Volkswagen's radiators are also made of aluminum. When connected together with water, an electric current will flow between the aluminum and cast iron of the engine block, causing corrosion.

In addition, if any phosphates are present in the coolant, insoluble aluminum phosphate will form. The aluminum phosphate can settle into the radiator, clogging it and preventing it from properly cooling the engine. This is why it is important that the proper coolant be used in Volkswagen engines.

As the name implies, antifreeze coolant also protects the vehicle's cooling system from freezing in subzero temperatures. It also increases the boiling point of the cooling liquid for added protection from boil-over.

DIFFERENT TYPES OF VW COOLANT
Because of the possibility of the formation of aluminum phosphate, antifreeze used in Volkswagen engines must be phosphate-free and also silicate-free.

Volkswagen models manufactured between 1993 and 1999 use Volkswagen antifreeze coolant called G11. This is blue/green in color.

From 1993 through 2002, a new type of coolant called G12 was used in all Volkswagen models. This was pink in color.

From model year 2003 and onward, G12 antifreeze was modified and is now a purple color, but is still called G12

TYPES OF VOLKSWAGEN ANTIFREEZE COOLANT

CAUTION: Blue/green G11 must NEVER be mixed with pink/purple G12 antifreeze. Such contamination can be identified by its brown color. The mixture of G11 and G12 will cause a foamy deposit to appear in the radiator's expansion tank. The coolant must be drained immediately and must be thoroughly flushed with water to remove all traces before refilling with the proper coolant.

(VW Part Number G 012 A8F A4). Early pink G12 can be mixed with later purple G12.

How often should I change the coolant?
It is interesting to note that Volkswagen has no recommended interval for replacing the antifreeze in its vehicle's cooling systems. In fact, after 1999, the cooling system was considered to be filled at the factory with a permanent coolant.

Prior to 1999, Volkswagen had no set flushing requirement, although makers of antifreeze recommend that the antifreeze be changed once a year to refresh the corrosion inhibitors that are a part of the formulation. This is considered especially important if the engine block or heads are made of aluminum.

ANTIFREEZE MIX

The mixture of antifreeze in the cooling system should be 50 percent water and 50 percent antifreeze coolant, which has a freeze point of -35 degrees Fahrenheit (-38 degrees Celsius) and a boiling point of 226 degrees Fahrenheit (108 degrees Celsius). For protection to -40 degrees Fahrenheit, concentrations as high as 60 percent antifreeze can be used. Beyond this level of antifreeze, freezing protection actually decreases, as does the liquid's ability to transfer heat away from the engine. Volkswagen recommends that tap water not be used in its cooling systems, but suggests that only distilled water should be mixed with antifreeze to avoid possible harmful deposits.

COOLANT CHANGE PROCEDURE
1. The expansion tank mounted on the side of the fender is translucent so that the proper coolant level can be easily

The expansion tank mounted on the side of the fender is translucent so the proper coolant level can be easily checked. Carefully open the cap of the coolant expansion top. At normal operating temperature, the expansion tank and radiator are under pressure. Remove the cap slowly in case the system is still pressurized. *Author*

checked. The coolant level should always be checked when the engine is cold. The coolant level should be above the "min." mark on the tank.

2. Before draining the coolant, squeeze the major hoses by hand to ensure that they are springy and firm. Be prepared to replace any hose that you may find that is brittle or cracked.

    CAUTION: Do not work on a hot engine, as coolant can scald.

3. Carefully open cap of the coolant expansion top. By opening the expansion tank you will reduce the suction on the system and make the antifreeze coolant drain more quickly.

    CAUTION: At normal operating temperature the expansion tank and radiator are under pressure. Remove the cap slowly in case the system is still pressurized.

4. Position a drain pan under the radiator drain plug (if so equipped) or under the lower radiator hose. The drain pan should have a capacity of at least 3 gallons to hold all of the coolant without spilling. If you need to raise the front of the vehicle to fit the drain pan underneath, do so safely and support it with proper jack stands before continuing work.

5. Unscrew the radiator drain plug, or disconnect the clamp and pull the lower radiator hose off of the radiator to allow the antifreeze coolant to flow into the drain pan

    CAUTION: Antifreeze coolant is poisonous to humans and pets. Review safety section and dispose of and use antifreeze properly.

6. Remove the smaller coolant hose that attaches to the cylinder head to fully drain the remaining antifreeze from the engine into the drain pan.

    NOTE: This makes a mess!

Remove the smaller coolant hose that attaches to the cylinder head to fully drain the remaining antifreeze from the engine into the drain pan. *Author*

Position a drain pan under the radiator drain plug (if so equipped) or under the lower radiator hose. Unscrew the radiator drain plug, or disconnect the clamp and pull the lower radiator hose off of the radiator to allow the antifreeze coolant to flow into the drain pan. *Author*

CAUTION: Make sure the plug covering the access to timing marks on the flywheel is in place

7. Using a garden hose, fill the expansion tank with running water and flush the remaining coolant out of the system until the water runs clear.

Above: This makes a mess! CAUTION: Make sure the plug covering the access to timing marks on the flywheel is in place. *Author*

Below: Using a garden hose, fill the expansion tank with running water. *Author*

Flush the remaining coolant out of the system until the water runs clear. *Author*

8. After the water is clear, allow all of the water to flow out of the engine.

9. Reattach the coolant hoses and close the tap at the bottom of the radiator.

10. Fill the expansion tank with the proper 50/50 mixture of coolant (blue/green for Mk III, pink/purple for Mk IV) and allow the air bubbles in the system to work their way up to the expansion tank. Continue to add antifreeze until the level remains constant.

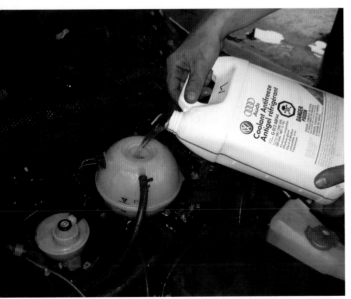

After the water is clear, allow all of the water to flow out of the engine. Reattach the coolant hoses and close the tap at the bottom of the radiator. Fill the expansion tank with the proper 50/50 mixture of coolant and allow the air bubbles in the system to work their way up to the expansion tank. Continue to add antifreeze until the level remains constant. Start engine. Continue topping the level of antifreeze in the expansion tank as the engine warms to normal operating temperature and air bleeds out of the system. *Author*

11. Start the engine and check for leaks. Allow the engine to run at low to moderate speeds while watching the level of the antifreeze in the expansion tank.

12. Continue topping the level of antifreeze in the expansion tank as the engine warms to normal operating temperature and air bleeds out of the system. NOTE: The dealer will probably use a pressure bleeder to remove all of the air from the system. Bleeding air out of the system by running the engine could take as long as a half an hour. Check the temperature gauge frequently to ensure that the car doesn't overheat.

CAUTION: As the engine warms, the electric fan can come on automatically. Make sure everything (including rags and you) are clear of the fan blades

Once the electric fan comes on, it is a good indication that the engine's thermostat has opened and that most of the air is out of the system.

13. Replace the cap on the expansion tank. Check the coolant level again, after a drive to ensure all of the air has been removed from the system and that the coolant is at the proper level.

SAFETY

- The cooling system contains antifreeze coolant that can scald when it is hot. Do not work on the cooling system until the engine has cooled for at least an hour.
- The cooling system is under pressure. Remove the cap from the expansion tank very carefully, wearing heavy gloves to avoid being scalded by hot pressurized coolant.
- Opening the expansion tank cap when the engine is hot may result in sudden boiling of the coolant in the tank. This can be very dangerous, as escaping steam could burn or scald.
- Avoid adding cold water to a hot engine. If you must add coolant when the engine is hot, make sure that the engine is running.
- When the engine is hot, the electric fan can come on at any time, even when the key is not in the ignition.
- Antifreeze is highly poisonous, yet its sweet odor may attract children or pets. Humans or animals that have ingested even small amounts of antifreeze coolant must see a doctor or veterinarian immediately. This could be a life-threatening emergency.
- Dispose of used antifreeze properly, in accordance with local, county, state, and federal regulations. Do not pour antifreeze onto the ground or allow it to run into storm drains, as it is poisonous and will pollute the ground water

10 REPLACE BRAKE PADS

DIFFICULTY: Moderate

MODELS: All

COST: $$

PARTS: New brake pads (front and/or rear)

TOOLS: Hand tools

Disc brakes are used on Golf and Jetta models. A disc brake consists of a disc, a caliper, and a set of pads. The brake disc is attached to the wheel. A clamping device, the caliper, squeezes the spinning disc to provide braking force. Pads made of high-friction material are located within the caliper and are the surfaces that actually squeeze against the disc.

Pads and rotors will eventually wear out. The point at which this happens varies, depending upon driving conditions, driving style, and the materials from which the brake pads are made. When the pads wear past acceptable thickness, they are relatively easy to replace.

Which pads do I use?

Brake pads come in a variety of materials (called compounds) and applications. Low-cost brake pads may not be sufficient for high-performance applications, in which high temperatures are reached. Conversely, pads designed for racing applications may not reach sufficient temperatures in street driving to become effective.

Choosing exactly the right pad is part science and part art, and in the absence of specialized information the safest thing is to get new original equipment pads from the Volkswagen dealer.

Brake Rotors

In addition to pad wear, the cast-iron brake rotors also wear and have limits beyond which they will need to be replaced. The specifications for the brake rotor thickness vary from year to year and model to model.

Also, if your brake rotors are heavily grooved or scored, you should visit a Volkswagen service technician to determine if they need replacement. Brake rotors should always be replaced in pairs on an axle.

Model-Specific Calipers and Pads

Volkswagen used several different combinations of front and rear brake calipers and pads in the third and fourth generation of the vehicle. The operations here are an example and your car may be different.

We strongly suggest you consult a shop manual dealing with your specific year and model before beginning any work on your braking system.

WARNING!

Brakes are not a good place to make mistakes. Make sure you understand the procedure before starting and work on one side at a time so that you can compare the side on which you are working to one that is correctly assembled. Remember, brake fluid is toxic, and it removes paint if it gets on the bodywork of the car. Be careful about any spills. It should not be necessary to disconnect the anti-lock brake system (ABS) sensor on most models.

PROCEDURE FOR CHANGING FRONT OR REAR BRAKE PADS

1. Loosen front wheel bolts for corner you will work on first.

2. Raise that corner with a jack and support safely with jack stands.

3. Remove the wheel from that corner.

4. Disconnect the wiring harness on those vehicles equipped with brake pad wear sensors.

Raise the vehicle and support it safely on jack stands. Remove the wheel. *Author*

The brake caliper is removed by unscrewing the two slide pins that hold it to the spindle. *Author*

5. Remove protective caps from brake caliper guide pins.

6. Remove both guide pins.

The inner wrench is a 15-millimeter and must be thinner than a standard wrench to fit between the caliper and its bracket. The outer wrench is a 13-millimeter. *Author*

After loosening the slide pins, the caliper can be pried away from the rotor. *Author*

7. Remove the brake caliper and hang it from a piece of wire attached to the suspension (DO NOT allow it to hang from the brake hose!).

8. Remove one of the worn brake pads from the brake caliper.

9. Check the fluid level in the brake fluid reservoir. If the level is near the top, pushing the pistons into the caliper may cause the brake fluid to overflow. Using a squeeze bottle, you may need to carefully remove and discard some of this brake fluid.

The brake pads can be removed and replaced with new ones. *Author*

The slide pins should be removed, cleaned, and regreased with axle grease. *Author*

Above: Using a special tool, the brake piston needs to be pressed back into the brake caliper. It must rotate clockwise as it is pushed in. *Author*

Right: This can also be accomplished with a C-clamp and some pliers, but is much easier with the special tool. *Author*

10. Press the piston of the pad you have removed into the brake caliper. There is a special Volkswagen tool to do this, tools are available from supply houses, or you can use a screwdriver. Be careful not to catch or damage the rubber seal on the edge of the piston. On the rear calipers, the piston must rotate clockwise as it is pressed into the caliper.

11. When the piston is far enough into the caliper, you should be able to put a new brake pad into place in the caliper.

12. Pull the second old brake pad out of the caliper and push the piston back to make room on that side for the new brake pad. Once both brake pads fit into the caliper, align them and replace any springs and clips that were present.

When the new pads are in place, slide the caliper back into position and reattach, using the newly greased slide pins. Remember to pump the brake pedal a few times after changing the brake pads to seat them before driving. *Author*

13. Slide the caliper back over the rotor and position it over the brake caliper mounting bracket.

14. Clean the guide pins and grease them with axle grease. Reattach the brake caliper, using the guide pins and reattach the guide pin protective caps.

15. Reattach the wire harness for the brake pad wear indicator sensor if so equipped.

16. Reattach wheel and lower car to ground.

17. Press the brake pedal several times to position the brake pads against the rotor.
   WARNING: failure to do this may result in little or no braking ability on the first stop

18. Check the fluid level in the reservoir and top up with fresh fluid as necessary.

19. Repeat with the brakes on the other wheels. Make sure you check your shop manual for the specific procedure for the front and rear pads of your car.

TORQUE ON BRAKE COMPONENT BOLTS

Brake caliper guide pins: 22 lb-ft
Brake caliper to bearing housing: 22 lb-ft
Wheel bolts: 89 lb-ft

CHAPTER 5 | **LIFE**

Air-cooled Volkswagen Beetles always had a huge following. In addition to car shows, swap meets, and nostalgia drag racing, the nature of VW's lightweight air-cooled engine and long travel suspension made them an excellent choice for travel across the desert. Off-road racing using the Beetle as a basis remains popular to this day, though truthfully so many specialized manufacturers of off-road parts exist that it is possible to build a VW off-road buggy using no Volkswagen parts. The Beetle itself has become an icon and with many of these cars now more than 40 years old, they are gracefully falling into the category of "collector" cars.

Water-cooled Volkswagens haven't yet quite reached the same level of veneration as their air-cooled older brothers, but they are getting close. In fact, in the club scene, there is a distinct split between the air-cooled and water-cooled ranks, to the point that each has its own clubs, meetings, and events to attend. Fortunately, there is a varied and active social scene for owners of late-model Volkswagens, and Golfs and Jettas are the cars that most Volkswagen owners own to enjoy.

CAR SHOWS

One thing that many Volkswagen owners like to do is show off their cars. There exist a variety of different classes in Volkswagen car shows. Some owners' idea of perfection is returning a car as near as possible to the condition it was in when it left the factory. Others want their Golf or Jetta to be unlike anyone else's and will gladly spend thousands of dollars to achieve exactly the right look and specification. In this customized category it's not unusual to see cars with extensive engine modifications, exceptional paint and interiors, and sometimes wild body modifications that express the owner's individuality. In many car clubs, originality is everything, but Volkswagen owners have always been a group that appreciates individual taste.

There are several advantages to attending car shows with your Volkswagen. You get to share your enthusiasm with a wide-ranging group of other people who probably will understand you when you start rhapsodizing over Volkswagen's narrow-angle VR6 engine. You might find you enjoy the car

Shows for water-cooled Volkswagens have become even more popular than those for their air-cooled ancestors. *Author*

There is a show class for everything from completely stock cars to cars that are highly modified. *Author*

show scene enough to travel to other cities and states to attend shows far away, seeing the friends that you make all over the country.

Unless you go really over the top in modifications, your "show" car can still be your daily driver. Best of all, because the third and fourth generation cars are still considered by most of the world as little more than ordinary used cars, you can enjoy Volkswagen heritage and camaraderie at a surprisingly reasonable cost.

DRIVING/TOURING

Sure, you may commute to work every day with your Volkswagen, but that's really not the same as going on a drive for the sheer fun of it.

Exploring back roads in a Golf or Jetta makes a lot of sense: they are small and nimble enough to handle well while getting great fuel economy. They are comfortable places to sit for long periods of time, and they have good climate control systems to keep you warm or cool. They have plenty

A drive in the country is a great way to appreciate your Volkswagen's handling capabilities. *Clewell*

The Golf and Jetta are looked at as a blank canvas by many Volkswagen enthusiasts. *Clewell*

of cargo space just in case you can't pass up a bargain at a rural yard sale.

Maybe best of all, after a long day of driving a Golf or Jetta to get to a weekend destination, you won't mind jumping back in the car for the trip home the next day.

IMPORT DRAG RACING

Back in the 1950s, just about everyone tried their hand at drag racing. Flathead Ford V-8 hot rods and later small-block Chevys ruled the quarter-mile strips. It was a cheap way to have some fun and prove your car was faster than someone else's.

Eventually, bracket racing became popular, where you declared a certain time that your car could run. As long as you

Whatever the type of competition in which you choose to compete, a roll bar adds safety. *Clewell*

weren't faster than your declared time (called "breaking out") and you kept beating your rivals, you would advance to the next round of racing. This kind of racing let cars of vastly different speeds compete against one another. The slowest car would be allowed to leave the starting line first, while the faster car had to wait before it got the green light to go. This made it possible for a car as slow as an original air-cooled Volkswagen Beetle to join in the fun, and they did so in large numbers.

Drag racing had its ups and downs over the following decades, but recently has had a resurgence of interest, thanks largely to an influx of imported sport-compact cars.

When the first front-wheel drive import sedans showed up at the drag strip, they weren't given much respect. With front-wheel drive, the weight transferred to the rear wheels on acceleration, exactly what you didn't need for a fast launch. But four-cylinder front-drivers were cheap to buy, and a new younger generation of drag racers worked hard to develop them into race cars.

In the early days of import drags, Volkswagens played a role, but over time the highly tuneable Honda Civic and Acura Integra became the cars to beat. By the mid-1990s, the sport-compact car segment's enthusiasm was well established nationwide.

Today, there is a strong and continuing interest in import drags and bracket racing. Water-cooled Volkswagens are still a part of this game and there is always a place for them to run, should this be of interest to you.

DYNAMOMETER PULLS

Another, perhaps less subtle, way to demonstrate your car's horsepower is by attaching it to a chassis dynamometer. The prices of these machines have come down and modern systems are computer controlled for a high degree of accuracy and simplicity in operation.

The car's drive wheels are placed upon rollers in the ground that in turn provide increasing resistance as the car accelerates through its gears. When the run is finished, the computer plots horsepower and torque at the wheels against engine speed. This is an excellent way to determine which new performance parts on your car are actually working. At a usual cost of $100 per hour, the cost is not insignificant, but can help you sort out problems at high speed under load, for example.

The competition part comes when a group of owners get together to see who can pull the highest horsepower numbers on the dyno. Some cars that show up at these events are designed strictly for power and are all but impossible to drive on the street. Numbers over 500-horsepower can be obtained from Volkswagen engines, usually for very short periods of time before something fails in a big way.

AUTOCROSSING

One of the joys of performance driving in a Volkswagen is the balance of engine, gearbox, brakes, suspension, and tires that these cars possess. It used to be only sports cars that had this kind of balance, and in the early days sports cars would show up to race around cones placed on a twisting course on a large parking lot.

Autocrossing changed significantly when the first Volkswagen Rabbits appeared. Suddenly you didn't need a cranky old British sports car to go fast. The VW GTI pushed the game further still; it was practically built for autocrossing, and today it's rare to see a "real" sports car for all of the sedans, coupes, and sport compacts.

In autocrossing, the cars run through a pylon-demarked course one at a time against the clock. The top speeds are rarely more than 45–50 miles per hour, and it is a relatively safe and easy way to learn more about the handling of your car at its limits. If you exceed those limits and hit a cone or go off-course, there will be little more than pride that is damaged. The keys to autocrossing are experience and car control, and you will be amazed at how well and how quickly some of your fellow competitors can negotiate the course.

The cars are divided into classes, depending upon engine size and speed potential, and entry fees are quite reasonable (usually less than $25 for a day full of fun). Safety requirements usually include an approved safety helmet (loaner helmets may be available) and the stock seat belts. There may be a technical inspection to ensure your car is mechanically safe before you are allowed to hit the course.

The best car with which to start autocrossing is probably the one you already own. You'll want to put the tire pressures up a bit (maybe 5–8 psi) to keep the tires from rolling under, and remove all the loose items from the interior and the trunk so that they won't fly about as you throw the car through the course.

When you first start out in this sport, you have to concentrate hard just to stay on course and not hit cones. Later, after you gain some proficiency, you will want to look into specialized autocross tires (the area that will bring the biggest immediate improvement) and possibly some suspension upgrades to make your car handle even better. If you make too many modifications, however, you may get moved into a modified class, where the competition becomes fairly intense.

After you become a regular at local autocross competitions, you might want to run in regional and even national events. The major organizer of such activities is the Sports Car Club of America (SCCA). Autocrossing has its own national championships, where the competition is as fierce as one might imagine. For more information, check out www.scca.com to see where you might want to be more involved.

Autocrossing is a great way to safely discover the limits of your car's handling. *Hallstrom*

Pushing the car to its limits at an autocross is safe and fun. *Dan Engle*

Aaron Jongbloedt
Network administrator
Minneapolis, Minnesota

Aaron was looking for a car with a zero to 60 mile per hour time of less than 7 seconds, with a manual transmission that cost less than $7,000. He had caught the autocross bug and wanted a car with which he could compete, but one that was practical enough to use as his daily driver. "I stumbled across VWs when I first borrowed a friend's severely neglected Corrado G60. I absolutely fell in love with the power and the handling. Then I found my Mark III GTI VR6. It fit the bill perfectly and wasn't the stereotypical sports car. I was after the "wolf in sheep's clothing" theme."

Aaron has taken his car to local autocrosses and even a few track days, where he has done well at embarrassing bigger and faster cars. "The VR6 is a heavy pig with way too much weight in the nose. The front end really pushes (understeers) in the corners and the rear gets really light under heavy braking and can get away from you," says Aaron. "Adding a Quaife limited-slip differential really helped that problem and really changed the whole dynamic of the car." Aaron has also found that there are some advantages to having a good power-to-weight ratio: "The best part about racing this car is having Corvette owners being disgruntled as they get passed by an econo-hatchback!"

Although the car is still used as a commuter, Aaron has some future plans. "I am pulling the air conditioning and installing a Schrick Variable Geometry intake manifold, along with gasket matching the intake and exhaust manifolds, and ceramic coating the exhaust headers. The battery is moving to the trunk for better weight distribution and I'll be running 225/45-15 Kumho V710 autocross tires on lighter rims." It's clear enough that Aaron wants to stick with his GTI VR6 and develop it further. Corvettes better watch out!

CHAPTER 5 | LIFE

TRACK DAYS

The next step up from autocrossing is the track day, often sponsored by a club or racing organization. Usually held on an off weekend at a racetrack, these events will give you a chance to drive your Volkswagen on a real racetrack as fast as you can go. Many times a track day will also be a part of a "high performance driver education" program that is designed to help drivers become more comfortable with driving at high speed on a real racetrack. This is helpful, because the first few times out on a track can be daunting for the driver.

At most track days, drivers are split into groups, depending upon their experience levels. Some groups may even have instructors who will ride with you to help you learn the track and how to get the most out of your car. If this is an option, take advantage of it, as there is always something that you will learn from a more experienced driver. An instructor can point out where the corner workers are stationed and help with learning the all-important "line" around the racetrack. This is the path that will result in the fastest lap times and something you will spend lap after lap trying to perfect.

At track days, passing other cars is only allowed in specific, safe places (such as on a long straight) and if you are too aggressive or act in a dangerous manner, you can bet someone will pull you aside and talk with you.

Because you are moving the bar up a notch or two when you attend a track day, there are a few things about which you need to think. It is unlikely that your insurance company will cover any damages that you inflict on your car while running a track day. And, because you are running at high speed on a racetrack, there is always a possibility that you could slide off the course and hit a guardrail, or worse.

A track day provides a higher-speed test of you and your car. *Thrill Photos*

Road racing requires a car that is fully prepared to racing specifications. In other words, a serious commitment of time and money. *Jon Roy*

What's more, you may or may not be voiding your new car's warranty by driving it at speed on a racetrack. This sometimes is considered to be abuse, and if you check the fine print, you'll find that car companies frown on such usage.

You'll also want to make sure your car is in superb mechanical condition. Diving into turn one is not the time to remember that you should have changed the front brake pads. Bleeding the brakes before each track day weekend, changing oil more frequently, uprating to stickier tires and stiffer shock absorbers, adding additional safety equipment (a roll bar and competition safety belts wouldn't be out of place), and keeping your car meticulously maintained are things you'll be doing, once you get serious about running track days.

The good news is that running your car flat-out against the clock on a famous racetrack is a bunch of fun. There are several national organizations specializing in track days, and even your local car club may have an occasional event. Entry fees can range from $150 to over $500, so it isn't a cheap sport, but it is a way to legally drive at the limit and find out what your Volkswagen can really do. Obviously, a car like a GTI VR6 is going to be a lot more fun on the track than a Jetta GL with its slow 2.0-liter four-cylinder engine. Thankfully, Volkswagen has made other versions of the Golf and Jetta that were quick and fun in both the third and fourth generations.

ROAD RACING

After you've run enough track days, it may be that you will want to compete wheel-to-wheel against other drivers. When you've reached this stage, it's time to face some harsh realities. The car you will be taking to the track will not be suitable for driving on the street. It may not even be legal to drive on public roads.

Most racing organizations require you to remove the air bag systems before you are allowed to race wheel-to-wheel and, depending where you live, that could get you into trouble with motor vehicle regulations. In addition, the full roll cage and competition belts will make getting in and out of the car a pain. After removing the sound deadening and interior, the noise will also be unpleasant. You'll likely be running in a

class that allows at least some modifications, so the car's suspension will be too low to drive on ordinary bumpy city streets and the exhaust will be far too loud.

All of this means that you'll need a way to get your car to and from the racetrack, and that means a trailer and another vehicle large enough to tow it and your race car. Most racers, even at the entry level of the sport, are using enclosed trailers. Although they are heavier than an open trailer, requiring an even bigger tow vehicle, they do provide a ready changing room, a place to get out of the rain and a safe place to lock up your tools and parts when going to and from the track. On the other hand, it's easy to hide a low-built open trailer in the bushes next to your house, something that is much harder to do with a bulky and oh-so-visible enclosed unit.

The tow vehicle will probably be some sort of pickup truck or sport utility vehicle, which will require its own insurance and preventative maintenance if it is to be reliable on long trips.

As for insuring your race car, you can get "pit and paddock" insurance that will cover it while it is at home in your garage, on its way to the track, or sitting in the paddock between track sessions. The only time it's not covered is when it's most likely to be damaged: while it's on the track.

If you want to try your hand at track racing your Volkswagen, the first thing you should do is attend a professional driving school. Although these are expensive ($1,500–$4,500), they will give you a chance to find out if you even like the feeling of racing side-by-side against another driver who is trying to beat you.

Driving schools usually provide all the necessary safety gear you'll need and, aside from a healthy credit card, require little from a prospective racer. After attending a pro school, you will be a bit further ahead in your quest for a racing license.

There are several organizations that promote "amateur" road racing in the United States. For example, the SCCA's Club Racing program is how the vast majority of racers in the United States get their start.

The SCCA has its own driver's school, but you must supply your own race car, which must pass a comprehensive technical inspection in order to be allowed on the track. For most, this means building or buying a race car before they ever actu-

Kirk Knestis finds his Golf III to be surprisingly reliable; he competes in a variety of motorsports. *Edward Pipala*

Dr. Kirk Knestis
Senior Evaluation Scientist
University of North Carolina

Building a car that can be used for a variety of different types of motorsport events is quite a challenge. But that's what Kirk Knestis, a research scientist in North Carolina, has tried to do with his 2.0-liter Golf III.

"My background, including rallying and hillclimbs in addition to road racing, steered me toward a car that I could use for a variety of events," said Kirk.

Most people looking for a race car would dismiss the softly sprung and somewhat underpowered GL as inferior to the VR6-powered version of the GTI. Knestis however had a plan.

"I had experience with VWs and knew them to be reliable and able to handle abuse, so when the Sports Car Club of America moved the 2.0-liter Golf III down a class where it was likely to be competitive, I jumped at the first good example I could find."

That was in 2003, and Kirk decided to run his car in the highly restrictive Showroom Stock category, which didn't allow much modification to the soft suspension and plush interior. Halfway through the 2004 season, he decided to switch the car to the popular Improved Touring category, which allows suspension upgrades and a stripped interior. But even then Kirk was faced with a compromise.

"I wanted to keep my car registered for legal use on public roads, to allow me to drive it to events and to use it for rallies," explains Kirk. This meant that unlike many of his competitors, he retained the catalytic converter and door glass, making the car street legal, but dooming it to be farther off the pace than a fully dedicated track car.

Still, the car was both reliable and fun, allowing Kirk to participate in two race-licensing schools and to compete in nine SCCA regional races, a rallycross, two hillclimbs, four Track Days, three NASA sprint races, a 3.5-hour NASA endurance race, and both a 12-hour and a 13-hour endurance race, all during a busy two-year period. The only mechanical failures in all of that competition? A loose shift linkage at a rallycross and a minor rear wheel bearing problem at the 12-hour endurance race.

There is a risk involved in motorsport, as Kirk is acutely aware. In September 2005, he rolled his multipurpose Golf III at a rally, totaling the car's body. Still, this unfortunate mishap has given him a chance to build a better car based upon what he learned from the first one. His plan is to have his new Golf III ready in time for a pair of upcoming endurance races.

"We will run a variety of other events this season, though our schedule has been delayed by the time necessary to make repairs, and will likely be abbreviated by a budget diminished by the costs of rebuilding," said Kirk.

ally get any track experience to find out if this is what they really want to do. You can also rent race cars, sometimes for less than $1,000 for a weekend, and it's a good way to go through a driver's school, with someone else worrying about keeping the car running.

Another organization, The National Auto Sports Association (NASA) offers wheel-to-wheel racing and has several touring car groups in which a third or fourth generation Golf or Jetta could compete. More information can be found at www.NASAProRacing.com, where the various classes and license requirements are specified. Other clubs that have their own racing series include the Midwest Council of Sports Car Clubs (www.mcscc.org) and Waterford Hills Road Racing (www.waterfordhills.com).

If you attend a few races either as a spectator or, better yet, as a volunteer worker, you'll see lots of Volkswagen Golfs. These will almost invariably be first and second generation cars and most will be running in the Improved Touring (IT) category. This class allows significant suspension modifications and some minor changes to the intake and exhaust of the engine. It is a cost-effective way to go racing, and Volkswagens have always been competitive in their classes.

Unfortunately, the third and fourth generation cars haven't brought the same level of enthusiasm, and these cars are quite rare in the amateur racing classes. One reason is that turbocharged cars are not allowed in the popular IT category, eliminating the popular 1.8T engine from competing. The VR6 engine, while eligible, has proven to be somewhat expensive to modify for more performance, while the 2.0-liter four-cylinder is fairly underpowered for the weight of the Golf.

As the first and second generation cars continue to get older and the third and fourth generation cars get cheaper on the used market, one can expect to see more of them taking to the track in the hands of Volkswagen enthusiasts.

PERFORMANCE RALLYING AND RALLYCROSS

If you don't mind getting your car dirty, there is another form of motoring competition that is especially appealing. You may be familiar with the sport from television coverage of the World Rally Championship (WRC) or from playing video games.

Performance rallying consists of driving your car over timed stretches of closed roads as fast as you can. That road might be a gravel track through the forest and it might be raining or snowing or you might be running late at night. This is an extraordinary driver's challenge, so much so that a second team member, the navigator or co-driver, helps keep the team from getting lost and warns the driver of upcoming dangers and obstacles. Also, cars need to be extensively prepared for safety and durability, so you'll need help with that, too. There is significant extra cost involved in bringing a navigator and service crew with you to help keep you and your car going during the event.

As with club racing, the first and second generation Volkswagen Golf has been a longtime choice of rally competitors. The cars were tough and rugged and were fast enough to sometimes surprise the all-wheel drive cars that dominate the sport. An all-wheel drive R32 would seem to be a good choice for this sport, but the lack of any support and special rally parts from Volkswagen of America makes it unlikely that a serious effort will be undertaken.

Until 2004 the SCCA was the organizer of performance rallies in the United States, but that duty has now been taken over by Rally America (www.Rally-America.com), an organization committed to a full calendar of professional and club-level events.

One part of rallying that the SCCA kept is rallycross. This is like an autocross held on loose surfaces and requires much less preparation than all-out performance rallying. The cars can be as simple as your daily driver or a full-house rally weapon, and there are different classes for each level of preparation. The SCCA's rallycross program features more than 150 events around the country and includes a national championship event at the end of the season.

The costs of competing in this form of motorsports are modest, probably in line with serious autocrossing. Specialized rally tires are often used to give grip on a variety of surfaces. The pounding the car takes over jumps and bumps may wear out the shock absorbers and suspension and damage the exhaust system, unless these items are uprated and skid plates are fitted. For those who live in winter climates, RallyCross competition on snow and ice adds yet another dimension to the driver's challenge.

CHAPTER 6 CUSTOMIZE

Just as the original air-cooled Volkswagen Beetle became a medium of self-expression for its owner, few Golf and Jetta enthusiasts are satisfied leaving their cars as they came from the factory. Both the Golf and Jetta are the perfect canvas for the owner who wants a distinctive look, better roadholding, or more performance from the water-cooled engine.

This slightly modified hood changes the whole appearance of this GTI. *Author*

help you achieve your dreams. This is good news: it means that all of the tough engineering and sourcing of minute parts can be left to the professionals. What's more, the broad experience of both Volkswagen owners and VW part manufacturers means that you'll never be at a loss for someone to ask for advice and help if you get stuck while working on your project car.

As with any project, there are pitfalls to be avoided, but the fact that so many enthusiasts have been down the same road ahead of you makes the whole process that much easier.

SLIPPERY SLOPE

The biggest problem that comes from modifying any car, but one that applies especially to Golfs and Jettas, is the danger of being seduced into the wrong direction by well-meaning but often uninformed "experts." This is often the result of the lack of any clear plan of what you want your car to do when you are finished with its modifications.

There aren't many limits when you begin customizing your Volkswagen Golf or Jetta. *Clewell*

There is literally no end to the number and types of modifications you can make to your Golf or Jetta. Owners have found everything from an example of postmodern art, a symbol of counterculture revolution, a fire-breathing drag racer, an outlaw street racer, a canyon-carving touring car, a road race demon, or a World Rally Championship contender under the sheet metal skin of their eager Volkswagens.

Because these cars have been so popular for so many years, a wide variety of companies and manufacturers wait to

Modifications can run from mild to wild. *Clewell*

If you want to build a car to drive on a racetrack during track days, it is likely that it won't be very comfortable on the frost heaves and potholes you encounter on your daily commute to and from work. Likewise, if you build an engine whose purpose is to blow the doors off of Honda Civics at import drag racing events, there is little chance that this peaky engine will be fun or reliable when you drive it on the street.

Each type of event requires its own levels of specialization and getting talked into ultrastiff road racing springs or a super-hot camshaft can lead to results that aren't what you had in mind. Fortunately, the nature of Golfs and Jettas is such that you can make your changes gradually, upgrading performance or appearance as time, money, and the need arises.

The key is to look before you leap; always ask yourself before bolting on the next superperformance goody if this really brings you closer to your target of the ultimate Golf or Jetta.

SOME PRACTICAL REALITIES

The third and fourth generations of Golfs and Jettas were built from 1993 and onward. The earlier first and second generation cars had relatively simple fuel injection and ignition systems that were easy to modify for more performance. They also were equipped with safety belts and little else in the way of passive occupant protection in the event of an accident, so changing steering wheels, seats, and even dashboards was a straightforward proposition.

By the mid-1990s however, Volkswagens were required to meet ever more stringent exhaust emission and safety regulations, and this resulted in much higher levels of sophistication when it came to engine management and passive restraints.

The result has been cars that are faster and more reliable, but whose sophistication often stands in the way of the traditional shade-tree mechanic approach to performance and appearance upgrades.

In many states and countries, removing or disabling air bags or other passive restraint devices, removing catalytic converters, dramatically altering emission-related components, or even changing the ride height beyond certain limits is illegal. That may mean, depending where you live and on the age of your car, that building that weekend racetrack demon that you can still drive to work on Monday morning may not be possible.

The good news is that clever tuners have come up with ways of working within the confines of engine management computers to liberate more horsepower from Volkswagen's family of engines while still maintaining a semblance of environmental responsibility and reliability. Sometimes this can be as easy as reprogramming the on-board engine management computer with a new electronic "chip" that tells the engine how to produce more power. In other cases, liberating even more power can require changes like less-restrictive exhausts systems, bigger fuel injectors, hotter camshafts, and even larger turbochargers and intercoolers.

It often does no good to make these kinds of changes without the background and experience to know how each change will affect the other components in the engine and drivetrain. Extensive engine modifications are beyond the scope of this book, but there certainly are plenty of Volkswagen specialists who can build just about anything you could ever want.

Underhood modifications must still meet local exhaust emissions regulations. *Hallstrom*

Chad Erickson runs SCI Performance, a shop specializing in water-cooled Volkswagens. *Author*

Chad Erickson
Owner/ Head Technician
SCI Performance
Minneapolis, Minnesota

Chad Erickson grew up around Volkswagens. "My father was a Volkswagen mechanic in the 1960s and 1970s and eventually ended up teaching automotive technology at a local technical college."

As a youngster, Chad was always hanging around the garage helping his dad keep the family's used cars on the road. When he was 16, he got his first car. Naturally it was a Volkswagen, although in this case it was a water-cooled, first generation Scirocco. That car actually led him to his current career.

"I had done an engine swap and had stopped by the local VW dealer to buy some parts. They had a particular problem with a fuel injection system that I had solved in my own VW, so I helped them out."

Before Erickson had even graduated from college, he was working at the Volkswagen dealership. He stayed there for 5 years before opening his own shop 10 years ago. SCI Performance has become a haven for VW and Audi performance enthusiasts in the Midwest and his crowded facility, formerly a repair shop for air-cooled VW's, also serves as a meeting place for the local Volkswagen club. Erickson likes the look, feel, and quality of Audis and Volkswagens and won't work on anything else.

"Cars have become so complex that nobody can know everything about every car. You have to specialize and try to know as much as possible about one type of car."

For Chad Erickson and SCI Performance, the choice of Volkswagen was never in question.

WHICH ONE?

You've probably already made your choice between the roomy and practical four-door Jetta sedan and the sportier (but often equally practical) Golf or GTI hatchback, or even the fun-filled cabriolet. Each of these body-styles has its plusses and minuses. Jettas are a bit heavier and longer than the Golf. The Cabriolet has a chassis that is less stiff, compromising its ultimate handling performance.

If you are a building a touring car with impeccable road manners, it's hard to imagine a better starting point than a GTI; a lot of the upgrades you'll want are already a part of the package. If you are building an all-out track car, you could start with a base Golf GL because almost every part of the drivetrain and suspension is going to be changed or modified anyway. If you need to use your car to haul the kids to school, but want to have some fun along the way, the Jetta can be built into a very sophisticated performance machine.

Underneath, the Golf, GTI, and Jetta are basically the same, giving you a very broad spectrum of choices.

The light weight of the two-door Golf body shell makes it an excellent starting point for a project car. *Hallstrom*

Many Volkswagen fans desire a customized look. *Clewell*

Interiors can be redone to reflect the owner's taste. *Clewell*

BODY AND PAINT

From calm and sophisticated to wild and wacky, the range of possibilities for interior and exterior makeovers are practically unlimited. Some want their cars to have the suave elegance of a high-end European exotic. Others want the look and feel of a World Rally Championship contender. Some upgrades and modifications like body kits, underbody neon lights, imaginative paint jobs and gullwing doors are strictly for show, while others like front and rear spoilers, sport seats, and auxiliary lights can and do improve the driving experience.

If you want to make changes to the interior, you will run into safety concerns. The air bag system in the steering wheel and proper mounting of aftermarket sport seats is a serious matter. The factory engineers have spent literally thousands of hours to make sure everything holds together in a serious collision and your changes and modifications should do nothing that compromises their efforts. Other than that, your imagination should be your guide.

As we've already said, Volkswagens have always been blank canvases for their artist owners. The Golf and Jetta are no exception, and you need only to attend a Volkswagen show to see the gamut of what people are willing to do to individualize their cars.

WHEELS AND TIRES

The first performance upgrade you should make to your Golf or Jetta is performance tires. So much of the correct tire choice is going to depend on how and where you drive your vehicle. Your car's original tires were chosen by the manufacturer to be a broad compromise of wet, dry, and snow traction; long tread life; low tread noise; ride comfort; and low rolling resistance. For many, wheels and tires are an important style statement; for others, the performance that they can bring is the real concern.

Above: Plus sizing puts larger-diameter wheels on a car without changing the overall tire diameter. *The Tire Rack*

Right: Even the appearance of a daily driver can be improved with custom wheels. *The Tire Rack*

Opposite bottom: Changing wheels and tires can give a car a new look. *The Tire Rack*

You may wish to enhance some areas of performance at the expense of some others when you choose tires for your car. Maximum dry performance, for example, comes from "summer" tires or even street-legal racing tires. These won't work in the snow and ice of winter, and many serious enthusiasts have a separate set of tires for winter.

Increasing the rim diameter (so-called "plus" sizing) from 15-inch to 16-inch or 17-inch will allow you to run lower-aspect-ratio tires that have shorter sidewalls and are more responsive. Sometimes, especially when no other suspension upgrades have been made, the response of a low-aspect-ratio tire can be too quick, making the car darty and unpleasant to drive. And remember, just because all the tuner cars in the enthusiast magazines are running 18-inch wheels and tires doesn't mean that it's the right setup for your car.

Fortunately, there is a company with a vast database on wheel and tire upgrades which is willing to share its information. The people at Tire Rack of South Bend, Indiana, are more than willing to share their expertise either by phone (888-541-1777) or on their web site (www.tirerack.com) to make the decision-making process easier.

Volkswagen brakes are adequate for street use, but may need to be upgraded if the performance of the vehicle is improved, especially for track duty. *Clewell*

BRAKES

Although Volkswagen's brakes on its standard cars are adequate for stock levels of performance, they begin to look less so as horsepower and performance increase. And the stock brakes are inadequate if you are doing any kind of track work. Fortunately, the upgrades are straightforward.

The first step is to replace the brake pads with new pads that use high-performance friction materials. These resist the heat of repeated use from high speed, such as you might do on a racetrack. There are several choices to make. Full competition pads for an all-out racing car may not heat up enough in normal driving to be useful on the street, while intermediate level pads may not give adequate fade resistance on the track.

You should expect performance pads to be noisier than stock pads and possibly more prone to producing brake dust that will coat your wheels. They also might wear your car's brake rotors more quickly. Brake rotors can also be upgraded to higher quality units, or even to rotors that have cooling slots machined into them. The slots can also be beneficial in removing water from the rotor in the wet.

Replacing the standard rubber brake lines with lines covered with braided stainless steel can result in a firmer, more predictable brake pedal feel. The rubber lines can flex under the thousands of pounds of line pressure inside the brake system, and the braided stainless-steel line resists this flex.

For really high performance applications, replacing the front, rear, or both front and rear brake calipers with aftermarket units can dramatically improve the car's braking performance. Calipers can even be a style statement, as evidenced by the red and blue brake calipers the factory fitted on some of its sporty fourth generation models.

Several companies make complete bolt-on braking systems for Golfs and Jettas, and buying a full system will save you having to engineer individual components from scratch.

These systems come with everything you need, including discs, calipers, pads, and braided-steel lines. A less expensive alternative would be to find used brake calipers from a higher-end model at an auto recycler and fit them to your car. Best to stay away from used discs unless you check them carefully for cracks, cupping, and thickness.

SUSPENSION

Upgrading the suspension is something that will have a huge and noticeable effect on how your vehicle handles. The third generation cars were particularly vilified for their sloppy and soggy handling, and changing this situation is straightforward and satisfying.

First, some basics. In general, lowering a car will lower its center of gravity and help it handle better. That's why Volkswagen lowered the Golf when it built the GTI. There are a limits, however. If you drive your car on the street and lower it to the

Lowering a car will help it corner better. *Clewell*

Adding negative camber (tilting the top of the tire inward) can help prevent it from rolling under during hard cornering. *Clewell*

" . . . even with the Sport Luxury package, the Jetta delivers too much rock and roll for our tastes."

—Car and Driver, *November 2001*

As a car leans into a corner, its outside tires tend to tuck under, reducing the amount of tread that is in contact with the road. To reduce this effect, the suspension can be set with negative camber at an alignment shop. Tires with negative camber lean inward at the top and can be expected to wear their inside shoulders more rapidly. Under hard cornering the initial negative camber will help the outside tires remain more upright, improving grip.

The amount of adjustment available from the stock camber adjustments is usually about 1 degree negative. To get more than this (2–3 degrees negative is common on race cars) the upper shock mount can be replaced with a special "camber plate" that allows the top of the shock to be moved inward to provide additional camber.

At the same time the shop sets your camber, they can also adjust the toe at the front and rear. The stock specifications of zero toe-in at the front and slight toe-out at the rear (not adjustable) give good stability and handling balance. Caster angle is not adjustable on these vehicles.

The suspension must absorb road imperfections and help isolate the cabin from jarring impacts. It does this in part by isolating the suspension components from the chassis through rubber bushings. As these bushings age, they get softer and looser, making the suspension sloppier. Replacing them with high-performance bushings that are stiffer than stock not only restores the car's handling, but can actually make it crisper and more precise when entering a curve. The perfect time to do this is when the suspension is apart for an upgrade to stiffer springs and shock absorbers.

point where the chassis hits speed bumps or scrapes going into driveways, you will probably eventually damage something.

Aside from the potential damage, excessively lowering a Golf or Jetta results in two undesirable outcomes. The first is that the half shafts that drive the front wheels will eventually run at excessive angles, causing them to wear prematurely. The second is that when lowered too far, the geometry of the suspension introduces significant "bump-steer" which can cause squirrelly handling whenever the car hits a bump.

Lowering is best accomplished by fitting shorter springs. Because the amount of suspension travel is reduced when the car is lowered, these springs must also be stiffer, to prevent all of the travel from being used up when the car hits a bump. Stiffer springs require stiffer shock absorbers to control their motion on rebound.

Stiffer springs will also change the handling balance and could result in a car that is unstable at the cornering limits. For this reason it's a good idea to buy springs in matched sets of fronts and rears, so that the proper handling balance can be maintained. Spring and shock absorber packages are available from a variety of suspension specialists. If you want to drop your car's ride height by more than about an inch, you will need shortened shock absorbers, which will come with the whole package.

Stiffer springs will reduce body roll in a corner. To further reduce lean and to change the handling balance, stiffer anti-roll bars can be fitted to your car. Anti-roll bars (sometimes called "sway" bars) are torsional springs that mount across the car and resist body lean. As with springs, changing anti-roll bars can have a beneficial or detrimental effect on the handling balance and should be matched to make an entire suspension package.

A "stress bar" (in red) can help stiffen the vehicle by tying together the tops of the struts. *Author*

In addition, the rubber engine mounts (which also support the transmission) can deteriorate with age, and replacing them with new stock items or high-performance mounts can also improve the vehicle's crisp feel.

Early Volkswagen Golfs and Rabbits had bodies that were prone to twisting under heavy cornering loads. This tendency was much reduced in the third and fourth generation of Golfs and Jettas, but the stiffness of the body and chassis can still be improved through the use of "stress bars." These are tubular structures that bolt across the chassis to reinforce the shock absorber and suspension mounts and help prevent the chassis from twisting when the car is cornered at its limits. Although not as critical as it was in previous generations of Golfs, the front and rear stress bars will help stiffen the chassis and allow the suspension to do its job.

WHICH ENGINE TO TUNE?

You basically have four choices when it comes to third and fourth generation Golf and Jetta powerplants: the 2.0-liter four-cylinder, the 2.8-liter VR6 six-cylinder, the 1.8-liter turbocharged and intercooled four-cylinder, and the 1.9-liter TDI diesel engine. Each has its strengths and weaknesses, and there were improvements and modifications made by the factory over the life of each of these motors. Let's look at each one and its potential for performance tuning.

2.0-Liter Four-cylinder

When this engine came out, it was largely dismissed for its relatively low power output (115 horsepower) and economy-car nature. It was the only engine available in a Golf in the United States, even in the GTI from 1993 until 1995. The engine was significantly revised in 1999, although it retained its 115-horsepower rating.

In reality, the 2.0-liter four-cylinder engine had some things going for it. First of all, it was the first Golf engine with a crossflow cylinder head. This meant that the intake ports were located on one side of the head while the exhaust ports were on the opposite side. Previous four-cylinder Volkswagen engines had the intake and exhaust ports on the same side of the head. Separating the hot exhaust from the cool intake charge and providing long intake runners was beneficial in many ways.

The crossflow head was specifically designed for the U.S. market, where its broad torque range and good fuel efficiency was especially appreciated. This was never designed as a high-speed, high-performance engine, however, and sometime in 1996 Volkswagen changed from a forged crankshaft to a cast-iron one that was at least two pounds heavier and not quite as strong. It isn't a problem for a street-driven car, but is a limitation for those looking for race-level performance.

The big news for the 2.0-liter in the third generation Golf and Jetta was the use of a new Bosch Motronic engine management system. Motronic controlled ignition timing and fuel injection by using a series of stored computerized "maps" for every operating condition. It wasn't long before tuners came out with "chips" for the Motronic system to liberate more performance from the 2.0-liter engine.

Where the 2.0-liter engine in the third generation was closely related to what had come earlier (and can even be easily swapped into previous generation chassis), the next iteration was quite different. Some of the changes included:

- Lower engine block (220-millimeter versus 236.5-millimeter)
- No distributor and intermediate shaft
- Coil-pack ignition
- No front engine mount
- Oil pump built into the front of the engine means crankshaft won't interchange with Mk III engines
- Cast-iron crankshaft (like later Mk III engines)
- Water pump in block instead of external
- Different style of oil pan
- Cylinder head bolts are 10-millimeter instead of 11-millimeter
- The changes make the potential for engine swaps into previous generations of Golfs and Jettas daunting. They also did nothing to improve the performance potential of Volkswagen's base engine.

Improving the 2.0-liter four-cylinder engine for better performance must be done with the engine's limitations in mind. Although supercharging and turbocharging of this engine has been done, you would be better served putting your efforts into a car whose engine bay already included a 1.8T engine.

For all of that, the 2.0-liter cars are inexpensive on today's market and tuning one is a cheap endeavor. With careful attention to detail, as much as 130 horsepower can be liberated by choosing the right combination of aftermarket parts. These would include:

- Chip for the engine management computer
- Less restrictive exhaust (cat-back)
- Less restrictive air filter on intake
- Performance three-angle valve job
- Porting the cylinder head
- Fitting a performance camshaft and uprated valve springs
- Underdrive accessory pulley
- Lightened flywheel

Not all of these changes would need to be done at one time. Just the first three bolt-on projects—the less restrictive intake and exhaust and the chip—would make a noticeably faster and more fun 2.0-liter engine, without hurting engine reliability or breaking any laws regarding exhaust emissions.

"The 1.8T made four-cylinder Volkswagens cool again in 1999, but the majority of cars still leave the dealer lot with eight valves."

—European Car, February 2003

"The lowliest of VW's U.S. engines can be worth the trouble to modify."

—European Car, July 2004

CHIPPING FOR PERFORMANCE

It seems too good to be true—simply plug an aftermarket computer chip in place of the stock one in your car's engine management computer and liberate huge amounts of extra horsepower. You have to ask: If it were that simple, wouldn't the car manufacturers do it already? The answer is yes and no. If you are a car manufacturer, keeping wild-eyed performance enthusiasts happy is just one of your many, often conflicting, priorities. Fuel economy, low exhaust emissions, reliability, and keeping the bean counters and production people happy are all part of the mix when building cars.

The tools the chip tuners use to get more performance include: removal of any electronic speed limiters, increasing the redline of the rev limiter, advancing spark timing at different throttle settings, and adjusting the air/fuel mixture for additional power, sometimes at the expense of lower fuel economy or higher exhaust emissions. All this is done by creating new "maps" that the engine management uses to make the engine operate.

Replacing the chip on the circuit board is often done by mailing your circuit board to a specialist, who makes the replacement and sends it back to you. This means your car could be out of commission for several days. The engine management systems used in the fourth generation Volkswagen cars no longer require the physical replacement of a memory chip in the engine controller, as software can be flashed into the computer's memory via the on-board diagnostic system (OBD-I or OBD-II depending on year of manufacture) much the same way as the dealer updates the engine's software during routine service. This is called serial programming and is the way modern cars are chipped for performance.

VR6 Six-Cylinder

When Volkswagen's sporty Corrado coupe ended production and its silky 2.8-liter VR6 finally found its way into the Golf III, performance enthusiasts had something to cheer about. Although the VR6 had been available in the four-door Jetta GLX from 1993, the lighter and more nimble Golf GTI VR6 really showcased the six-cylinder's abilities.

With 172-horsepower, the stock engine could crank out zero-to-60-mile per hour times near 7 seconds, serious performance-car territory in the mid-1990s. But naturally, there were those for whom the GTI VR6 was just a starting point, and performance tuning was quickly applied to Volkswagen's narrow angle marvel.

Like the 2.0-liter four-cylinder, the VR6 responds well to the usual tuning techniques. However, because the engine is already at a high state of tune and has reasonably good intake breathing and a free-flowing exhaust, the gains made from tuning upgrades just won't be as great.

The search for more power for the VR6 starts with reprogramming the engine management computer ("chipping") to find a few extra horsepower and to take advantage of the other modifications to come. These include a cat-back exhaust system, and a less restrictive air intake system. Actually, you can simply remove the trumpet-shaped air-silencer from inside of the stock air-filter box and not only gain some flow, but also make the engine growl of the VR6 more pronounced.

Likewise, an aftermarket variable geometry intake manifold that automatically adjusts the length of the intake runners at low and high speed can be fitted to the VR6 engine. Doing so will give a smooth rush of power across the entire rpm range.

The VR6 also responds well to a change in camshafts (intake and exhaust), but this is a project that requires significant mechanical skill. The VR6 is an interference engine, meaning the valves will hit the pistons if the cam timing isn't exactly correct, so unless you have lots of experience, you might leave the camshafts to a professional mechanic.

In 2002, Volkswagen found a way to stuff 24-valves into the cylinder head of the VR6 engine, resulting in 200 horsepower. The four-valve VR6 engine responds well to reprogramming of the engine management system and improvements to the intake and exhaust systems.

Opening up the exhaust system helps the engine make more power. *Hallstrom*

Tim McKinney
Automotive photographer and writer
Ithaca, New York

Tim McKinney has a job most car enthusiasts dream about. He is a professional photographer, whose specialty is shooting cars. Not only has this given him a chance to travel to automotive events all over the world, it has also given him the opportunity to use his own personal car as a magazine project car, testing new parts and modifications and writing about them for an envious readership.

One such project was a 1995 Jetta GLX.

"The Jetta was a bit of serendipitous luck," explains Tim. "It was four years old with only 16,000 miles on it, literally driven by a lady owner only on weekends."

Tim had been impressed by the sight of Volkswagen factory-backed rally cars sliding past the lenses of his cameras at Pro Rally events in the late 1980s, and he wanted to find out what the fuss was about.

Although he enjoyed the car's ability to eat up miles on his frequent photography assignments, it wasn't long before he started to make modifications. A pair of European Golf H3 headlights and matching hood cleaned up the front appearance. The engine was modified with Schrick 268 camshafts and a VGi variable intake manifold. A Bosal header and exhaust system also helped the engine breathe. A Peloquins limited-slip differential put that extra power to the ground and H&R's coil-over suspension kept everything connected to the ground in corners. New SSR wheels hid an upgrade to bigger brakes from a later model Jetta. Now the car would not only eat up Interstate miles, it would blast down back roads.

Tim went on to drive his hot rod Jetta for 120,000 troublefree miles before recently replacing it with a 2003 Saab Vector.

"It's a great car, too, but unlike the huge interest my Jetta generated among VW enthusiasts, not as many Saab fans come up to me to talk about my car."

As with the 2.0-liter engine, both supercharging and turbocharging kits are available for the VR6 engine. Depending upon how much boost pressure is used (and how long you want the engine to survive) much more horsepower (80–100 more is typical) can be found, dropping the zero-to-60-mile per hour times into the low 5-second range or lower. These kits aren't cheap ($2,500 is a good starting point) and require significant underhood mechanical skills. They also may not be legal in every state.

On the lunatic fringe, twin turbo setups have given more than 400 horsepower from the 24-valve VR6 engine, but such highly tuned engines are extremely fragile.

> "Although the VR6 is no stranger to turbos, the systems we've seen are usually custom-built, one-off programs, things that are more of a suggestion than a fully fledged kit."
>
> —European Car, January 2005

Volkswagen did the tuners one better when in 2004 it introduced its 240-horsepower R32 model. The engine capacity was increased to 3.2-liters and the compression ratio went from 10.5:1 to 11.25:1. Variable valve timing for the intake and exhaust camshafts provided excellent torque and drivability over a broad range of engine speeds. The intake and exhaust systems were both extensively modified from the normal 24V VR6 engine to help make the car a performance enthusiast's dream.

1.8T

The biggest problem with Volkswagen's VR6 engine was the cost of making performance upgrades. The components were expensive, and as the car was already highly tuned from the factory, the gains to be had weren't huge.

When the 1.8T engine appeared in the fourth generation of the Golf and Jetta, it wasn't met with much initial enthusiasm. The five-valve-per cylinder turbocharged and intercooled engine came from the Audi A4, where it was introduced in 1997. The New Beetle used the engine when it was introduced in 1998 (on the fourth generation Golf platform), although that

This turbocharged VR6 engine made more than 400 horsepower on the dynamometer. *Author*

150-horsepower engine used a smaller turbocharger, intercooler, and injectors than that of the Audi's engine.

The 1.8T finally found its way into Golfs and Jettas in 2001. In the Audi TT (which also shared the fourth generation Golf platform) this 1,781-cc engine produced 180 horsepower. Initially in the Golf GTI, the 1.8T engine was the same basic configuration of the 180-horsepower Audi engine, but used its engine management software to dial back its output to 150 horsepower at 5,700 rpm and 155 lb-ft of torque at 1,750 rpm. That changed in 2002, when Volkswagen upgraded the 1.8T to 180 horsepower and added a six-speed manual transmission to the mix. This was more like it, and the GTI 1.8T could compete with the Japanese cars that were becoming the mainstay of the sport-compact car craze.

Tuning the 1.8T engine ended up to be far easier than any previous Volkswagen engine had been. The engine management computer in the 150-horsepower cars limited turbocharger boost to 0.6-bar (8.8-psi) while the 180-horsepower cars had a limit of 0.8-bar (11.8 psi). Clearly, the 150-horsepower cars can be upgraded to 180 horsepower simply by changing the software in the engine management system.

A larger exhaust system will liberate an additional 10 horsepower, albeit with slightly more noise. Although you can spend money on a stainless steel exhaust, most tuners say that the exhaust temperature of the turbocharged 1.8T engine is so high that it burns off most water vapor quickly, and that a standard steel exhaust system will last just fine in this application.

Most tuners also agree that the stock intake air box does a very good job, requiring little more than a low-restriction air filter to give good performance.

Interestingly, the stock intercooler (a device that cools the intake air after it has been compressed by the turbocharger), while not restrictive, is small and can heat up to the point where performance drops after running hard over a period of time. The solution is to fit a bigger intercooler, like one from the 225-horsepower Audi TT.

DIVERTER VALVE

The 1.8T engine uses a diverter valve to protect the throttle plate from getting hammered by boost pressure when the throttle is closed. This valve uses a vacuum source to sense when the throttle plate is closed, and it bleeds away the boost pressure. When higher-than-stock turbocharger boost pressures are used, the diaphragm in the diverter valve can fail, leaving the engine without boost. The solution is to install a heavy-duty aftermarket diverter valve.

Getting more than about 200 horsepower from the 1.8T engine is possible, but becomes much more involved. As with the 225-horsepower Audi TT, a larger turbocharger and intercooler and higher-flow fuel injectors are needed, and custom engine management software will be required. The stock clutch will probably need an upgrade at this point. Over 300 horsepower will require new forged pistons and connecting rods and a range of engine modifications. At the limits, more than 500 horsepower can be pulled from the 1.8T engine in highly modified form.

1.9 TDI Diesel

Most owners of diesel Golfs and Jettas are looking for economical operation and not performance and speed. The modifications that these owners make are primarily for enhanced reliability and to overcome some of the problems that have shown up over time. Still, as demonstrated by Audi's recent efforts with turbocharged diesel engines at the 24-hour race at Le Mans, the potential for diesel performance is an area that might bear fruit in the future.

"At the track, the TDI trails the slowest gasoline Jettas by more than a second, but with copious low-end torque routed through a responsive five-speed manumatic transmission, it tends to feel quicker than the 11.3-second 0-to-60 mph time suggests."

—Car and Driver, March 2004

TRANSMISSION UPGRADES

Although the stock transmission is reasonably durable under ordinary use, it can suffer if it is driven roughly. Volkswagen recommends synthetic gear oil in its transmissions, and this will help protect the gears and synchronizers.

When cornering hard under power, the inside front tire is lightly loaded and can begin to spin. When this happens, the differential in the transmission sends all of the power to this lightly loaded tire. To send power to the tire that is still in contact with the ground a slip-limiting device is needed for the differential and final drive. A variety of different slip-limiting devices are available for Volkswagens. Fitting them is beyond the scope of this book, but they can make a big difference in lap times and are really required for serious track work.

Other upgrades can improve the quality of gear shifts in your Volkswagen. Replacing the stock shift plate on the transmission with a "short-shift" kit (or one from an Audi

"Like the German manufacturer's earlier engines, it isn't hard to make more power from the 1.8T, provided the proper recipe is followed."

—Grassroots Motorsports, February 2006

A short shift kit from an Audi TT will shorten the shift throws on Mark IV cars with manual transmissions. *Author*

TT on fourth generation cars) will shorten the throws and make shifting more precise. Earlier cars will also benefit from weighted shift rods. They don't change the length of the throws, but make the shifter assembly feel more solid and robust.

Volkswagen used rivets to hold the ring gear to the differential carrier in the final drive. These rivets can fail and cause significant damage inside of the transmission. The solution is to drill out all of the rivets and have them replaced by hardened bolts. This isn't cheap, but can help prevent a bigger failure if you drive your car hard.

It is also important to note that reverse gear is not synchronized in these gearboxes, and shifting to reverse while the car is rolling forward can jam the manual transmission into reverse, requiring significant repair. The answer is to always make sure you are at a stop before shifting into reverse.

SIX PERFORMANCE UPGRADE PROJECTS

Finding the right wheels for your Golf or Jetta is a combination of personal taste and proper engineering. *Hallstrom*

1 TIRE AND WHEEL UPGRADE

 DIFFICULTY: Easy

 MODELS: All Mk IV models

 **COST:** $$$–$$$$

 PARTS: Wheels, tires, wheel bolts (if needed)

TOOLS: Floor jack, jack stand, tire lug wrenche, torque wrench, small hook, tire pressure gauge, never-seize compound, spray wax

The first step to higher performance is upgrading the wheels and tires that came on your Volkswagen. By now, the original equipment tires that came with your car are probably worn and need replacing. By choosing a replacement tire that emphasizes specific performance characteristics, you can dramatically improve the handling and performance of your car. Not insignificantly, by changing wheels and by "plus-sizing" you can customize your car's appearance.

TIRE SPEED RATING

The maximum speed a tire can withstand depends upon the load the tire is carrying. For this reason, tires carry load index and speed rating information in their size designations. A typical Volkswagen tire for example, 195/65 R15 91H carries a load index of 91 and an H speed rating. When replacing tires, your new tires should at least match the original load index number and speed rating. The speed ratings are:

Speed Rating	Top Speed	
	Mph	Kph
S	112	180
T	118	190
U	124	200
H	130	210
V	149	240
Z	above 140	above 240
W	168	270
Y	186	300

When Z-rated tires were introduced, it was up to the vehicle and tire manufacturer to certify for each specific vehicle at what speed above 149 miles per hour the tires would be safe. More recently, W and Y speed ratings have been added. Typically these will be listed as 285/35 ZR19 99Y, indicating that the tires are approved for speeds above 149 miles per hour (the Z-Rating) and that at a load index of 99, a maximum speed of 186 miles per hour is allowed. When the Y-rating is included in parenthesis (285/35 ZR19 (99Y)) it indicates that the tires have been tested in excess of the 186-mile per hour speed capability.

Make sure that the wheels' bolts fit properly and that the offset is correct so that the wheels don't hit suspension elements or the inner fenders. This is especially important if the car has been lowered. *Clewell*

After you've chosen which tires and wheels you want to use, you will need to check on a few things that your tire supplier should be able to help determine.

Will you need new wheel bolts to match the wheels that you are using? Will you need any wheel spacers to move the wheels away from the brake calipers and help everything fit? If so, do the wheel spacers mean you will need longer wheel bolts? What tire pressure does your tire supplier recommend for a starting point for your application? Armed with the answers to these questions, changing the wheels and tires is about as difficult as the Tire Rotation procedure we talked about in Chapter 4.

WHEEL AND TIRE CHANGE PROCEDURE

1. Using a small screwdriver or wire with a hook in it, remove the caps (if so equipped) covering the vehicle's wheel bolts.

2. Using a lug wrench, loosen the wheel bolts on one side of the car.

3. Raise one whole side of the vehicle using the floor jack and then support it on jack stands. Make sure the vehicle is in gear and that the parking brake is set. Block the wheels on the opposite side of the vehicle to ensure it cannot roll away. Lift the vehicle only under the proper lifting points under the car.

4. Remove the wheel bolts and remove both wheels from one side of the car. Sometimes the wheel will stick to the hub. You may need to hammer with a rubber mallet on the inside of the tire to get the wheel to loosen from the hub. This can be prevented in the future using the spray wax hint below.

5. Inspect the tread area and sidewalls of both tires carefully. Abnormal wear might include cupping of the outside shoulders or uneven wear of the blocks. This might indicate a suspension alignment problem and should be checked by a mechanic or alignment shop.

6. Put the new wheels and tires onto the hubs, including any spacer plates that are required for your wheel application.

NOTE: Because Volkswagen uses wheel bolts instead of studs and lug nuts, it is sometimes difficult to hold the wheel in place while starting the first bolt. You can try sitting next to the wheel and putting your foot under the tire to lever it up into position.

HINT: If you smear a bit of anti-seize compound (available at auto parts stores) onto the wheel bolts, it will make them easier to take off next time.

HINT: Spraying some wax onto the back side of the wheel flange (where it meets with the hub) will make it easier to take the wheel off next time. Just be sure you don't get any spray wax onto the brake rotors or brake pads.

7. Tighten the wheel bolts with the wrench (make them just snug at this point).

8. Spin the wheels on the hubs and make sure there is no rubbing of the wheel on the brakes or suspension or of the tire on the fender or the suspension components. Turn the front wheels with the steering wheel to full right and left lock and check again for interference.

9. Lower the car off of the jack stands.

10. Tighten the wheel bolts. The wheel bolts should be tightened in a diagonal pattern. Imagine the five bolts are arrayed around a clock face. Starting with a bolt at the top of the wheel (in the 12 o'clock position), tighten 12, then 7, then 2, then 10, then 4. If you don't have a torque wrench, make the bolts tight. If you do have a torque wrench, the torque value for all wheel bolts is 89 lb-ft (120 N-m).

11. Check the air pressures and adjust to the recommended levels, which can be found on a placard inside the vehicle door jams, glove box lid, or trunk lid, or given by your tire supplier.

12. Repeat the procedure on the other side of the vehicle.

13. Once the car is back on its new wheels and tires, check carefully for interference with the wheels, tires, and body. Take the car for a CAREFUL test drive and listen for any scrapes or rubs when you go over bumps. Any strange noises should be investigated immediately to ensure that the new wheels and tires are not rubbing the body, brakes, or suspension.

TIRE AND WHEEL PACKAGES

Package	Tire Size	Wheel Size	Offset (mm)
Standard	195/65 R15 91H	6J 15	38
Optional	205/55 R16 91H	6-1/2 J16	42
Optional	225/45 R17 90/91H	7 J17	38
Optional	225/55 R18 90/91Z	7-1/2 J18	38

Note: Bolt circles for VW models are 4-100 mm or 5-100 mm depending upon year and model

2 BRAKE UPGRADE

DIFFICULTY: High

MODELS: All models

COST: $$$–$$$$

PARTS: Performance brake pads, brake rotor, braided stainless steel brake hoses, brake calipar kits, DOT 4 Super brake fluid

TOOLS: 11-millimeter wrench (front), 7-millimeter wrench (rear) pressure or vacuum brake bleeding system or small diameter plastic hose, wrenches, rags, floor jack, jack stands, tire lug wrench, torque wrench

Three levels of performance upgrades will make your brakes more effective:

Upgrade to higher performance brake pads and new rotors
Upgrade to braided stainless steel brake hoses
Upgrade to new brake calipers, pads, rotors, and hoses (usually available together in a high-performance brake kit)

Pads and Rotors

1. Raise the vehicle and support with jack stands.

2. Remove the wheel at the corner on which you will be working.

Brake calipers on the Jetta GLI of 2004 were painted red. *Author*

3. Disconnect the wiring harness on those vehicles equipped with brake pad wear sensors.

4. Remove protective caps from brake caliper guide pins.

5. Remove both guide pins.

6. Remove the brake caliper and hang it from a piece of wire attached to the suspension. (DO NOT allow it to hang from the brake hose!)

7. Remove one of the worn brake pads from the brake caliper.

8. Check the fluid level in the brake fluid reservoir. If the level is near the top, pushing the pistons into the caliper may cause the brake fluid to overflow. Using a squeeze bottle, you may need to carefully remove and discard some of this brake fluid.

9. Press the piston of the pad you have removed into the brake caliper. There is a special Volkswagen tool to do this, tools are available from supply houses, or you can use a screwdriver. Be careful not to catch or damage the rubber seal on the edge of the piston.

10. When the piston is far enough into the caliper, you should be able to put a new brake pad into place in the caliper.

11. Pull the second old brake pad out of the caliper and push the piston back to make room on that side for the new brake pad. Once both new brake pads fit into the caliper, align them and replace any springs and clips that were present.

12. On ventilated front brakes, remove the brake caliper bracket from the spindle housing.

13. Remove the countersunk screw from the front of the brake rotor (you may need to use some penetrating oil) and pull the rotor off of the hub.

14. Put the new rotor into place and replace the countersunk screw.
    HINT: you might put a bit of anti-seize on its threads to make it easier to remove next time.

15. Replace the brake caliper bracket onto the spindle.

16. Slide the caliper back over the rotor and position it over the brake caliper mounting bracket.

17. Reattach the brake caliper using the guide pins and reattach the guide pin protective caps.

18. Reattach the wire harness for the brake pad wear indicator sensor if so equipped.

19. Reattach wheel and lower car to ground.

Larger wheels provide extra space for bigger brake rotors and more robust calipers. *Clewell*

20. Press the brake pedal several times to position the brake pads against the rotor.

   WARNING: Failure to do this may result in little or no braking ability on the first stop.

21. Check the fluid level in the reservoir and top up with fresh fluid as necessary.

22. Repeat with the brakes on the other wheels. Make sure you check your shop manual for the specific procedure for the front and rear pads of your car.

Brembo brakes are a popular tuning upgrade for Volkswagen models. *Hallstrom*

Brake Hoses

This can be done while changing pads and rotors. You should buy your upgraded stainless-steel brake hoses from a reputable supplier. DO NOT BEND or kink the stainless-steel brake hoses.

   1. Working one wheel at a time, carefully remove the brake line by removing the bolt where the hose enters the caliper.

   CAUTION: Brake fluid will spill—make sure you have a container to catch it.

2. Keep careful track of which sealing washers were in which position.

3. Remove the other end of the brake hose from the brake line.

4. Assemble the new braided stainless-steel hoses in the same way as the original hoses. Use new sealing washers and make sure that they are in the same positions as they were originally.

5. Repeat with the other wheels and then bleed the entire braking system following the procedure outlined in Chapter 4.

Upgraded Calipers

Follow the above procedures to place larger calipers and rotors onto your vehicle. Buy your brake upgrades as a kit, so the new components will be matched to the vehicle's existing brake master cylinder and ABS system. Be aware that larger brakes may not fit your original diameter wheels and may require bigger wheels for clearance.

Stock rotors look small when plus-sized wheels are fitted. *Hallstrom*

3 SUPENSION UPGRADE

DIFFICULTY: High

MODELS: All models

COST: $$$–$$$$

PARTS: Front and rear performance springs, shock absorbers, new front strut bearings

TOOLS: floor jack, jack stands, tir lug wrench, torque wrench, 16- and 21-millimeter deep sockets, 17- and 21-millimeter wrenches, 5- and 7-millimeter Allen wrenches, T20 Torx socket, strut spring compressor

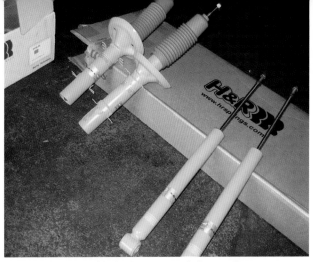

The front and rear Bilstein shocks also come in matched sets. *Author*

Changing springs and anti-roll bars is an involved project, but one that can be tackled at home if you have the right tools. As you will be working under the car, it is considerably easier if you have access to a lift so that you don't have to lie under the car as you are removing and replacing components. As always, make sure your car is well supported by jack stands before doing any work under the car.

Working with the coil springs that support the weight of your car can be dangerous. When they are mounted on the strut units they possess significant potential energy, enough to cause damage and injury should the springs get away from you.

To release this energy, a coil spring compressor is used. These come in various types. Some use long threaded rods with hooks to compress the spring, while others use hydraulic or air pressure. If you have never used spring compressors before, read all of the instructions carefully and have someone with experience demonstrate the proper technique to you. Whenever the springs are in the compressor and off of the strut, treat them as an unexploded bomb that is ready to go off.

The fourth generation cars differ from the third generation cars in the way in which their rear suspension is arranged. On the third generation cars, the rear springs are concentric around the rear strut and a spring compressor will be needed to remove them. On the fourth generation cars, the rear spring is separate from the strut shock unit and can be carefully removed without a compressor. At the front of both cars, a spring compressor is necessary to remove the concentric coil springs from the strut unit.

Coil springs should be replaced in sets to help maintain the handling balance. Stiffening just one end can result in a handling imbalance that may be unsafe. Consult your parts supplier.

SUSPENSION UPGRADE PROCEDURE
Rear suspension (Mark IV)

1. Jack up rear of car and support with jack stands.

2. Remove both rear wheels.

Upgraded springs come in sets. Both the front and rear springs should be changed at the same time to maintain the proper handling balance. *Author*

After raising the car and safely supporting it on jack stands, remove the rear wheels. *Author*

CHAPTER 6 | **CUSTOMIZE**

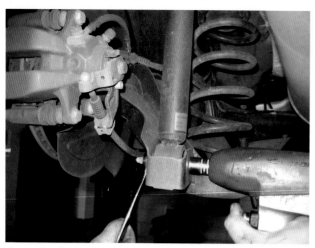

Place a jack under the shock mount of the side you will do first and raise it about an inch. Remove the bolt holding the lower end of the rear shock absorber. *Author*

Remove the bolts holding the upper end of the rear shock absorber in place and remove the shock. *Author*

3. You must change one side at a time or the entire rear axle will fall out.

4. Place a floor jack under the bottom of the shock absorber bracket on the side you will change first.

5. Gently lift the suspension an inch or so, but do not lift the car from the jack stands.

6. Remove the two upper shock mount bolts from inside the wheel well.

7. Remove the lower shock mount bolt where it goes through the bracket.

8. Carefully lower the floor jack. The shock absorber will come loose and the coil spring will extend until it falls out of its perch.

9. Remove the coil spring and the shock absorber.

Drop the floor jack holding the lower shock mount and lever the shock out of its lower mount. At this point, the rear coil spring will probably fall out of its perch. *Author*

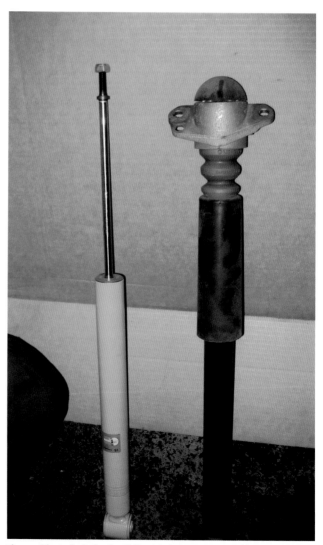

The new Bilstein shock absorber (left) needs the upper mount and bump stop from the original equipment shock absorber (right). *Author*

Remove the nut at the top of the original shock absorber and remove the mount and rubber bump stop. *Author*

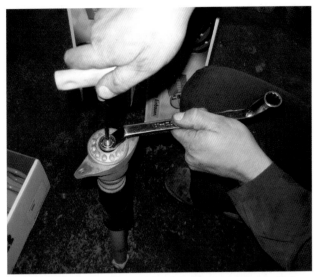

Place the upper mount onto the new shock and use the new nut that came with the new shock absorber. Tighten this 17-millimeter nut to 18 ft-lbs, using a 5-millimeter Allen wrench at the top of the shock absorber shaft to keep it from moving. *Author*

10. Using a 16-millimeter deep socket, remove the nut from the top of the rear shock absorber mount and remove the mount from the old shock.

11. Place the mount on the new shock and using the new nut that came with the new shocks, start it onto the threaded top of the shock by hand.

12. Using a 5-millimeter Allen wrench, hold the shock absorber rod in place while you tighten the 17-millimeter nut with a wrench and then a torque wrench to 18 lb-ft.

    NOTE: The 5-millimeter Allen wrench and 17-millimeter nut are used by Bilstein; other manufacturers may use other sizes.

13. Push the top mount back up into the wheel well and attach it with its bolts.

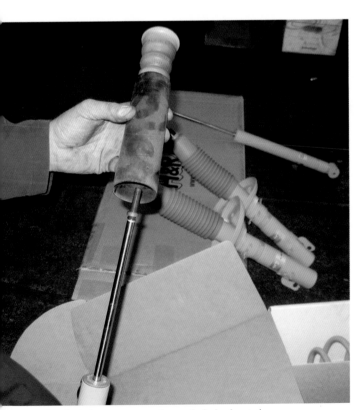

Transfer the bump stop over to the new shock absorber. *Author*

Remount the top shock mount in the rear fender well. *Author*

Place the rubber isolator from the original rear spring onto the smaller end of the new spring. *Author*

Repeat on the other side of the rear of the car. *Author*

Slide the new spring into place. *Author*

16. Repeat this process for the opposite side.

17. After you are finished and the car is back on its wheels, check the tightness of the upper shock mount bolts.

Front Suspension (all)
1. Raise both front wheels and place the car onto jack stands.

2. Remove both front wheels.

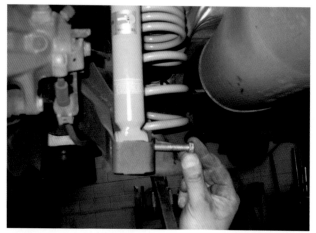

Push the bottom end of the shock absorber into its mount (you may need to use the floor jack to lift the shock mount slightly) and thread the bolt through the bottom mount and shock eye. Tighten to 30 ft-lbs. *Author*

14. Place the new coil spring onto the perch and carefully use the floor jack to move the rear axle back into position until you can thread the lower bolt through the shock absorber and mount. Tighten this bolt to 30 lb-ft.

15. Tighten the upper shock mount bolts.

Raise the front of the vehicle and support securely with jack stands. Remove the front wheels. The coil springs are mounted on the front MacPherson struts. The original equipment strut/spring assembly must be removed and disassembled, as the original strut mount will be used when installing the new strut/spring assembly. *Author*

5. Remove the bolt and nut from the spindle where it attaches to the bottom of the strut.

Use a Torx T20 driver to remove the brake-wear sensor and move it out of the way. *Author*

3. Use a T20 Torx socket or driver to remove the brake wear sensor and push it out of the way.

4. Remove the brake caliper by removing the guide pins and sliding the caliper off of the strut. Do not allow the caliper to hang from its brake hose; use some wire to hold it into place.

The cable for the anti-lock brake sensor will also need to be removed from its clip on the strut. *Author*

Remove the bolt and nut from the spindle where it attaches to the bottom of the strut. *Author*

Remove the front anti-roll bar link where it attaches to the suspension arm. *Author*

Spray some penetrating lubricant into the strut and spindle housing and let it soak for a few minutes. *Author*

6. Spray some lubricant into the strut and spindle housing and let it soak for a few minutes.

7. Carefully, using a flat screwdriver bit on your socket drive (or the special VW tool 3424), pry the housing apart where it is split.

Gently tap the spindle away from the strut tube. *Author*

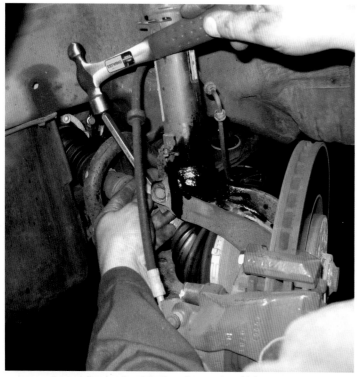

Use a small wedge-shaped chisel or a flat screwdriver blade on your ratchet to pry apart the housing on the spindle where it is split. *Author*

The strut tube should end up free from the spindle. *Author*

8. Pull the spindle housing downward, sliding the strut out of the housing.

Remove the plastic cap from the top of the strut mount under the hood. *Author*

9. Open hood and remove plastic cover plate from top of strut (if so equipped).

10. Hold onto the strut from underneath and, working under the hood, use a 7-millimeter Allen wrench to hold the rod of the strut in place and use a 21-millimeter wrench to loosen the nut and stop plate at the top of the strut (alternatively this can usually be accomplished with an air impact wrench and a 21-millimeter deep socket).

Use a 21-millimeter deep socket to loosen the nut and stop plate at the top of the strut. Hold onto the strut from underneath, remove the nut, and then withdraw the strut assembly from under the car. *Author*

On the workbench, carefully attach a spring compressor to the strut and compress the coil spring. *Author*

11. Pull the strut unit away from under the car.
   WARNING! Do not remove the upper strut mount nut without a spring compressor.

12. Use a spring compressor to compress the coil spring until the upper spring seat is free.

13. Use a 7-millimeter Allen wrench to hold the shaft and carefully remove the 21-millimeter nut.

14. Remove all of the components, keeping them in order as they come apart.

15. CAREFULLY remove pressure on the spring compressor and release the old spring.

Using a 21-millimeter deep socket, remove the nut holding the strut to the upper strut mount. Remove the spring from the strut and carefully remove the spring compressor from the spring. *Author*

Set aside the old strut tube and place the new strut tube onto the workbench. Slide the new spring over the new strut, making sure the bottom of the spring engages into the spring pocket. *Author*

16. Slide the new shock absorber into the strut tube.

17. Slide the new coil spring over the strut tube. Make sure the fit end engages with the bottom of the strut tube.

18. Compress the new spring with the spring compressor.

Use the spring compressor to compress the new spring. *Author*

19. **NOTE:** It is a good idea to use a new strut bearing assembly when upgrading to high performance springs and shocks.

20. Place the strut bearing onto the top of the strut, and using the new nut that came with the shock, tighten to 44 lb-ft.

21. Carefully remove the spring compressor and reinstall the strut assembly.

22. The torque on the top mount should be 44 lb-ft.

Put a new strut bearing onto the top of the strut and reattach the strut mount, using the new nut that came with the strut and tighten it to 44 ft-lbs. Carefully remove the spring compressor. *Author*

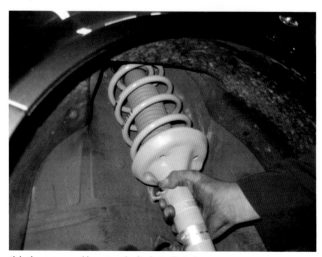

Slide the strut assembly up into the fender well. *Author*

Attach the stop plate and nut at the top of the strut. Torque to 44 ft-lbs. *Author*

When the strut is seated into the spindle, remove the wedge chisel and slide the retaining bolt into place. Tighten this bolt, and then reattach the anti-roll bar link and brake sensor cables. *Author*

Repeat on the other side. Remember: Replacing the front springs means that a front-end alignment will be necessary. *Author*

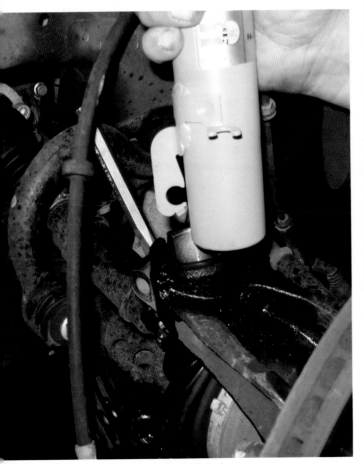

Slide the bottom of the strut into the spindle. *Author*

23. Repeat on the other side.

24. Replacing the front springs necessitates a realignment of the front end. This should be done before the car is driven any significant distance.

4 ENGINE MANAGEMENT SOFTWARE UPGRADE

DIFFICULTY: Easy

MODELS: All Mk IV models

COST: $$$

PARTS: New engine managemnt chip

TOOLS: none

Strangely enough for a do-it-yourself project, this isn't really something that you can do yourself, yet it can provide a significant upgrade in performance. Serial programming the engine management computer's flash memory takes place using an upgrade program running on a laptop that connects to the vehicle through the On-Board Diagnostic (OBD) port located in the driver's side footwell.

This operation is usually performed by a tuning shop that has the necessary software and contract from a supplier. The laptop works with the on-board computer, changing maps that control fuel, ignition, and boost pressure, along with increasing the engine's rev limiter and removing the electronic speed limiter. It takes about 15 minutes to accomplish the programming.

Some shops also have the capability to install a "trial" version of the upgraded software. This improves performance for a period of time (usually five hours of engine operation) to let the prospective customer know what they can expect from the chip upgrade.

Mark III Volkswagens can also benefit from chipping, except in this case the engine management computer must be removed from the vehicle and shipped to the tuning company, where an actual physical computer chip with all of the upgraded software will be substituted for the original one on the computer's motherboard.

Reprogramming the engine management system of third generation cars requires the engine management computer to be removed from the car and sent away for a new chip to be installed. *Author*

The computer used to reprogram the flash memory in the engine management system interfaces with the vehicle through the onboard diagnostic (OBD-II) port, located in the driver's side footwell. *Author*

INTAKE AIR BOX UPGRADE

DIFFICULTY: Easy

MODELS: All models

COST: $$–$$$

PARTS: High performance air filter, high-flow air intake

TOOLS: Hand tools

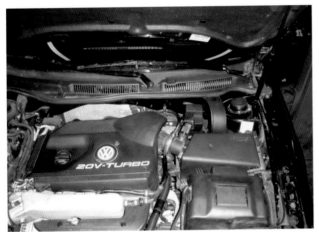

The stock air intake system for a 1.8T is quite good, pulling cool air from behind the bumper on the left front of the vehicle. *Erickson*

Although the stock 1.8T intake system flows well, some owners will want to upgrade their system with one that is freer breathing. For other engine variations, the cold-air intake can provide significant benefits.

1. Remove the engine cover.

2. Remove the pipe leading from the engine intake manifold to the mass-airflow sensor.

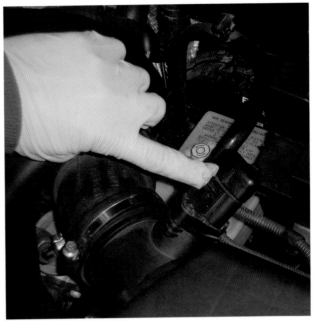

Remove the electrical connection to the mass-airflow sensor. *Erickson*

3. Disconnect the positive and negative terminals of the battery.

4. Remove the electrical connection to the mass-airflow sensor.

5. Remove the battery and battery tray.

Above: Remove the battery and the battery tray. *Erickson*

Left: The pipe leading from the engine intake to the mass-airflow sensor must be removed. *Erickson*

123

The entire air filter housing is removed next. *Erickson*

Remove the mass-airflow sensor from the stock air filter housing. *Author*

6. Remove the entire air filter housing.

7. Unbolt the cold air intake for the stock air filter housing from the bracket on the fender.

8. Remove the mass-airflow sensor from the stock air filter housing.

9. Remount the mass-airflow sensor onto the engine air intake using the supplied hose.

The cold air intake for the stock air filter unbolts from a bracket on the fender. *Erickson*

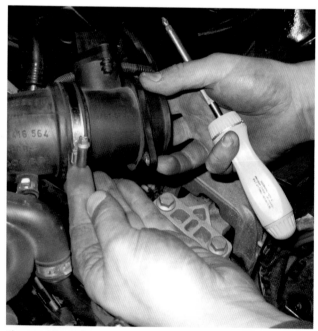

The mass-airflow sensor is remounted using the hose in the GHL Motorsports kit. *Author*

The new air intake tube attaches to the mass-airflow sensor with a coupler. *Author*

10. Attach the new cold air intake hose to the other side of the mass-airflow sensor with the supplied coupler.

11. Thread the new cold air intake hose through the bottom the fender beneath the headlight.

The new air intake tube attaches to the same bracket on the fender. *Author*

12. Attach the new cold air intake hose to the bracket on the fender.

13. Working under the car, attach the preoiled K&N air filter to the new cold air hose under the left-front fender behind the bumper.

Tighten the clamps on the coupler only after positioning the mass-airflow sensor and new intake tube. *Author*

The new K&N filter comes preoiled. *Author*

The air filter attaches under the left side fender, behind the front bumper. *Author*

The engine air pump has its own K&N filter. *Author*

14. Replace the battery tray and install the battery.

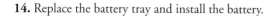

15. Place the small K&N air filter on the hose that leads to the air pump and secure this hose and filter out of the way with cable ties.

16. Replace the engine cover.

Replace the battery tray and reinstall the battery. *Author*

The new cold air intake fits cleanly in the space previously taken up by the air filter housing. *Author*

6 CAT-BACK EXHAUST SYSTEM UPGRADE

 DIFFICULTY: Moderate

 MODELS: All models

 COST: $$$–$$$$

 PARTS: New cat-back exhaust system

 TOOLS: Floor jack, jack stand, hand tools, saw

Replacing the exhaust system from the catalytic converter to the back of the car will help reduce engine backpressure (increasing performance); it will also change the exhaust note to one that is deeper and more authoritative. We aren't looking to make the car noisier, just changing the tone of its exhaust.

1. Raise the car and support it on jack stands.

2. Cut the exhaust pipe between the front and rear mufflers. Some models have a small indent on the stock pipe to indicate where to cut.

The rear muffler is held on with brackets at its front and rear. *Author*

3. Remove the bolts that hold the rear muffler mount to the rear of the chassis.

Raise the car and support it on jack stands. Cut the exhaust pipe between the front and rear mufflers in the position shown. *Author*

CHAPTER 6 | **CUSTOMIZE**

127

Loosen the bolts on the sleeve that attaches the front muffler to the pipe from the catalytic converter. Remove the four bolts that hold the muffler bracket to the chassis floorpan and slide the muffler off of the converter pipe, removing it with the bracket. *Author*

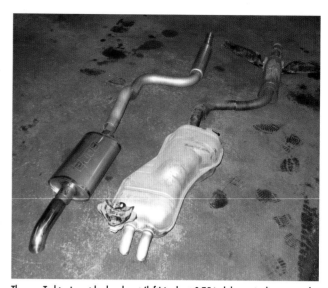

The new Techtonics cat-back exhaust (left) is about 0.75 inch larger in diameter and weighs about 13 pounds less than the stock system (right). *Author*

Remove the bolts that hold the rear of the rear muffler mount to the chassis. *Author*

4. Slide the front of the rear muffler off of its mount and then twist and pull the rear muffler until it is clear of the rear axle and slides out from under the car.

5. Loosen the bolts on the sleeve between the front muffler and the catalytic converter.

6. Remove the four bolts that hold the muffler cross bracket to the chassis.

7. Slide the muffler and coupler off of the pipe from the catalytic converter.

8. Remove the front muffler from its cross bracket.

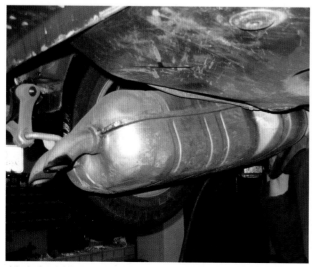

Slide the front of the rear muffler off of its front mount and remove it from the vehicle. *Author*

Remove the front muffler from its bracket. *Author*

Attach the new muffler to the front muffler bracket. *Author*

Slide the rubber rear muffler mount off of the old rear muffler. *Author*

9. Attach the new muffler to the cross bracket.

10. Slide the coupler onto the front of the new muffler.

11. Slide the coupler and muffler back onto the catalytic converter pipe and reattach the four bolts that hold the cross bracket to the chassis.

Slide the coupler back onto the new front muffler pipe. Use new bolts. *Author*

Reattach the rear muffler mount to the vehicle. *Author*

12. Slide the rubber mount off the rear of the rear muffler.

13. Reattach the rear mount to the rear of the chassis.

14. Make sure the new rear muffler is pointing the proper direction (it has an arrow that indicates flow that should point to the rear).

Slide the coupler and muffler back onto the pipe from the catalytic converter. Reattach the four bolts that hold the bracket onto the chassis floorpan. *Author*

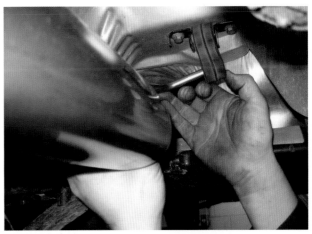

Slide the muffler clamp over the front end of the new muffler (check to make sure it is facing the right way) and slide it into the old front mount. *Author*

Slide the rear muffler over the exhaust pipe and snug the muffler clamp. Do not fully tighten it yet. *Author*

15. Slide the front mount and clamp for the rear muffler over the end of the muffler and slide the muffler onto the exhaust pipe and the clamp onto the rubber mount attached to the chassis. Snug but do not tighten yet.

16. Place the rear muffler clamp over the rear of the muffler, slide the exhaust tip into the muffler, and slide the clamp into the mount at the rear of the vehicle.

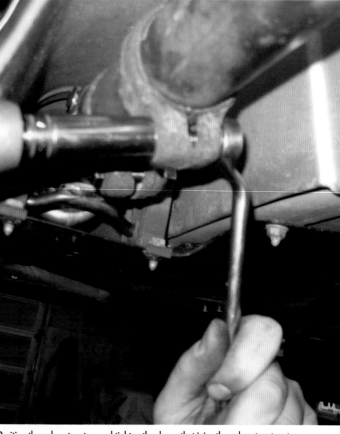

Position the exhaust system and tighten the sleeve that joins the exhaust system to the pipe from the catalytic converter. *Author*

17. Position the muffler and exhaust system before tightening any of the clamps.

Place the rear muffler clamp over the end of the rear muffler and slide it into the rear mount. Slide the muffler tip into the muffler and snug (do not fully tighten) the muffler clamp to hold it in place. *Author*

Above: Rotate the muffler so that it has sufficient clearance from the rear coil spring. To avoid rattles, move the exhaust system around so that it doesn't strike any part of the chassis. *Author*

Left: After the exhaust system is in place, attach clips to the muffler mounts to keep them from shifting. *Author*

18. Rotate the muffler so that it has clearance with the rear coil spring and the exhaust tip so that it points straight downward (on Golf models).

19. Shake the exhaust pipe and muffler to make sure it doesn't rattle. Tighten all of the clamps and bolts and then shake it again.

20. Attach the supplied clips to the muffler mounts to prevent the muffler from sliding back and forth. Check one more time to make sure nothing rattles.

Align the rear tip, and then tighten all of the clamps and mounting bolts. Tighten the bolt holding the front muffler to the cross bracket last. *Author*

CHAPTER 7 | DATA

SPOTTER'S GUIDE
THIRD GENERATION (1993–1998)

Golf GL (1993–1998)

The base version of the Golf III changed little during its six years of production. It was available as a two-door and four-door hatchback and can be identified by:

- 14-inch steel wheels with hubcaps
- GL badge below left taillight
- Body color grille
- Black side mirrors
- Cloth interior
- Five-speed manual transmission (four-speed automatic was an option)
- Power glass sunroof was optional
- In 1997, grille and front air dam were slightly revised

The third generation Golf GL. *VWOA*

Golf GTI 2.0 (1993, 1995 Golf Sport, 1996–1998)

The 115-horsepower GTI 2.0 was a sheep in wolf's clothing; not a bad car but not an appropriate successor to the GTI name. It arrived in 1993, but wasn't available in 1994. In 1995, the GTI 2.0 was actually called the Golf Sport, but the next year was given the GTI nameplate. The GTI 2.0 can be distinguished by:

- GTI badges under right taillight and on left side of front grille
- Close-ratio five-speed manual transmission
- Power steering
- Integrated fog lights
- Body-color outside mirrors
- 14-inch alloy wheels
- Roof-mounted antenna
- Standard air conditioning
- Eight-speaker AM/FM cassette
- Height-adjustable sport seats

The third generation GTI 2.0. *VWOA*

Thankfully, the third generation GTI eventually got a powerful VR6 engine. *VWOA*

Golf GTI VR6 (1995–1998)

The addition of the 2.8-liter VR6 engine to the GTI gave it real performance. The GTI VR6 can be distinguished by:

- VR6 badge on the front grille
- GTI badge under the right taillight
- 15-inch alloy wheels
- Roof-mounted antenna
- Integrated fog lights
- Body-color outside mirrors
- Body-color moldings and bumpers
- Standard air conditioning
- Power sunroof
- Rear spoiler
- Eight-speaker AM/FM cassette
- Height-adjustable sport seats
- Leather seating is optional

The Golf Trek, K2, and Jazz were special-market versions of the Golf GL aimed at a young and active segment of Volkswagen buyers.

Golf Trek (1997–1998)

The Golf Trek was essentially a Golf GL with the following special additions:

- Height-adjustable driver seat
- Four-door hatchback
- Remote trunk release
- Trek 21-speed mountain bike
- Roof-mount bike carrier
- Fog lights
- Alloy wheels
- Rear spoiler
- Roof antenna
- Sport seats
- Cargo net
- TREK badge on right rear under taillight

Trek models can be identified by the "TREK" badge on the rear. *Author*

Golf K2 (1997–1998)

The Golf K2 was essentially a Golf GL with the following special additions:

- Height-adjustable driver seat
- Four-door hatchback
- Remote trunk release
- K2 skis or snowboard
- Roof-mount ski carrier
- Alloy wheels
- Fog lights
- Rear spoiler
- Roof antenna
- Sport seats
- Cargo net

K2 badge on right rear under taillight

Golf Jazz (1997–1998)

The Golf Jazz was essentially a Golf GL with the following special additions:

- Height-adjustable driver seat
- Remote trunk release
- Alloy wheels
- Fog lights
- Rear spoiler
- Roof antenna
- Eight-speaker stereo with six-disc CD changer
- Style seats
- Jazz badge on left rear of trunk

Golf GTI VR6 Driver's Edition (1997)

A special version of the GTI VR6 appeared in 1997. In addition to standard VR6 equipment it included:

- Seven-spoke 15-inch alloy wheels
- Red-painted brake calipers
- Bright finish twin tailpipes
- Yellow, Jazz Blue, Red, White, and Black exterior colors
- Sport cloth interior with choice of red, blue, or yellow trim
- Red accents in cabin
- GTI doorsill plate

The 1997 GTI VR6 Driver's Edition *VWOA*

Third generation Jetta GL. *VWOA*

Jetta GL (1993–1998)

The base version of the Jetta came reasonably well equipped and was Volkswagen's sales leader. It was available as a four-door sedan and can be identified by:

- 14-inch steel wheels with hubcaps
- GL badge below left taillight
- Body-color grille
- Black side mirrors
- Cloth interior
- Five-speed manual transmission (four-speed automatic was an option)
- Power glass sunroof was optional
- In 1996 grille and front air dam were slightly revised

Jetta GLS (1994–1998)

The Jetta GLS added a few extra comfort and convenience features:

- Air conditioning
- GLS rear badge
- Power sunroof
- Body-color side mirrors
- Cruise control
- Power windows
- Split folding rear seats
- CD changer

Third generation Jetta GLS. *VWOA*

Jetta GLX (1993–1998)

The GLX was the flagship of the Jetta III line and came with a 2.8-liter VR6 engine. It was well equipped with:

- Traction control
- Power windows
- Cruise control
- Rear spoiler
- Body-color side mirrors and bumpers
- Leather seats
- Fog lights
- 15-inch alloy wheels (BBS in 1994–1995, seven-spoke alloy wheels 1996–1998)
- GLX badge on right rear trunk lid

The Jetta Trek, K2, and Jazz were special-market versions of the Jetta GL aimed at a young and active segment of Volkswagen buyers.

Jetta Trek (1996–1998)
The Jetta Trek was essentially a Jetta GL with the following special additions:
- Height-adjustable driver seat
- Trek 21-speed mountain bike
- Roof-mount bike carrier
- Fog lights
- Alloy wheels
- Rear spoiler
- Sport seats
- TREK badge on right rear of trunk lid

Jetta K2 (1997–1998)
The Jetta K2 was essentially a Jetta GL with the following special additions:
- Height-adjustable driver seat
- Four-door hatchback
- K2 skis or snowboard
- Roof-mount ski carrier
- Alloy wheels
- Fog lights
- Rear spoiler
- Sport seats
- K2 badge on right rear of trunk lid

Jetta Jazz (1997–1998)
The Jetta Jazz was essentially a Jetta GL with the following special additions:
- Height-adjustable driver seat
- Alloy wheels
- Fog lights
- Rear spoiler
- Eight-speaker stereo with six-disc CD changer
- Style seats
- Jazz badge on left rear of trunk

Jetta GT (1997)
The Jetta GT was similar in content and appearance to the Jetta GLX, but came with the 2.0-liter four-cylinder engine instead of the 2.8-liter VR6 engine. It included:
- Sport seats
- Alloy wheels
- Rear spoiler
- Fog lights
- Body-color mirrors and bumpers
- GT badge on right rear trunk lid

Jetta TDI (1998)
The Jetta TDI was a diesel-powered version of the Jetta III GL with a turbocharged direct injection diesel engine. It was equipped with:
- Steel wheels with hub caps
- TDI badge on right rear trunk lid

Third generation Jetta TDI. *Author*

FOURTH GENERATION
Golf GL (1999–2005)
The base GL version of the fourth generation of the Golf included standard features like side air bags and anti-lock brakes. It was available as a two-door and four-door hatchback. An immobilizer alarm system was standard beginning in 2000. and side curtain air bags were standard beginning in 2001. Standard equipment on a GL included:
- Height-adjustable driver's seat
- Adjustable steering column
- Air conditioning
- Cruise control
- Power steering
- Anti-lock brakes
- Fold-down rear seats with headrests
- 15-inch steel wheels
- A GL badge on the rear hatch

The fourth generation Golf GL *VWOA*

Golf GL TDI (2001–2005)
The TDI added a 1.9-liter turbocharged direct injected diesel engine to the base GL specification. A TDI badge was placed on the right rear trunk lid.

The fourth generation Golf was available with a TDI diesel. *VWOA*

Golf GLS (1999–2005)

The Golf GLS was available with the base 2.0-liter four-cylinder engine as a four-door hatchback. It added options like:

- Power sunroof
- Heated seats
- Leather upholstery
- 15-inch alloy wheels

Golf GLS. *VOLKSWAGEN AG*

Golf GLS TDI (2001–2005)

The TDI added a 1.9-liter turbocharged direct injected diesel engine to the GLS specification. A TDI badge was placed on the right rear trunk lid.

Golf GLS 1.8T (2001–2005)

The turbocharged and intercooled 20-valve 1.8T engine was available in the Golf GLS beginning in 2000. It added:

- 16-inch alloy wheels
- Front sport seats
- Power sunroof
- Automatic climate control
- Windshield wiper rain sensor (not all years)
- Trip computer (not all years)
- Fog lights
- Sport suspension
- 1.8T badge to rear hatchback
- Anti-slip regulation (ASR)
- Electronic differential lock (EDL)

Golf GTI 1.8T (2001–2005)

The 2001 1.8T engine produced 150 horsepower, but in subsequent years the engine produced 180 horsepower. The available equipment was very similar to the Golf GLS 1.8T listed above, and the GTI badge was placed on the rear hatchback. The letter "I" was red to denote the 1.8T engine.

Golf GTI 1.8T *Author*

Golf GTI 337 (2002)

In the middle of 2002, a special edition of the Golf, called the VW GTI 337, was introduced. Only 1,500 cars were made available to U.S. buyers, and the car had significant upgrades that appealed to enthusiasts. These included:

- 180-horsepower 1.8T turbocharged engine
- Six-speed transmission
- Lowered sport suspension
- 18-horsepower BBS RC wheels
- Brake system from Audi's TT
- Red brake calipers
- Michelin Pilot Sport 225/40-ZR18 tires
- Recaro racing bucket seats
- Monsoon CD/cassette eight-speaker sound system
- Front air dam
- Rear deck hatch spoiler
- Leather-trimmed steering wheel and shifter with red stitching
- Special edition golf-ball shift knob
- Only available in Silver

Golf GTI 20th Anniversary (2003)

In 2003, a special 20th Anniversary Edition of the GTI appeared. It was equipped with:

- Lowered sport suspension
- 18-inch alloy wheels
- 225/40ZR18 performance tires
- Monsoon CD stereo system
- Rear spoiler
- Front air dam
- Aerodynamic side skirts
- Single chrome exhaust
- Recaro front sport seats
- Golf-ball shifter
- Stainless steel pedals
- Power sunroof
- Automatic climate control
- Projector fog lights
- Antislip regulation (ASR)
- Electronic differential lock (EDL)
- 20th Anniversary GTI plaque

The 20th Anniversary Edition of the GTI. *VWOA*

20th Anniversary cars had their own special badges. *VWOA*

GTI VR6 (4th generation). *Author*

Jetta GL (4th generation) sedan and wagon. *VOLKSWAGEN AG*

Golf GTI GLX VR6 (1999–2003)

The VR6-powered GTI GLX remained the Golf flagship until 2003. In 2003, the engine was upgraded with four valves per cylinder. In its upgraded form, it produced 200 horsepower. A six-speed manual transmission was standard (the VR6 never was offered with an automatic transmission in the GTI), and 17-inch alloy wheels and items like Climatronic climate control and Electronic Stability Program (ESP).

Golf R32 (2004–2005)

The R32 was a very special version of the GTI, with a 3.2-liter VR6 engine and 4MOTION all-wheel drive. Other notable features included:

- Six-speed manual transmission
- 4MOTION all-wheel drive
- Blue four-piston brake calipers
- Multilink sport suspension
- Sport seats
- Heated front seats
- 18-inch alloy wheels
- Side skirts
- Front spoiler
- Rear spoiler
- Power sunroof
- Monsoon stereo system
- Windshield wiper rain sensor
- Dual exhaust
- Projector fog lights
- Automatic climate control
- Trip computer
- Antislip regulation (ASR)
- Electronic differential lock (EDL)
- Electronic Stability Program (ESP)
- R32 badges

The 2004 R32 was VW's weapon against the Subaru WRX and Mitsubishi Evo. *VWOA*

The dash of the R32 might be the nicest instrument panel ever placed in a production Volkswagen. *VWOA*

Jetta GL (1999–2004)

The base GL version of the fourth generation of the Jetta included standard features like side air bags and anti-lock brakes. It was available as a four-door sedan and, beginning in 2001, as a four-door station wagon. An immobilizer alarm system was standard beginning in 2000, and side curtain air bags were standard beginning in 2001. Standard equipment on a GL included:

- Height-adjustable driver's seat
- Adjustable steering column
- Air conditioning
- Cruise control
- Power steering
- Anti-lock brakes
- 15-inch steel wheels
- A GL badge on the trunk lid

Jetta GL TDI (2001–2004)

The TDI added a 1.9-liter turbocharged direct injected diesel engine to the base GL specification. A TDI badge was placed on the right rear trunk lid.

Jetta TDI (4th generation). *Author*

Jetta GLS 2.0 (1999–2004)

The GLS added:

- Power sunroof
- 15-inch alloy wheels
- Optional leather interior
- Optional Monsoon stereo system

Jetta GLS TDI (2001–2004)

The TDI added a 1.9-liter turbocharged direct injected diesel engine to the GLS specification. A TDI badge was placed on the right rear trunk lid.

Jetta GLS TDI. *VOLKSWAGEN AG*

Jetta GLS 1.8T (2001–2004)

The addition of the 1.8-liter turbocharged and intercooled 20-valve four-cylinder engine to the Jetta GLS also brought a six-speed manual transmission, anti-slip regulation (ASR), and electronic differential lock (EDL), along with an optional five-speed automatic transmission.

Jetta Wolfsburg Edition. *VWOA*

Jetta GLX (1999–2003)

The Jetta GLX was available with the 2.8-liter VR6 engine with a five-speed (and later a six-speed) manual transmission. A five-speed automatic transmission was also available, as was a GLX wagon. Options included 17-inch alloy wheels and a sport suspension. Standard features of the GLX included:

- 16-inch alloy wheels
- Monsoon stereo system
- Leather upholstery
- Power sunroof
- Traction control
- Electronic Stability Program

Rear view of the Jetta Wolfsburg. *VWOA*

Jetta GLI (2004)

The 2004 Jetta GLI was initially available with the 2.8-liter VR6 engine, but beginning in February 2004, came only with the 1.8-liter turbocharged and intercooled 20-valve four-cylinder engine. That version had the following standard features:

- Six-speed manual transmission
- Red brake calipers
- Lowered sport suspension
- Sport seats
- Monsoon stereo system
- Power sunroof
- Anti-slip regulation (ASR)
- Electronic differential lock (EDL)
- 18-inch alloy wheels
- Rear spoiler
- Front spoiler
- Side skirts
- Fog lights
- Dual exhaust pipes

Jetta Wolfsburg (2003)

The Jetta Wolfsburg Edition sedan of 2003 added the following to the Jetta GLS 1.8T model:

- Optional Monsoon stereo system
- 16-inch BBS alloy wheels
- Rear spoiler
- Dual exhaust pipes

Jetta GLS VR6 (1999–2002)

The Jetta GLS was also available with the 2.8-liter VR6 engine. This had most of the same standard features and options as the Jetta GLS 1.8T version.

2004 Jetta GLI. *VWOA*

SPECIFICATIONS

DIMENSIONS
Third Generation

	Golf	Jetta	GTI	Cabriolet
Length (inches)	160.4	160.4	160.4	173.4
Width (inches)	66.7	66.7	66.7	66.7
Height (inches)	56.2	56.2	56.0	56.1
Wheelbase (inches)	97.4	97.4	97.2	97.4
Track F/R (inches)	57.5/57.0	57.5/57.0	57.5/57.6	57.5/57.0

Fourth Generation

	Golf	Jetta	GTI	Cabriolet
Length (inches)	163.3	163.3	160.4	172.3
Width (inches)	68.3	68.3	66.7	68.3
Height (inches)	56.7	56.7	56.0	56.9
Wheelbase (inches)	98.9	98.9	97.4	98.9
Track F/R (inches)	59.6/58.8	59.6/58.8	57.5/57.6	59.6/58.8

CONFIGURATION
Third Generation
Golf—Two-door/four-door hatchback

GTI—Two-door hatchback

Cabriolet—Two-door convertible

Jetta—Four-door sedan

Layout: Front engine, front-wheel drive

Transmission: Five-speed manual, four-speed automatic (optional)

Suspension:
  Front—MacPherson struts with coil springs
  Rear—Torsion beam axle with trailing arms and coil springs

Steering: Rack and pinion

Brakes: Front disc, rear disc with ABS

Fourth Generation
Golf—Two-door/four-door hatchback

GTI—Two-door hatchback

Cabriolet—Two-door convertible

Jetta—Four-door sedan

R32—Two-door hatchback

Layout: Front engine, front-wheel drive (R32 4MOTION all-wheel drive)

Transmission: Five-speed or six-speed manual, four-speed or five-speed automatic (optional)

Suspension:
  Front—MacPherson struts with coil springs

Rear—Torsion beam axle with trailing arms and coil springs (R32 multilink independent)

Steering: Rack and pinion

Brakes: Front disc, rear disc with ABS

ENGINES
2.0-liter Four-Cylinder (1993–1998)
Type: Inline four-cylinder

Material: Cast-iron block, aluminum cylinder head

Valves: 8

Displacement: 1,984 cc (121 cubic inches)

Bore: 3.25 inches (82.5 millimeters)

Stroke: 3.65 inches (92.8 millimeters)

Compression Ratio: 10.0:1

Horsepower: 115 horsepower @ 5,400 rpm

Torque: 122 lb-ft @ 3,200 rpm

2.0-liter Four-Cylinder (1999–2005)
Type: Inline four-cylinder

Material: Cast-iron block, aluminum cylinder head

Valves: 8

Displacement: 1,984 cc (121 cubic inches)

Bore: 3.25 inches (82.5 millimeters)

Stroke: 3.65 inches (92.8 millimeters)

Compression ratio: 10.0:1

Horsepower: 115 horsepower @ 5,200 rpm

Torque: 122 lb-ft @ 2,600 rpm

The 2.0-liter four-cylinder from a 3rd generation Jetta. *Author*

1.9-liter TDI Diesel (1998–2001)
Type: Inline four-cylinder, turbocharged direct injection

Material: Cast-iron block, aluminum cylinder head

Valves: 8

Displacement: 1,896 cc (116 cubic inches)

Bore: 3.13 inches (79.5 millimeters)

Stroke: 3.76 inches (95.5 millimeters)

Compression ratio: 19.5:1

Horsepower: 90 horsepower @ 3,750 rpm

Torque: 149 lb-ft @ 1,900 rpm

1.9-liter TDI-PD Diesel (2002–2005)
Type: Inline four-cylinder, turbocharged direct injection
Material: Cast-iron block, aluminum cylinder head
Valves: 8
Displacement: 1,896 cc (116 cubic inches)
Bore: 3.13 inches (79.5 millimeters)
Stroke: 3.76 inches (95.5 millimeters)
Compression ratio: 19.5:1
Horsepower: 90 horsepower @ 3,750 rpm
Torque: 155 lb-ft @ 1,900 rpm

2.8-liter VR6 (1993–1998)
Type: 15-degree V-6
Material: Cast-iron block, aluminum cylinder head
Valves: 12
Displacement: 2,792 cc (170 cubic inches)
Bore: 3.19 inches (81 millimeters)
Stroke: 3.56 inches (90.3 millimeters)
Compression ratio: 10.0:1
Horsepower: 172 horsepower @ 5,800 rpm
Torque: 177 lb-ft @ 4,200 rpm

2.8-liter VR6 (1999–2002)
Type: 15-degree V-6
Material: Cast-iron block, aluminum cylinder head
Valves: 12
Displacement: 2,792 cc (170 cubic inches)
Bore: 3.19 inches (81 millimeters)
Stroke: 3.56 inches (90.3 millimeters)
Compression ratio: 10.0:1
Horsepower: 174 horsepower @ 5,800 rpm
Torque: 181 lb-ft @ 3,200 rpm

2.8-liter VR6 24V (2003–2005)
Type: 15-degree V-6
Material: Cast-iron block, aluminum cylinder head
Valves: 24
Displacement: 2,792 cc (170 cubic inches)
Bore: 3.19 inches (81 millimeters)
Stroke: 3.56 inches (90.3 millimeters)
Compression ratio: 10.5:1
Horsepower: 200 horsepower @ 6,200 rpm
Torque: 195 lb-ft @ 3,200 rpm

3.2-liter VR6 24V (2004–2005 R32)
Type: 15-degree V-6
Material: Cast-iron block, aluminum cylinder head
Valves: 24
Displacement: 3,189 cc (195 cubic inches)
Bore: 3.31 inches (84 millimeters)
Stroke: 3.78 inches (95.9 millimeters)
Compression ratio: 11.25:1
Horsepower: 240 horsepower @ 6,250 rpm
Torque: 236 lb-ft @ 2,800–3,200 rpm

The powerful 3.2-liter engine of the R32. *VWOA*

A cutaway drawing shows the detail of the VR6 engine. *VWOA*

1.8-liter Turbo-four-cylinder (2001)
Type: Inline four-cylinder, turbocharged and intercooled
Material: Cast-iron block, aluminum cylinder head
Valves: 20
Displacement: 1,781 cc (108.7 cubic inches)
Bore: 3.19 inches (81.1 millimeters)
Stroke: 3.40 inches (86.4 millimeters)
Compression ratio: 9.5:1
Horsepower: 150 horsepower @ 5,700 rpm
Torque: 155 lb-ft @ 1,750–4,600 rpm

1.8-liter Turbo four-cylinder (2002–2005)
Type: Inline four-cylinder, turbocharged and intercooled
Material: Cast-iron block, aluminum cylinder head
Valves: 20
Displacement: 1,781 cc (108.7 cubic inches)
Bore: 3.19 inches (81.1 millimeters)
Stroke: 3.40 inches (86.4 millimeters)
Compression ratio: 9.5:1
Horsepower: 180 horsepower @ 5,500 rpm
Torque: 174 lb-ft @ 1,950 rpm

TYPICAL PERFORMANCE (VWOA AND VARIOUS SOURCES)

	0–60 mph (sec)	Top Speed (mph)	EPA Miles Per Gallon City/Highway
Golf 2.0-liter	9.8	120	24/31
Golf Cabriolet	9.9	116	23/30
GTI 2.0-liter	9.8	120	24/31
GTI VR6	7.6	146	20/28
GTI 1.8T	7.4	130	23/30
R32	6.4	153	19/26
Jetta GL 2.0	10.1	120	24/31
Jetta 1.9 TDI	11.3	115	42/49
Jetta VR6	7.8	130	19/28
Jetta 1.8T	7.7	130	24/31

SUGGESTED MAINTENANCE SCHEDULE

2.0-liter Four-Cylinder Engine

Change engine oil	every 5,000 miles (8,000 km)
Change oil filter	every 5,000 miles (8,000 km)
Rotate tires	every 10,000 miles (16,000 km)
Check CV boots	every 10,000 miles (16,000 km)
Check brake pads	every 10,000 miles (16,000 km)
Check manual transmission oil level	every 20,000 miles (32,000 km)
Replace pollen filter	every 20,000 miles (32,000 km)
Check power steering	every 40,000 miles (32,000 km)
Change spark plugs	every 40,000 miles (64,000 km)
Replace air filter	every 40,000 miles (64,000 km)
Check timing belt	every 40,000 miles (64,000 km)
Replace timing belt	every 80,000 miles (128,000 km)
Change brake fluid	every two years
Change antifreeze	every three years

1.9 TDI Diesel Four-Cylinder Engine

Change engine oil	every 5,000 miles (8,000 km)
Change oil filter	every 5,000 miles (8,000 km)
Drain water separator	every 5,000 miles (8,000 km)
Check timing belt	every 10,000 miles (16,000 km)
Rotate tires	every 10,000 miles (16,000 km)
Check CV boots	every 10,000 miles (16,000 km)
Check brake pads	every 10,000 miles (16,000 km)
Check manual transmission oil level	every 20,000 miles (32,000 km)
Replace fuel filter	every 20,000 miles (32,000 km)
Replace pollen filter	every 20,000 miles (32,000 km)
Check power steering	every 40,000 miles (32,000 km)
Replace air filter	every 40,000 miles (64,000 km)
Replace timing belt	every 40,000 miles (64,000 km)
Replace timing belt tensioner	every 80,000 miles (128,000 km)
Change brake fluid	every two years
Change antifreeze	every three years

1.8-liter Turbocharged Four-Cylinder Engine

Change engine oil	every 5,000 miles (8,000 km)
Change oil filter	every 5,000 miles (8,000 km)
Rotate tires	every 10,000 miles (16,000 km)
Check CV boots	every 10,000 miles (16,000 km)
Check brake pads	every 10,000 miles (16,000 km)
Check timing belt	every 20,000 miles (32,000 km)
Check manual transmission oil level	every 20,000 miles (32,000 km)
Replace pollen filter	every 20,000 miles (32,000 km)
Check power steering	every 40,000 miles (32,000 km)
Change spark plugs	every 40,000 miles (64,000 km)
Replace air filter	every 40,000 miles (64,000 km)
Replace timing belt	every 60,000 miles (96,000 km)
Replace V-belt	every 80,000 miles (128,000 km)
Replace timing belt tensioner	every 100,000 miles (160,000 km)
Change brake fluid	every two years
Change antifreeze	every three years

The timing belt on this 1.8T engine failed, causing all of this damage. Timing belts on 1.8T engines should be changed religiously every 60,000 miles. *Author*

2.8-Liter VR6 Engine

Change engine oil	every 5,000 miles (8,000 km)
Change oil filter	every 5,000 miles (8,000 km)
Rotate tires	every 10,000 miles (16,000 km)
Check CV boots	every 10,000 miles (16,000 km)
Check brake pads	every 10,000 miles (16,000 km)
Check manual transmission oil level	every 20,000 miles (32,000 km)
Replace pollen filter	every 20,000 miles (32,000 km)
Check power steering	every 40,000 miles (64,000 km)
Change spark plugs	every 40,000 miles (64,000 km)
Replace air filter	every 40,000 miles (64,000 km)
Replace V-belt	every 80,000 miles (128,000 km)
Change brake fluid	every two years
Change antifreeze	every three years

3.2-Liter VR6 R32

Change engine oil	every 5,000 miles (8,000 km)
Change oil filter	every 5,000 miles (8,000 km)
Rotate tires	every 10,000 miles (16,000 km)
Check CV boots	every 10,000 miles (16,000 km)
Check brake pads	every 10,000 miles (16,000 km)
Check manual transmission oil level	every 20,000 miles (32,000 km)
Replace pollen filter	every 20,000 miles (32,000 km)
Change Haldex clutch oil	every 40,000 miles (64,000 km)
Check power steering	every 40,000 miles (64,000 km)
Change spark plugs	every 40,000 miles (64,000 km)
Replace air filter	every 40,000 miles (64,000 km)
Replace V-belt	every 80,000 miles (128,000 km)
Change brake fluid	every two years
Change antifreeze	every three years

PRICES FOR PARTS

The following are some typical street prices for parts. These are what you might expect to pay if you order the parts online or purchase them from a discount parts supplier. They are for comparison use only.

Part	1997 Golf III GL 2.0-liter	2001 Golf GLS 1.8T	2002 Jetta GLX VR6
Headlight assembly	$123	$143	$123
Taillight assembly	$70	$16	$16
Front brake disc	$38	$66	$66
Front brake pads	$52	$75	$75
Clutch disc	$72	$148	$196
Water pump	$43	$72	$76
Axle assembly (front)	$102	$119	$106
Oil filter	$6	$4	$6
Timing belt	$19	$44	——
Catalytic converter	$184	$332	$306
Fuel injector	$100	$123	$147
Oxygen sensor	$85	$94	$194
Tie rod end	$26	$31	$31

VIN DECODER

The vehicle identification number (VIN) is a set of 17 characters assigned by manufacturers to identify every individual vehicle that they manufacture. Volkswagen's VIN can be found on a plate mounted at the base of the windshield on the driver's side (left) and can be seen through the windshield. The characters are decoded as:

Position	Description	Information
1	**Country of origin**	

3= Mexico W= Europe 9= Brazil

2 Manufacturer
V=Volkswagen

3 Vehicle Type
W= Passenger car

4 Series

5 Engine

6 Restraint System
5= Active belts with driver air bag
6= Front and side air bags
8= Active belts with dual air bags

7&8 Model
9M= Jetta sedan
1E= 1995 Cabriolet
1H= 1993–95 Golf/ Jetta
1J= Golf, GTI, Jetta wagon, R32

9 NHTSA Check digit
0–9 or X, determined by NHTSA

10 Model Year

P= 1993	R= 1994	S= 1995
T= 1996	V= 1997	W= 1998
X= 1999	Y= 2000	1= 2001
2=2002	3= 2003	4=2004
5=2005		

11 Assembly Plant
4= Curitiba, Brazil
H= Hannover, Germany
8= Dresden, Germany
M= Puebla, Mexico
D= Bratislava, Slovakia
P= Model, Germany
E= Emden, Germany
W= Wolfsburg, Germany

12–17 Serial Number
Production number of the specific vehicle

RESOURCES LIST

VOLKSWAGEN CLUBS AND WEB GROUPS
Samba: (www.TheSamba.com)
Vortex: (www.vortex.com)
Volkswagen Club of America: (www.vwclub.org)
Volkswagen of America: (www.vw.com)

WHEELS AND TIRES
Discount Tire Direct: (800) 483-7555
  (DiscountTireDirect.com)
The Tire Rack: (888) 981-3952 (www.tirerack.com)

SUSPENSION
Bilstein: (704) 663-7563 (www.Bilstein.com)
Eibach Springs: (951) 256-8300 (www.eibach.com)
Energy Suspension: (949) 361-3935
  (www.energysuspension.com)
Ground Control: (530) 677-8600
  (www.ground-control.com)
H&R Springs: (888) 827-8881 (www.hrsprings.com)
Koni: (859) 586-4100

BRAKES
Brembo Brakes: (800) 325-3994 (www.brembo.com)
Carbotech USA: (877) 899-5024 (www.carbotecheng.com)
Classic Tube (brake hoses): (800) 882-3711
  (www.stopflex.com)
Hawk Performance: (800) 542-0972
  (www.hawkperformance.com)
Stoptech Brake Conversions: (310) 325-4799
  (www.stoptech.com)

RACING AND MOTORSPORTS ORGANIZERS
Eastern Motor Racing Association: (718) 948-7971
  (www.emraracing.org)
Import Drag Racing (www.nopi.com)
Midwest Council of Sports Car Clubs: (815) 434-9999
  (www.mcscc.org)
National Auto Sport Association: (510) 232-6272
  (www.nasaproracing.com)
Sports Car Club of America: (www.scca.com)
Waterford Hills Road Racing: (www.waterfordhills.com)

VW TUNERS AND PARTS SUPPLIERS
ABD Racing: (www.abdracing.com)
ABT Tuning: (916) 716-1674 (www.abt-tuning.com)
APR: (334) 502-5181 (www.goapr.com)
Autotech Sport Tuning: (949) 240-4000
BSI Racing: (386) 677-5778 (www.bsiracing.com)
Euro Sport Accessories: (714) 630-1555
  (www.eurosport.com)
Electrodyne/Racing Dynamics: (703) 823-0202
  (www.racdyn-usa.com)
Giac USA: (www.GIACusa.com)
Neuspeed: (800) 423-3623 (www.neuspeed.com)
New Dimensions Ltd.: (408) 980-1691
  (www.ndimports.com)
Quaife America (limited slip differentials): (949) 240-4000
  (www.quaifeamerica.com)
Revo Technik: (805) 544-0061 (www.revotechnik.com)
Shine Racing Services: (508) 660-7974 (www.srsvw.com)
Techtonics Tuning: (503) 843-2700
  (www.techtonicstuning.com)
VF-Engineering: (714) 528-0066 (www.vf-engineering.com)
Virtual World Parts: (888) 389-7278 (www.parts4vws.com)

REFERENCES AND MANUALS
*Volkswagen Jetta, Golf, GTI, Cabrio Service Manual
  1993–1999* (1999) Bentley Publishers,
  ISBN: 0-8376-0366-8 (www.BentleyPublishers.com)
Volkswagen Jetta, Golf, GTI Service Manual 1999–2005
  (2005) Bentley Publishers, ISBN: 0-8376-1251-9
  (www.BentleyPublishers.com)
Water Cooled Volkswagen Performance Handbook, by Greg
  Raven (1999) MBI Publishing Company,
  ISBN: 0-7603-0491-2 (www.mbipublishing.com)
Thirty Years of the Volkswagen Golf & Rabbit, by Kevin
  Clemens (2006) Iconografix Inc., ISBN 1583881581
  (www.Inconografixinc.com)
Standard Catalog of Volkswagen, by John Gunnell
  (2004) KP Books, ISBN: 0-87349-761-9

VOLKSWAGEN GOLF/JETTA BUYER'S CHECKLIST 1993-2005

Photocopy these pages and take them with you when you go and look at a used Golf or Jetta. Use them as a guide to help make sure you check everything carefully before buying.

FIRST IMPRESSIONS

—— Can I live with the color?

—— Is the car exceptionally dirty inside or out?

—— Are the seats ripped, torn, stained?

—— Was the previous owner a smoker?

—— Does the car have a trailer hitch? Was it used for towing?

—— Does it have a manual or automatic transmission? Which do I want?

—— Is this a car that I would like to own?

EXTERIOR

—— Is there any major body damage from a collision?

—— Is there any minor body damage from a collision?

—— Is all of the window glass intact?

—— Is the roof, hood, or trunk dimpled from hailstones?

—— Do the bumpers, fenders, and doors fit properly with no big gaps or interference?

—— Does the paint on any of the panels not match?

—— Has the car been repainted—are there signs of masking along the edges of the windshield molding?

—— Look for significant rust:

___ On a Golf where the glass meets the hatch

___ On a Golf where the hatch meets the license plate holder

___ Are the license plate lights rusted out?

___ Under the fender wells

___ Around the fuel filler neck and where it meets the fender

___ Around the front shock absorber strut towers

___ Along the lower radiator support

___ Along the point where the windshield pillars meet the body

___ At the bottom of the doors

___ At the bottom of the door handles

___ Where the bottom of the rocker panels meet the floor of the car

—— Look carefully at the tires:

___ Are they all the same brand?

___ Are they all the same size?

___ Are any of the tires damaged or irregularly worn?

___ Are there cracks in the sidewall or tread area of any of the tires?

___ Do any of the tires appear to have low air pressure?

___ Do the rims match each other, and are they original to the car?

___ Are the rims damaged or suffering from curb rash?

___ Look at the inside of the front wheels. The presence of large amounts of grease here probably signals a split outer constant velocity joint boot.

INTERIOR

—— Open each of the doors. Do they open properly? Are they hard to open? Do the keys work properly on each door?

—— Is the driver's seat excessively worn or ripped?

—— Some cars have had problems with heated seats shorting out and causing fires. Any sign of this?

—— When you sit in the driver's seat, is it firm and supportive, or soggy and misshapen?

—— Are the rubber pads on the pedals heavily worn, despite low mileage on the odometer?

—— Do the seat belts pull out and retract smoothly?

—— Does the car have floor mats? Are they ripped or worn?

—— Is the carpet under the floor mats wet or mildewed?

—— Has the sunroof leaked onto the headliner causing stains?

—— Does the headliner have rips or is it sagging?

—— Is there any evidence that the air bags have been deployed or removed from the vehicle?

—— Check the trunk. Is it dry and clean? No sign of water leaks? Are the spare tire and jack properly located and secured?

UNDER THE HOOD

—— Does the hood release work properly? Does the hood open easily?

—— Does everything look clean and tidy?

—— Are there any extra wires or wires spliced into the standard wiring harness?

—— Do the vacuum lines have any splits and cracks?

—— Are all of the accessory drive belts installed?

—— Are there any signs of fluid leaks?

—— Do the battery terminals have heavy green or white corrosion products covering them?

—— Does the radiator overflow bottle have the correct coolant color for the model year? (1993–1999: Green; 1999–2002: Pink; 2002–2005: Purple)

—— Does the brake fluid look clear and not cloudy?

—— Pull out the engine oil dipstick. Is the oil at the proper level? Is the oil dirty or clean? (A milky or chocolaty appearance of the oil could mean it is contaminated with coolant, possibly indicating a blown cylinder head gasket.)

—— Open the oil filler cap. Does it look dirty and gritty under the cap?

START THE CAR

—— Has the ignition switch been tampered with or damaged?

—— When you switch on the ignition, before cranking the engine, do all of the proper indicator lights on the dash illuminate?

—— Start the engine. If it has been sitting for a long time, there may be a slight tapping noise for 5–10 seconds, as oil reaches the hydraulic valve lifters. This is normal. If there are any loud knocks or grinding noises, shut off the engine immediately.

—— Does the engine turn over sluggishly or does it crank well prior to starting?

—— Check the instrument panel. The "Check Engine" and ABS warning lights should go out after a few seconds.

—— If the car has an oil pressure gauge, it should read a normal level while the car is warming up.

—— The car should idle smoothly without any driver input. If the weather is cold and the engine hasn't warmed yet, it should idle slightly faster, around 1,000–1,200 rpm.

—— Allow the engine to warm up while you test the electrical system:

___ Turn on the headlights and get out of the car to make sure all of the lights are working.

___ Check the directional signals in both directions.

___ Try the windshield wipers by pulling back on the stalk to activate the windshield washers. Avoid running the wipers across a dry windshield.

___ Switch on the heater blower and check that the air blows from the proper vents on all of the settings.

___ Switch on the air conditioning and let it run for several minutes. The engine speed should remain constant with the A/C on. Make sure that the A/C blows very cold air after it has run for a minute or two.

___ Turn on the radio/CD player and make sure that all of the speakers are working properly. Put a CD in the player to see if it is working.

___ Switch on the rear window defogger and make sure that the light illuminates.

___ Do the mirror controls work properly?

___ Do all of the electric windows go up and down properly?

___ Does the electric sunroof open and shut properly without any grinding or squeaking noises?

___ Do the heated seats work properly?

TEST DRIVE

—— Before going on a test drive, make sure that the car is properly registered and is carrying the proper insurance.

—— After the engine has warmed, step on the brake pedal and place the automatic transmission in drive, or press the clutch and select first gear.

—— Are there any strange grinding noises? Does the engine still idle smoothly?

—— When you drive away, does the engine pick up speed smoothly, without hesitation?

—— On a manual transmission car, does the clutch grab, or does it slip as you try to accelerate? Is it hard to shift between gears with some grinding occurring? Does the clutch release in the middle of its travel, or is it too close to the floor or too high? Is it hard to shift into reverse?

—— On an automatic transmission car, are there any unusual whirring noises from the transmission? Does it take a long time to shift gears or are shifts too abrupt?

—— Does the steering feel direct and precise? Are there any vibrations coming through the steering system? Does the steering make noise when the wheels are turned? Does the vehicle pull to one side or the other or feel vague? Are there any clunks or tightness in the steering?

—— Apply the brakes firmly. Is there any pulsing in the brake pedal (not the anti-lock system). Do the brakes feel firm or squishy? Does it pull to one side while braking? Are there any scraping noises while braking? Does the ABS light stay off while driving the car?

—— Come to a stop. Pull up the handbrake and try to drive away. ——

—— Does the handbrake prevent the car from moving?

—— Drive the car on a variety of road surfaces. Does it feel well controlled and firm? Does the body continue to bounce after hitting a bump? Does the car have too much body roll when cornering? Are there any growling or knocking noises coming from the front end that might be a bad wheel bearing or CV joint?

—— Check out the cruise control. It should engage and disengage smoothly, without any jerkiness or surprises.

—— Is the engine temperature running in the normal range? Is the oil pressure in the normal range at speed and while the car is idling?

—— Try a few hard accelerations (carefully) and look in the rearview mirror (or have someone look out the rear window) to see if there is any blue smoke, indicating an excessively worn engine. If the engine stumbles or runs roughly and the "Check Engine" light illuminates, it could indicate:

___ Dirty or clogged fuel injectors

___ A defective coil pack (on VR6s and 1.8Ts)

___ A malfunctioning oxygen sensor

___ Worn-out spark plugs or plug wires

___ A malfunctioning mass airflow sensor in the fuel injection system

___ A vacuum leak caused by a cracked vacuum or loose or cracked fuel injector seals

DOCUMENTATION

—— Does the owner have a clear title for the vehicle?

—— Do the numbers on the title match the vehicle identification number (VIN) on the top of the dash?

—— Is the person who is selling you the car the person to whom it is titled?

—— Is the car currently registered in your state?

—— Before purchasing the car, it's a good idea to do a VIN history search (see Chapter 7) to make sure that car hasn't been in a major accident or been damaged by flood.

—— Ask the owner for service records. They should cover the maintenance from when the car was new.

—— If required in your area, ask for proof that the vehicle has recently passed an exhaust emissions test.

A SECOND OPINION

Try not to buy the car the first time you see it. Go back and see it a second time and take it to a reputable shop for a prepurchase inspection. If the seller refuses to let you do this, move on to the next car. An inspection will cost you both time and money, but could mean real savings in the future. In the best case, the mechanic will confirm all of the things you found while using this checklist.

APPENDIX B | STANDARD EQUIPMENT AND OPTIONS

MODEL YEAR: 1993

Model	Standard Equipment	Options
Golf GL	Five-speed manual transmission Four-wheel disc brakes Halogen headlamps Antitheft alarm Cup holders Height-adjustable driver seat Remote trunk release	Four-speed automatic transmission Anti-lock brakes (ABS) Power glass sunroof Air conditioning Cruise control
Golf GTI	Close-ratio five-speed manual transmission Power steering Four-wheel disc brakes Halogen headlamps Integrated fog lights Body-color grille Body-color outside mirrors Alloy wheels Air conditioning Eight-speaker AM/FM cassette Height-adjustable sport seats Height-adjustable steering wheel	
Jetta GL	5-speed manual transmission Four-wheel disc brakes Halogen headlamps Cup holders Remote trunk release	4-speed automatic transmission Anti-lock brakes (ABS) Air conditioning Cruise control Power glass sunroof
Jetta GLS	Five-speed manual transmission Four-wheel disc brakes Anti-lock brakes (ABS) Halogen headlamps Air conditioning Cup holders Cruise Control Remote trunk release Power glass sunroof Power windows Split folding rear seat CD changer	Four-speed automatic transmission
Jetta GLX	2.8-liter VR6 engine Four-speed automatic transmission Four-wheel disc brakes Anti-lock brakes (ABS) Traction control Halogen headlamps Fog lights Dual front air bags Air conditioning Cup holders Cruise Control Remote trunk release Power glass sunroof Power windows Split folding rear seat CD changer Rear spoiler Leather seats 15-inch BBS alloy wheels	Five-speed manual transmission

MODEL YEAR: 1994

Model	Standard Equipment	Options
Golf GL	Five-speed manual transmission Four-wheel disc brakes Halogen headlamps Antitheft alarm Cup holders Height-adjustable driver seat Dual front air bags Remote trunk release	Four-speed automatic transmission Anti-lock brakes (ABS) Power glass sunroof Air conditioning Cruise control

Model	Standard Equipment	Options
Jetta GL	Five-speed manual transmission Four-wheel disc brakes Halogen headlamps Cup holders Remote trunk release	Four-speed automatic transmission Anti-lock brakes (ABS) Air conditioning Cruise control Power glass sunroof
Jetta GLS	Five-speed manual transmission Four-wheel disc brakes Anti-lock brakes (ABS) Halogen headlamps Air conditioning Cup holders Cruise Control Remote trunk release Power glass sunroof Power windows Split folding rear seat CD changer	Four-speed automatic transmission
Jetta GLX	2.8-liter VR6 engine Five-speed manual transmission Four-wheel disc brakes Anti-lock brakes (ABS) Traction control Halogen headlamps Fog lights Dual front air bags Air conditioning Cup holders Cruise control Remote trunk release Power glass sunroof Power windows Split folding rear seat CD changer Rear spoiler Leather seats 15-inch BBS alloy wheels	Four-speed automatic transmission

MODEL YEAR: 1995

Model	Standard Equipment	Options
Golf GL	Five-speed manual transmission Four-wheel disc brakes Halogen headlamps Antitheft alarm Cup holders Height-adjustable driver seat Dual front air bags Height-adjustable front seatbelts Daytime running lights Remote trunk release	Four-speed automatic transmission Anti-lock brakes (ABS) Power glass sunroof Air conditioning Cruise control
Golf GTI VR6	2.8-liter VR6 engine Five-speed manual transmission Sport front shocks Gas rear shocks Halogen headlamps Fog lights Electronic traction control "Plus" front axle Four-wheel disc brakes Anti-lock brakes (ABS) 15-inch alloy wheels Sport seats Height-adjustable front seatbelts Daytime running lights Remote trunk release Air conditioning Power windows Cruise control Antitheft alarm	Four-speed automatic transmission Power glass sunroof

Model	Standard Equipment	Options
Golf Sport		
	2.0-liter inline four-cylinder	Four-speed automatic transmission
	Five-speed manual transmission	Power glass sunroof
	Sport front shocks	
	Gas rear shocks	
	Halogen headlamps	
	Fog lights	
	Electronic traction control	
	"Plus" front axle	
	Four-wheel disc brakes	
	Anti-lock brakes (ABS)	
	15-inch alloy wheels	
	Sport seats	
	Height-adjustable front seatbelts	
	Daytime running lights	
	Remote trunk release	
	Air conditioning	
	Power windows	
	Cruise control	
	Antitheft alarm	
Golf Cabriolet		
	2.0-liter four-cylinder	Four-speed automatic transmission
	Five-speed manual transmission	CD changer
	Six-layer convertible top	Seven-spoke alloy wheels
	Heated rear window	Partial leather upholstery
	Halogen headlights	
	Body-color grille	
	Body-color outside mirrors	
	Body-color bumpers	
	Integrated roll bar	
	Folding rear seat	
	Dual air bags	
	Four-wheel disc brakes	
	Anti-lock brakes (ABS)	
	Height-adjustable steering wheel	
	Cloth ports seats	
	Power windows	
	Cruise control	
	Eight-speaker stereo	
	Power locking with alarm	
Jetta GL		
	Five-speed manual transmission	Four-speed automatic transmission
	Four-wheel disc brakes	Anti-lock brakes (ABS)
	Halogen headlamps	Air conditioning
	Cup holders	Cruise control
	Remote trunk release	Power glass sunroof
Jetta GLS		
	Five-speed manual transmission	Four-speed automatic transmission
	Four-wheel disc brakes	
	Anti-lock brakes (ABS)	
	Halogen headlamps	
	Air conditioning	
	Cup holders	
	Cruise control	
	Remote trunk release	
	Power glass sunroof	
	Power windows	
	Split folding rear seat	
	CD changer	
Jetta GLX		
	2.8-liter VR6 engine	Four-speed automatic transmission
	Five-speed manual transmission	
	Four-wheel disc brakes	
	Anti-lock brakes (ABS)	
	Traction control	
	Halogen headlamps	
	Fog lights	
	Dual front air bags	
	Air conditioning	
	Cup holders	
	Cruise control	
	Remote trunk release	
	Power glass sunroof	
	Power windows	
	Split folding rear seat	
	CD changer	
	Rear spoiler	
	Leather seats	
	Alloy wheels	

MODEL YEAR: 1996

Model	Standard Equipment	Options
Golf GL		
	Five-speed manual transmission	Four-speed automatic transmission
	Four-wheel disc brakes	Anti-lock brakes (ABS)
	Halogen headlamps	Power glass sunroof
	Antitheft alarm	Air conditioning
	Cup holders	Cruise control
	Height-adjustable driver seat	
	Dual front air bags	
	Height-adjustable front seatbelts	
	Daytime running lights	
	Remote trunk release	
Golf GTI VR6		
	2.8-liter VR6 engine	Four-speed automatic transmission
	Five-speed manual transmission	Power glass sunroof
	Sport front shocks	
	Gas rear shocks	
	Halogen headlamps	
	Fog lights	
	Electronic traction control	
	"Plus" front axle	
	Power steering	
	Four-wheel disc brakes	
	Anti-lock brakes (ABS)	
	15-inch alloy wheels	
	Sport seats	
	Height-adjustable front seatbelts	
	Daytime running lights	
	Remote trunk release	
	Air conditioning	
	Power windows	
	Cruise control	
	Antitheft alarm	
Golf GTI 2.0		
	2.0-liter inline Four-cylinder	Four-speed automatic transmission
	Five-speed manual transmission	Power glass sunroof
	Sport front shocks	
	Gas rear shocks	
	Halogen headlamps	
	Fog lights	
	Electronic traction control	
	"Plus" front axle	
	Power steering	
	Four-wheel disc brakes	
	Anti-lock brakes (ABS)	
	14-inch alloy wheels	
	Sport seats	
	Height-adjustable front seatbelts	
	Daytime running lights	
	Remote trunk release	
	Air conditioning	
	Power windows	
	Cruise control	
	Antitheft alarm	
Golf Cabriolet		
	2.0-liter Four-cylinder	Four-speed automatic transmission
	Five-speed manual transmission	CD changer
	Six-layer convertible top	Seven-spoke alloy wheels
	Heated rear window	Partial leather upholstery
	Halogen headlights	
	Body-color grille	
	Body-color outside mirrors	
	Body-color bumpers	
	Integrated roll bar	
	Folding rear seat	
	Dual air bags	
	Four-wheel disc brakes	
	Anti-lock brakes (ABS)	
	Height-adjustable steering wheel	
	Cloth sports seats	
	Power windows	
	Cruise control	
	Eight-speaker stereo	
	Power locking with alarm	
Jetta GL		
	Five-speed manual transmission	Four-speed automatic transmission
	Four-wheel disc brakes	Anti-lock brakes (ABS)
	Halogen headlamps	Air conditioning
	Cup holders	Cruise control
	Remote trunk release	Power glass sunroof
	Power steering	

Model	Standard Equipment	Options
Jetta Trek		
	Five-speed manual transmission	Four-speed automatic transmission
	Four-wheel disc brakes	Anti-lock brakes (ABS)
	Halogen headlamps	Air conditioning
	Cup holders	Cruise control
	Remote trunk release	Power glass sunroof
	Power steering	
	Trek 21-speed mountain bike	
	Roof-mount bike carrier	
	Fog lights	
	Rear spoiler	
	Style seats	
Jetta GLS		
	Five-speed manual transmission	Four-speed automatic transmission
	Four-wheel disc brakes	Bose audio system
	Anti-lock brakes (ABS)	
	Power Steering	
	Halogen headlamps	
	Air conditioning	
	Cup holders	
	Cruise Control	
	Remote trunk release	
	Power glass sunroof	
	Power windows	
	Split folding rear seat	
	CD changer	
Jetta GLX		
	2.8-liter VR6 engine	Four-speed automatic transmission
	Five-speed manual transmission	Bose Audio system
	Four-wheel disc brakes	
	Anti-lock brakes (ABS)	
	Traction control	
	Power steering	
	Halogen headlamps	
	Fog lights	
	Dual front air bags	
	Air conditioning	
	Cup holders	
	Cruise control	
	Remote trunk release	
	Power glass sunroof	
	Power windows	
	Split folding rear seat	
	CD changer	
	Rear spoiler	
	Leather seats	
	Alloy wheels	

MODEL YEAR: 1997–1998

Model	Standard Equipment	Options
Golf GL		
	Five-speed manual transmission	Four-speed automatic transmission
	Four-wheel disc brakes	Anti-lock brakes (ABS)
	Halogen headlamps	Power glass sunroof
	Antitheft alarm	Air conditioning
	Cup holders	Cruise control
	Height-adjustable driver seat	
	Dual front air bags	
	Height-adjustable front seatbelts	
	Daytime running lights	
	Remote trunk release	
Golf Trek		
	Five-speed manual transmission	Four-speed automatic transmission
	Four-wheel disc brakes	Anti-lock brakes (ABS)
	Halogen headlamps	Power glass sunroof
	Antitheft alarm	Air conditioning
	Cup holders	Cruise control
	Height-adjustable driver seat	
	Dual front air bags	
	Height adjustable front seatbelts	
	Daytime running lights	
	Remote trunk release	
	Trek 21-speed mountain bike	
	Roof-mount bike carrier	
	Fog lights	
	Rear spoiler	
	Style seats	
Golf K2		
	Five-speed manual transmission	Four-speed automatic transmission
	Four-wheel disc brakes	Anti-lock brakes (ABS)
	Halogen headlamps	Power glass sunroof
	Antitheft alarm	Air conditioning
	Cup holders	Cruise control
	Height-adjustable driver seat	
	Dual front air bags	
	Height-adjustable front seatbelts	
	Daytime running lights	
	Remote trunk release	
	K2 skis or snowboard	
	Roof-mount ski carrier	
	Fog lights	
	Rear spoiler	
	Style seats	

Model	Standard Equipment	Options
Golf Jazz		
	Five-speed manual transmission	Four-speed automatic transmission
	Four-wheel disc brakes	Anti-lock brakes (ABS)
	Halogen headlamps	Power glass sunroof
	Antitheft alarm	Air conditioning
	Cup holders	Cruise control
	Height-adjustable driver seat	
	Dual front air bags	
	Height-adjustable front seatbelts	
	Daytime running lights	
	Remote trunk release	
	Fog lights	
	Rear spoiler	
	Style seats	
	Eight-speaker stereo with six-disc CD	
Golf GTI VR6		
	2.8-liter VR6 engine	Four-speed automatic transmission
	Five-speed manual transmission	Black leather upholstery
	Sport front shocks	CD changer
	Gas rear shocks	
	Halogen headlamps	
	Fog lights	
	Electronic traction control	
	"Plus" front axle	
	Power steering	
	Four-wheel disc brakes	
	Anti-lock brakes (ABS)	
	15-inch alloy wheels	
	Sport seats	
	Height-adjustable front seatbelts	
	Daytime running lights	
	Remote trunk release	
	Air conditioning	
	Power windows	
	Cruise control	
	Antitheft alarm	
	Power glass sunroof	
	Rear spoiler	
Golf GTI VR6 1997 DRIVER'S EDITION		
	2.8-liter VR6 engine	Four-speed automatic transmission
	Five-speed manual transmission	Black leather upholstery
	Sport front shocks	CD changer
	Gas rear shocks	
	Halogen headlamps	
	Fog lights	
	Electronic traction control	
	"Plus" front axle	
	Power steering	
	Four-wheel disc brakes	
	Anti-lock brakes (ABS)	
	Seven-spoke alloy wheels	
	Red-painted brake calipers	
	Twin tailpipes	
	Sport seats with special cloth	
	Height-adjustable front seatbelts	
	Red accents in interior	
	Daytime running lights	
	Remote trunk release	
	Air conditioning	
	Power windows	
	Cruise control	
	Antitheft alarm	
	Power glass sunroof	
	Rear spoiler	
Golf GTI 2.0		
	2.0-liter inline Four-cylinder	Four-speed automatic transmission
	Five-speed manual transmission	Power glass sunroof
	Sport front shocks	Black leather upholstery
	Gas rear shocks	CD Changer
	Halogen headlamps	
	Fog lights	
	Electronic traction control	
	"Plus" front axle	
	Power steering	
	Four-wheel disc brakes	
	Anti-lock brakes (ABS)	
	14-inch alloy wheels	
	Sport seats	
	Height-adjustable front seatbelts	
	Daytime running lights	
	Remote trunk release	
	Air conditioning	
	Power windows	
	Cruise control	
	Antitheft alarm	

Model	Standard Equipment	Options
Golf Cabriolet		
	2.0-liter Four-cylinder	Four-speed automatic transmission
	Five-speed manual transmission	CD changer
	Six-layer convertible top	Seven-spoke alloy wheels
	Heated rear window	Partial leather upholstery
	Halogen headlights	
	Body-color grille	
	Body-color outside mirrors	
	Body-color bumpers	
	Integrated roll bar	
	Folding rear seat	
	Dual air bags	
	Four-wheel disc brakes	
	Anti-lock brakes (ABS)	
	Height-adjustable steering wheel	
	Cloth sports seats	
	Power windows	
	Cruise control	
	Eight-speaker stereo	
	Power locking with alarm	
Jetta GL		
	2.0-liter Four-cylinder	Four-speed automatic transmission
	Five-speed manual transmission	Anti-lock brakes (ABS)
	Four-wheel disc brakes	Air conditioning
	Halogen headlamps	Cruise control
	Cup holders	Power glass sunroof
	Remote trunk release	
	Power steering	
Jetta Trek		
	Five-speed manual transmission	Four-speed automatic transmission
	Four-wheel disc brakes	Anti-lock brakes (ABS)
	Halogen headlamps	Air conditioning
	Cup holders	Cruise control
	Remote trunk release	Power glass sunroof
	Power steering	
	Trek 21-speed mountain bike	
	Roof-mounted bike carrier	
	Fog lights	
	Rear spoiler	
	Style seats	
Jetta K2		
	Five-speed manual transmission	Four-speed automatic transmission
	Four-wheel disc brakes	Anti-lock brakes (ABS)
	Halogen headlamps	Air conditioning
	Cup holders	Cruise control
	Remote trunk release	Power glass sunroof
	Power steering	
	K2 skis or snowboard	
	Roof-mounted ski carrier	
	Fog lights	
	Rear spoiler	
	Style seats	
Jetta Jazz		
	Five-speed manual transmission	Four-speed automatic transmission
	Four-wheel disc brakes	Anti-lock brakes (ABS)
	Halogen headlamps	Air conditioning
	Cup holders	Cruise control
	Remote trunk release	Power glass sunroof
	Power steering	
	Fog lights	
	Rear spoiler	
	Style seats	
	Eight-speaker stereo with six-disc CD	
Jetta GLS		
	Five-speed manual transmission	Four-speed automatic transmission
	Four-wheel disc brakes	Bose audio system
	Anti-lock brakes (ABS)	
	Power steering	
	Halogen headlamps	
	Air conditioning	
	Cup holders	
	Cruise control	
	Remote trunk release	
	Power glass sunroof	
	Power windows	
	Split folding rear seat	
	CD changer	

Model	Standard Equipment	Options
Jetta GLX		
	2.8-liter VR6 engine	Four-speed automatic transmission
	Five-speed manual transmission	Bose Audio system
	Four-wheel disc brakes	
	Anti-lock brakes (ABS)	
	Traction control	
	Power steering	
	Halogen headlamps	
	Fog lights	
	Dual front air bags	
	Air conditioning	
	Cup holders	
	Cruise control	
	Remote trunk release	
	Power glass sunroof	
	Power windows	
	Split folding rear seat	
	CD changer	
	Rear spoiler	
	Leather seats	
	Alloy wheels	
Jetta GT		
	2.0-liter Four-cylinder engine	Four-speed automatic transmission
	Five-speed manual transmission	Bose Audio system
	Four-wheel disc brakes	
	Anti-lock brakes (ABS)	
	Power steering	
	Halogen headlamps	
	Fog lights	
	Dual front air bags	
	Air conditioning	
	Cup holders	
	Cruise control	
	Remote trunk release	
	Power glass sunroof	
	Power windows	
	Split folding rear seat	
	CD changer	
	Rear spoiler	
	Leather seats	
	Alloy wheels	
Jetta TDI 1998		
	1.9-liter TDI diesel	Four-speed automatic transmission
	Five-speed manual transmission	Anti-lock brakes (ABS)
	Four-wheel disc brakes	Air conditioning
	Halogen headlamps	Cruise control
	Cup holders	Power glass sunroof
	Remote trunk release	
	Power steering	

FOURTH GENERATION

MODEL YEAR: 1999

Model	Standard Equipment	Options
Golf GL		
	2.0-liter Four-cylinder	Four-speed automatic transmission
	Five-speed manual transmission	CD changer
	Dual front and side air bags	
	Four-wheel disc brakes	
	Anti-lock brakes (ABS)	
	Air conditioning	
	Antitheft alarm	
	Power door locks	
	Power windows	
	Tilt/telescope steering wheel	
	15-inch steel wheels	
	Roof antenna	
	AM/FM stereo cassette	
Golf GL TDI		
	1.9-liter four-cylinder diesel	Four-speed automatic transmission
	Five-speed manual transmission	CD changer
	Dual front and side air bags	
	Four-wheel disc brakes	
	Anti-lock brakes (ABS)	
	Air conditioning	
	Antitheft alarm	
	Power door locks	
	Power windows	
	Tilt/telescope steering wheel	
	15-inch steel wheels	
	Roof antenna	
	AM/FM stereo cassette	

Model	Standard Equipment	Options	Model	Standard Equipment	Options
Golf GLS	2.0-liter four-cylinder Five-speed manual transmission Dual front and side air bags Four-wheel disc brakes Anti-lock brakes (ABS) Air conditioning Antitheft alarm Power door locks Power windows Tilt/telescope steering wheel 15-inch steel wheels Roof antenna AM/FM stereo cassette Cruise control Heated power side mirrors Front center armrest	Four-speed automatic transmission CD changer Power sunroof 15-inch alloy wheels Leather upholstery package Heated seats	**Golf Cabriolet**	2.0-liter Four-cylinder Five-speed manual transmission Six-layer convertible top Heated rear window Halogen headlights Body-color grille Body-color outside mirrors Body-color bumpers Integrated roll bar Folding rear seat Dual air bags Four-wheel disc brakes Anti-lock brakes (ABS) Height-adjustable steering wheel Cloth sports seats Power windows Cruise control Eight-speaker stereo Power locking with alarm	Four-speed automatic transmission CD changer Seven-spoke alloy wheels Partial leather upholstery
Golf GLS TDI	1.9-liter Four-cylinder diesel Five-speed manual transmission Dual front and side air bags Four-wheel disc brakes Anti-lock brakes (ABS) Air conditioning Antitheft alarm Power door locks Power windows Tilt/telescope steering wheel 15-inch steel wheels Roof antenna AM/FM stereo cassette Cruise control Heated power side mirrors Front center armrest	Four-speed automatic transmisison CD changer Power sunroof 15-inch alloy wheels Leather upholstery package Heated seats	**Jetta GL**	2.0-liter four-cylinder Five-speed manual transmission CD changer Dual front and side air bags Four-wheel disc brakes Anti-lock brakes (ABS) Air conditioning Antitheft alarm Power door locks Power windows Tilt/telescope steering wheel 15-inch steel wheels Roof antenna AM/FM stereo cassette	Four-speed automatic transmission
Golf GTI	2.0-liter four-cylinder five-speed manual transmission Dual front and side air bags Four-wheel disc brakes Anti-lock brakes (ABS) Air conditioning Antitheft alarm Power door locks Power windows Tilt/telescope steering wheel 16-inch alloy wheels Roof antenna AM/FM stereo cassette Cruise control Heated power side mirrors Front center armrest Leather trim interior Power sunroof Automatic climate control Windshield wiper rain sensor Trip computer Fog lights Sport suspension	CD changer four-speed automatic transmission	**Jetta GL TDI**	1.9-liter four-cylinder diesel Five-speed manual transmission Dual front and side air bags Four-wheel disc brakes Anti-lock brakes (ABS) Air conditioning Antitheft alarm Power door locks Power windows Tilt/telescope steering wheel 15-inch steel wheels Roof antenna AM/FM stereo cassette	Four-speed automatic transmission CD changer
Golf GTI VR6	2.8-liter VR6 Five-speed manual transmission Dual front and side air bags Four-wheel disc brakes Anti-lock brakes (ABS) Air conditioning Antitheft alarm CD changer Power door locks Power windows Tilt/telescope steering wheel 16-inch alloy wheels Roof antenna AM/FM stereo cassette Cruise control Heated power side mirrors Front center armrest Leather trim interior Power sunroof Automatic climate control Windshield wiper rain sensor Trip computer Fog lights Sport suspension Traction control		**Jetta GLS**	2.0-liter Four-cylinder Five-speed manual transmission Dual front and side air bags Four-wheel disc brakes Anti-lock brakes (ABS) Air conditioning Antitheft alarm Power door locks Power windows Tilt/telescope steering wheel 15-inch steel wheels Roof antenna AM/FM stereo cassette Cruise control Heated power side mirrors Front center armrest	2.8-liter VR6 Four-speed automatic transmission Power sunroof 15-inch alloy wheels Leather upholstery package Heated seats CD changer
			Jetta GLS TDI	1.9-liter Four-cylinder diesel Five-speed manual transmission Dual front and side air bags Four-wheel disc brakes Anti-lock brakes (ABS) Air conditioning Antitheft alarm Power door locks Power windows Tilt/telescope steering wheel 15-inch steel wheels Roof antenna AM/FM stereo cassette Cruise control Heated power side mirrors Front center armrest	Four-speed automatic transmission Power sunroof 15-inch alloy wheels Leather upholstery package Heated seats CD changer

Model	Standard Equipment	Options
Jetta GLX	2.8-liter VR6 Five-speed manual transmission Dual front and side air bags Four-wheel disc brakes Anti-lock brakes (ABS) Air conditioning Antitheft alarm CD changer Power door locks Power windows Tilt/telescope steering wheel 16-inch alloy wheels Roof antenna AM/FM stereo cassette Cruise control Heated power side mirrors Front center armrest Leather trim interior Power sunroof Automatic climate control Windshield wiper rain sensor Trip computer Fog lights Sport suspension Traction control	Four-speed automatic transmission

MODEL YEAR: 2000

Model	Standard Equipment	Options
Golf GL	2.0-liter Four-cylinder Five-speed manual transmission Dual front and side air bags Four-wheel disc brakes Anti-lock brakes (ABS) Air conditioning Immobilizer antitheft alarm Power door locks Power windows Tilt/telescope steering wheel 15-inch steel wheels Roof antenna AM/FM stereo cassette Heated power side mirrors Cruise control	Four-speed automatic transmission CD changer
Golf GL TDI	1.9-liter four-cylinder diesel Five-speed manual transmission Dual front and side air bags Four-wheel disc brakes Anti-lock brakes (ABS) Air conditioning Immobilizer antitheft alarm Power door locks Power windows Tilt/telescope steering wheel 15-inch steel wheels Roof antenna AM/FM stereo cassette Heated power side mirrors Cruise control	Four-speed automatic transmission CD changer
Golf GLS	1.8-liter Turbo four-cylinder Five-speed manual transmission Dual front and side air bags Four-wheel disc brakes Anti-lock brakes (ABS) Air conditioning Immobilizer antitheft alarm Power door locks Power windows Tilt/telescope steering wheel 15-inch steel wheels Roof antenna AM/FM stereo cassette Cruise control Heated power side mirrors Front center armrest Antislip regulation (ASR) Electronic differential lock (EDL)	Four-speed automatic transmission CD changer Power sunroof 15-inch alloy wheels Leather upholstery package heated seats Monsoon stereo system

Model	Standard Equipment	Options
Golf GLS TDI	1.9-liter Four-cylinder diesel Five-speed manual transmission Dual front and side air bags Four-wheel disc brakes Anti-lock brakes (ABS) Air conditioning Immobilizer Antitheft alarm Power door locks Power windows Tilt/telescope steering wheel 15-inch steel wheels Roof antenna AM/FM stereo cassette Cruise control Heated power side mirrors Front center armrest	Four-speed automatic transmission CD changer Power sunroof 15-inch alloy wheels Leather upholstery package Heated seats Monsoon stereo system
Golf GTI GLS	1.8-liter Turbo Four-cylinder Five-speed manual transmission Dual front and side air bags Four-wheel disc brakes Anti-lock brakes (ABS) Air conditioning Immobilizer antitheft alarm Power door locks Power windows Tilt/telescope steering wheel 16-inch alloy wheels Roof antenna AM/FM stereo cassette Cruise control Front sport seats Heated power side mirrors Front center armrest Power sunroof Automatic climate control Windshield wiper rain sensor Trip computer Fog lights Sport suspension Anti-slip regulation (ASR) Electronic differential lock (EDL)	CD changer Four-speed automatic transmission Monsoon stereo system Partial Leather trim
Golf GTI GLX	2.8-liter VR6 Five-speed manual transmission Dual front and side air bags Four-wheel disc brakes Anti-lock brakes (ABS) Air conditioning Antitheft alarm Power door locks Power windows Tilt/telescope steering wheel 16-inch alloy wheels Roof antenna AM/FM stereo cassette Cruise control Heated power side mirrors Front center armrest Leather trim interior Power sunroof Automatic climate control Windshield wiper rain sensor Trip computer Fog lights Sport suspension Traction control	CD changer
Golf Cabriolet	2.0-liter Four-cylinder Five-speed manual transmission Six-layer convertible top Heated rear window Halogen headlights Body-color grille Body-color outside mirrors Body-color bumpers Integrated roll bar Folding rear seat Dual air bags Four-wheel disc brakes Anti-lock brakes (ABS) Height-adjustable steering wheel Cloth sports seats Power windows Cruise control Eight-speaker stereo Power locking with alarm Heated power side mirrors	Four-speed automatic transmission CD changer Seven-spoke alloy wheels Partial leather upholstery

Model	Standard Equipment	Options

Jetta GL

2.0-liter Four-cylinder
Five-speed manual transmission
Dual front and side air bags
Four-wheel disc brakes
Anti-lock brakes (ABS)
Air conditioning
Immobilizer antitheft alarm
Power door locks
Power windows
Tilt/telescope steering wheel
15-inch steel wheels
Roof antenna
AM/FM stereo cassette
Heated power side mirrors
Cruise control

Options: Four-speed automatic transmission
CD changer

Jetta GL TDI

1.9-liter Four-cylinder diesel
Five-speed manual transmission
Dual front and side air bags
Four-wheel disc brakes
Anti-lock brakes (ABS)
Air conditioning
Immobilizer antitheft alarm
Power door locks
Power windows
Tilt/telescope steering wheel
15-inch steel wheels
Roof antenna
AM/FM stereo cassette
Heated power side mirrors
Cruise control

Options: Four-speed automatic transmission
CD changer

Jetta GLS

1.8-liter Turbo Four-cylinder
Five-speed manual transmission
Dual front and side air bags
Four-wheel disc brakes
Anti-lock brakes (ABS)
Air conditioning
Immobilizer antitheft alarm
Power door locks
Power windows
Tilt/telescope steering wheel
15-inch steel wheels
Roof antenna
AM/FM stereo cassette
Cruise control
Heated power side mirrors
Front center armrest
Antislip regulation (ASR)
Electronic differential lock (EDL)

Options: 2.8-liter VR6
Four-speed automatic transmission
Power sunroof
15-inch alloy wheels
Leather upholstery package
Heated seats
CD changer
Monsoon stereo system

Jetta GLS TDI

1.9-liter Four-cylinder diesel
Five-speed manual transmission
Dual front and side air bags
Four-wheel disc brakes
Anti-lock brakes (ABS)
Air conditioning
Immobilizer antitheft alarm
Power door locks
Power windows
Tilt/telescope steering wheel
15-inch steel wheels
Roof antenna
AM/FM stereo cassette
Cruise control
Heated power side mirrors
Front center armrest

Options: Four-speed automatic transmission
Power sunroof
15-inch alloy wheels
Leather upholstery package
Heated seats
CD changer
Monsoon stereo system

Jetta GLX

2.8-liter VR6
Five-speed manual transmission
Dual front and side air bags
CD changer
Four-wheel disc brakes
Anti-lock brakes (ABS)
Air conditioning
Immobilizer antitheft alarm
Power door locks
Power windows
Tilt/telescope steering wheel
16-inch alloy wheels
Roof antenna
AM/FM stereo cassette
Cruise control
Heated power side mirrors
Front center armrest
Leather trim interior
Power sunroof
Automatic climate control
Windshield wiper rain sensor
Trip computer
Fog lights
Sport suspension
Traction control

Options: Four-speed automatic transmission

Model	Standard Equipment	Options

Golf GL

2.0-liter Four-cylinder
Five-speed manual transmission
Dual front and side air bags
Four-wheel disc brakes
Anti-lock brakes (ABS)
Air conditioning
Immobilizer antitheft alarm
Power door locks
Power windows
Tilt/telescope steering wheel
15-inch steel wheels
Roof antenna
AM/FM stereo cassette
Heated power side mirrors
Cruise control

Options: Four-speed automatic transmission
CD changer

Golf GL TDI

1.9-liter Four-cylinder diesel
Five-speed manual transmission
Dual front and side air bags
Four-wheel disc brakes
Anti-lock brakes (ABS)
Air conditioning
Immobilizer antitheft alarm
Power door locks
Power windows
Tilt/telescope steering wheel
15-inch steel wheels
Roof antenna
AM/FM stereo cassette
Heated power side mirrors
Cruise control

Options: Four-speed automatic transmission
CD changer

Golf GLS

1.8-liter Turbo four-cylinder
Five-speed manual transmission
Dual front and side air bags
Four-wheel disc brakes
Anti-lock brakes (ABS)
Air conditioning
Immobilizer antitheft alarm
Power door locks
Power windows
Tilt/telescope steering wheel
15-inch steel wheels
Roof antenna
AM/FM stereo cassette
Cruise control
Heated power side mirrors
Front center armrest
Anti-slip regulation (ASR)
Electronic differential lock (EDL)

Options: Four-speed automatic transmission
CD changer
Power sunroof
15-inch alloy wheels
Leather upholstery package
Heated seats
Monsoon stereo system

Golf GLS TDI

1.9-liter four-cylinder diesel
Five-speed manual transmission
Dual front and side air bags
Four-wheel disc brakes
Anti-lock brakes (ABS)
Air conditioning
Immobilizer antitheft alarm
Power door locks
Power windows
Tilt/telescope steering wheel
15-inch steel wheels
Roof antenna
AM/FM stereo cassette
Cruise control
Heated power side mirrors
Front center armrest

Options: Four-speed automatic transmission
CD changer
Power sunroof
15-inch alloy wheels
Leather upholstery package
Heated seats
Monsoon stereo system

Golf GTI GLS

1.8-liter Turbo four-cylinder
Five-speed manual transmission
Dual front and side air bags
Four-wheel disc brakes
Anti-lock brakes (ABS)
Air conditioning
Immobilizer antitheft alarm
Power door locks
Power windows
Tilt/telescope steering wheel
16-inch alloy wheels
Roof antenna
AM/FM stereo cassette
Cruise control
Front sport seats
Heated power side mirrors
Front center armrest
Power sunroof
Automatic climate control
Windshield wiper rain sensor
Trip computer
Fog lights
Anti-slip regulation (ASR)
Electronic differential lock (EDL)

Options: CD changer
Four-speed automatic transmission
Monsoon stereo system
Partial leather trim
Sport suspension

Model	Standard Equipment	Options	Model	Standard Equipment	Options

Golf GTI GLX

2.8-liter VR6
Five-speed manual transmission
Dual front and side air bags
Four-wheel disc brakes
Anti-lock brakes (ABS)
Air conditioning
Antitheft alarm
Power door locks
Power windows
Tilt/telescope steering wheel
16-inch alloy wheels
Roof antenna
Monsoon stereo system
Cruise control
Heated power side mirrors
Front center armrest
Leather upholstery
Power sunroof
Automatic climate control
Windshield wiper rain sensor
Trip computer
Fog lights
Traction control

Options:
CD changer
17-inch alloy wheels
Sport suspension

Golf Cabriolet

2.0-liter four-cylinder
Five-speed manual transmission
Six-layer convertible top
Heated rear window
Halogen headlights
Body-color grille
Body-color outside mirrors
Body-color bumpers
Integrated roll bar
Folding rear seat
Dual air bags
Four-wheel disc brakes
Anti-lock brakes (ABS)
Height-adjustable steering wheel
Cloth sports seats
Power windows
Cruise control
Eight-speaker stereo
Power locking with alarm
Heated power side mirrors

Options:
Four-speed automatic transmission
CD changer
Seven-spoke alloy wheels
Partial leather upholstery

Jetta GL

2.0-liter four-cylinder
Jetta GL Wagon
Five-speed manual transmission
Dual front and side air bags
Four-wheel disc brakes
Anti-lock brakes (ABS)
Air conditioning
Immobilizer antitheft alarm
Power door locks
Power windows
Tilt/telescope steering wheel
15-inch steel wheels
Roof antenna
AM/FM stereo cassette
Heated power side mirrors
Cruise control

Options:
Four-speed automatic transmission
CD changer

Jetta GL TDI
Jetta GL TDI Wagon

1.9-liter four-cylinder diesel
Five-speed manual transmission
Dual front and side air bags
Four-wheel disc brakes
Anti-lock brakes (ABS)
Air conditioning
Immobilizer antitheft alarm
Power door locks
Power windows
Tilt/telescope steering wheel
15-inch steel wheels
Roof antenna
AM/FM stereo cassette
Heated power side mirrors
Cruise control

Options:
Four-speed automatic transmission
CD changer

Jetta GLS
Jetta GLS Wagon

1.8-liter Turbo four-cylinder
Five-speed manual transmission
Dual front and side air bags
Four-wheel disc brakes
Anti-lock brakes (ABS)
Air conditioning
Immobilizer antitheft alarm
Power door locks
Power windows
Tilt/telescope steering wheel
Roof antenna
AM/FM stereo cassette
Cruise control
Heated power side mirrors
Front center armrest
Antislip regulation (ASR)
Electronic differential lock (EDL)

Options:
2.8-liter VR6
Four-speed automatic transmission
Power sunroof
15-inch alloy wheels
Leather upholstery package
Heated seats
CD changer
Monsoon stereo system

Jetta GLS TDI
Jetta GLS TDI Wagon

1.9-liter four-cylinder diesel
Five-speed manual transmission
Dual front and side air bags
Four-wheel disc brakes
Anti-lock brakes (ABS)
Air conditioning
Immobilizer antitheft alarm
Power door locks
Power windows
Tilt/telescope steering wheel
15-inch steel wheels
Roof antenna
AM/FM stereo cassette
Cruise control
Heated power side mirrors
Front center armrest

Options:
Four-speed automatic transmission
Power sunroof
15-inch alloy wheels
Leather upholstery package
Heated seats
CD changer
Monsoon stereo system

Jetta GLX

2.8-liter VR6
Five-speed manual transmission
Dual front and side air bags
Four-wheel disc brakes
Anti-lock brakes (ABS)
Air conditioning
Immobilizer antitheft alarm
Power door locks
Power windows
Tilt/telescope steering wheel
16-inch alloy wheels
Roof antenna
Monsoon stereo system
Cruise control
Heated power side mirrors
Front center armrest
Leather upholstery
Power sunroof
Automatic climate control
Windshield wiper rain sensor
Trip computer
Fog lights
Traction control

Options:
CD changer
Four-speed automatic transmission
17-inch alloy wheels
Sport suspension

MODEL YEAR: 2002

Model	Standard Equipment	Options

Golf GL

2.0-liter four-cylinder
Five-speed manual transmission
Dual front and side air bags
Four-wheel disc brakes
Anti-lock brakes (ABS)
Air conditioning
Immobilizer antitheft alarm
Power door locks
Power windows
Tilt/telescope steering wheel
15-inch steel wheels
Roof antenna
AM/FM stereo cassette
Heated power side mirrors
Cruise control

Options:
Four-speed automatic transmission
CD changer

Model	Standard Equipment	Options

Golf GL TDI
- 1.9-liter four-cylinder diesel
- Five-speed manual transmission
- Dual front and side air bags
- Four-wheel disc brakes
- Anti-lock brakes (ABS)
- Air conditioning
- Immobilizer antitheft alarm
- Power door locks
- Power windows
- Tilt/telescope steering wheel
- 15-inch steel wheels
- Roof antenna
- AM/FM stereo cassette
- Heated power side mirrors
- Cruise control

Options:
- Four-speed automatic transmission
- CD changer

Golf GLS
- 1.8-liter Turbo four-cylinder
- Five-speed manual transmission
- Dual front and side air bags
- Four-wheel disc brakes
- Anti-lock brakes (ABS)
- Air conditioning
- Immobilizer antitheft alarm
- Power door locks
- Power windows
- Tilt/telescope steering wheel
- 15-inch steel wheels
- Roof antenna
- AM/FM stereo cassette
- Cruise control
- Heated power side mirrors
- Front center armrest
- Antislip regulation (ASR)
- Electronic differential lock (EDL)

Options:
- Five-speed automatic transmission
- CD changer
- Power sunroof
- 15-inch alloy wheels
- Leather upholstery package
- Heated seats
- Monsoon stereo system

Golf GLS TDI
- 1.9-liter four-cylinder diesel
- Five-speed manual transmission
- Dual front and side air bags
- Four-wheel disc brakes
- Anti-lock brakes (ABS)
- Air conditioning
- Immobilizer antitheft alarm
- Power door locks
- Power windows
- Tilt/telescope steering wheel
- 15-inch steel wheels
- Roof antenna
- AM/FM stereo cassette
- Cruise control
- Heated power side mirrors
- Front center armrest

Options:
- Four-speed automatic transmission
- CD changer
- Power sunroof
- 15-inch alloy wheels
- Leather upholstery package
- Heated seats
- Monsoon stereo system

Golf GTI GLS
- 1.8-liter Turbo four-cylinder
- Six-speed manual transmission
- Dual front and side air bags
- Four-wheel disc brakes
- Anti-lock brakes (ABS)
- Air conditioning
- Immobilizer antitheft alarm
- Power door locks
- Power windows
- Tilt/telescope steering wheel
- 16-inch alloy wheels
- Roof antenna
- AM/FM stereo cassette
- Cruise control
- Front sport seats
- Heated power side mirrors
- Front center armrest
- Power sunroof
- Automatic climate control
- Windshield wiper rain sensor
- Trip computer
- Fog lights
- Anti-slip regulation (ASR)
- Electronic differential lock (EDL)

Options:
- CD changer
- Five-speed automatic transmission
- Monsoon stereo system
- Partial Leather trim
- Sport suspension

Golf GTI 337
- 1.8-liter Turbo four-cylinder
- Six-speed manual transmission
- Dual front and side air bags
- Four-wheel disc brakes (Audi TT)
- Red brake calipers
- Anti-lock brakes (ABS)
- Air conditioning
- Immobilizer antitheft alarm
- Power door locks
- Power windows
- Tilt/telescope steering wheel
- Lowered port suspension
- 18-inch BBS alloy wheels
- 225/40ZR18 Michelin tires
- Roof antenna
- Monsoon CD stereo system
- Rear spoiler
- Front air dam
- Cruise control
- Front sport seats
- Golf-ball shifter
- Heated power side mirrors
- Front center armrest
- Power sunroof
- Automatic climate control
- Windshield wiper rain sensor
- Trip computer
- Fog lights
- Anti-slip regulation (ASR)
- Electronic differential lock (EDL)

Golf GTI GLX
- 2.8-liter VR6
- Six-speed manual transmission
- Dual front and side air bags
- Four-wheel disc brakes
- Anti-lock brakes (ABS)
- Air conditioning
- Antitheft alarm
- Power door locks
- Power windows
- Tilt/telescope steering wheel
- 16-inch alloy wheels
- Roof antenna
- Monsoon stereo system
- Cruise control
- Heated power side mirrors
- Front center armrest
- Leather upholstery
- Power sunroof
- Automatic climate control
- Windshield wiper rain sensor
- Trip computer
- Fog lights
- Traction control

Options:
- 17-inch alloy wheels
- Sport suspension
- CD changer

Golf Cabriolet
- 2.0-liter four-cylinder
- Five-speed manual transmission
- Six-layer convertible top
- Heated rear window
- Halogen headlights
- Body-color grille
- Body-color outside mirrors
- Body-color bumpers
- Integrated roll bar
- Folding rear seat
- Dual air bags
- Four-wheel disc brakes
- Anti-lock brakes (ABS)
- Height-adjustable steering wheel
- Cloth sports seats
- Power windows
- Cruise control
- Eight-speaker stereo
- Power locking with alarm
- Heated power side mirrors

Options:
- Four-speed automatic transmission
- CD changer
- Seven-spoke alloy wheels
- Partial leather upholstery

Jetta GL
Jetta GL Wagon
- 2.0-liter Four-cylinder
- Five-speed manual transmission
- Dual front and side air bags
- Four-wheel disc brakes
- Anti-lock brakes (ABS)
- Air conditioning
- Immobilizer antitheft alarm
- Power door locks
- Power windows
- Tilt/telescope steering wheel
- 15-inch steel wheels
- Roof antenna
- AM/FM stereo cassette
- Heated power side mirrors
- Cruise control

Options:
- Four-speed automatic transmission
- CD changer

Model	Standard Equipment	Options

Jetta GL TDI
Jetta GL TDI Wagon

	Standard Equipment	Options
	1.9-liter four-cylinder diesel Five-speed manual transmission Dual front and side air bags Four-wheel disc brakes Anti-lock brakes (ABS) Air conditioning Immobilizer antitheft alarm Power door locks Power windows Tilt/telescope steering wheel 15-inch steel wheels Roof antenna AM/FM stereo cassette Heated power side mirrors Cruise control	Four-speed automatic transmission CD changer

Jetta GLS
Jetta GLS Wagon

| | 1.8-liter turbo four-cylinder
Six-speed manual transmission
Dual front and side air bags
Four-wheel disc brakes
Anti-lock brakes (ABS)
Air conditioning
Immobilizer antitheft alarm
Power door locks
Power windows
Tilt/telescope steering wheel
Roof antenna
AM/FM stereo cassette
Cruise control
Heated power side mirrors
Front center armrest
Anti-slip regulation (ASR)
Electronic differential lock (EDL) | 2.8-liter VR6
Five-speed automatic transmission
Power sunroof
15-inch alloy wheels
Leather upholstery package
Heated seats
CD changer
Monsoon stereo system |

Jetta GLS TDI
Jetta GLS TDI Wagon

| | 1.9-liter Four-cylinder diesel
Five-speed manual transmission
Dual front and side air bags
Four-wheel disc brakes
Anti-lock brakes (ABS)
Air conditioning
Immobilizer antitheft alarm
Power door locks
Power windows
Tilt/telescope steering wheel
15-inch steel wheels
Roof antenna
AM/FM stereo cassette
Cruise control
Heated power side mirrors
Front center armrest | Four-speed automatic transmission
Power sunroof
15-inch alloy wheels
Leather upholstery package
Heated seats
CD changer
Monsoon stereo system |

Jetta GLX

| | 2.8-liter VR6
Six-speed manual transmission
Dual front and side air bags
Four-wheel disc brakes
Anti-lock brakes (ABS)
Air conditioning
Immobilizer antitheft alarm
Power door locks
Power windows
Tilt/telescope steering wheel
16-inch alloy wheels
Roof antenna
Monsoon stereo system
Cruise control
Heated power side mirrors
Front center armrest
Leather upholstery
Power sunroof
Automatic climate control
Windshield wiper rain sensor
Trip computer
Fog lights
Traction control | CD changer
Five-speed automatic transmission
17-inch alloy wheels
Sport suspension |

MODEL YEAR: 2003

Model	Standard Equipment	Options

Golf GL

| | 2.0-liter four-cylinder
Five-speed manual transmission
Dual front and side air bags
Side curtain air bags
Four-wheel disc brakes
Anti-lock brakes (ABS)
Air conditioning
Immobilizer antitheft alarm
Power door locks
Power windows
Tilt/telescope steering wheel
15-inch steel wheels
Roof antenna
AM/FM stereo cassette
Heated power side mirrors
Cruise control | Four-speed automatic transmission
CD changer |

Golf GL TDI

| | 1.9-liter four-cylinder diesel
Five-speed manual transmission
Dual front and side air bags
Side curtain air bags
Four-wheel disc brakes
Anti-lock brakes (ABS)
Air conditioning
Immobilizer antitheft alarm
Power door locks
Power windows
Tilt/telescope steering wheel
15-inch steel wheels
Roof antenna
AM/FM stereo cassette
Heated power side mirrors
Cruise control | Four-speed automatic transmission
CD changer |

Golf GLS

| | 1.8-liter turbo four-cylinder
Five-speed manual transmission
Dual front and side air bags
Four-wheel disc brakes
Anti-lock brakes (ABS)
Side curtain air bags
Air conditioning
Immobilizer antitheft alarm
Power door locks
Power windows
Tilt/telescope steering wheel
15-inch alloy wheels
Roof antenna
AM/FM stereo cassette
Cruise control
Heated power side mirrors
Front center armrest
Antislip regulation (ASR)
Electronic differential lock (EDL)
Power sunroof | Five-speed automatic transmission
CD changer
Monsoon stereo system
Heated seats
Leather upholstery package |

Golf GLS TDI

| | 1.9-liter four-cylinder diesel
Five-speed manual transmission
Dual front and side air bags
Four-wheel disc brakes
Anti-lock brakes (ABS)
Side curtain air bags
Air conditioning
Immobilizer antitheft alarm
Power door locks
Power windows
Tilt/telescope steering wheel
15-inch alloy wheels
Roof antenna
AM/FM stereo cassette
Cruise control
Heated power side mirrors
Front center armrest
Power sunroof | Four-speed automatic transmission
CD changer
Monsoon stereo system
Heated seats
Leather upholstery package |

Model	Standard Equipment	Options

Golf GTI 1.8T

1.8-liter turbo four-cylinder
Five-speed manual transmission
Dual front and side air bags
Four-wheel disc brakes
Anti-lock brakes (ABS)
Air conditioning
Side curtain air bags
Immobilizer antitheft alarm
Power door locks
Power windows
Tilt/telescope steering wheel
16-inch alloy wheels
Roof antenna
AM/FM stereo cassette
Cruise control
Front sport seats
Heated power side mirrors
Front center armrest
Power sunroof
Anti-slip regulation (ASR)
Electronic differential lock (EDL)
Dual exhaust system

Options:
Six-disc CD changer
Five-speed automatic transmission
Monsoon stereo system
Partial Leather trim
Sport suspension
17-inch alloy wheels
Electronic Stability Program

Golf GTI 20th Anniversary

1.8-liter turbo four-cylinder
Six-speed manual transmission
Dual front and side air bags
Side curtain air bags
Four-wheel disc brakes
Red brake calipers
Anti-lock brakes (ABS)
Air conditioning
Immobilizer antitheft alarm
Power door locks
Power windows
Tilt/telescope steering wheel
Lowered sport suspension
18-inch alloy wheels
225/40ZR18 performance tires
Roof antenna
Monsoon CD stereo system
Rear spoiler
Front air dam
Aerodynamic side skirts
Single chrome exhaust
Cruise control
Recaro front sport seats
Golf-ball shifter
Stainless steel pedals
Heated power side mirrors
Power sunroof
Automatic climate control
Projector fog lights
Anti-slip regulation (ASR)
Electronic differential lock (EDL)
20th Anniversary GTI plaque

Options:
Electronic stability program
Six-disc CD changer

Golf GTI VR6

2.8-liter VR6 24V
Six-speed manual transmission
Dual front and side air bags
Side curtain air bags
Four-wheel disc brakes
Anti-lock brakes (ABS)
Sport suspension
Sport seats
Air conditioning
Immobilizer antitheft alarm
Power door locks
Power windows
Tilt/telescope steering wheel
17-inch alloy wheels
Roof antenna
AM/FM-CD stereo system
Cruise control
Heated power side mirrors
Front center armrest
Dual chrome exhaust
Automatic climate control
Trip computer
Electronic stability program (ESP)

Options:
CD changer
Windshield wiper rain sensor
Leather upholstery
Heated front seats
Monsoon stereo system
Power sunroof
Electronic climate control

Jetta GL
Jetta GL Wagon

2.0-liter four-cylinder
Five-speed manual transmission
Dual front and side air bags
Side curtain air bags
Four-wheel disc brakes
Anti-lock brakes (ABS)
Air conditioning
Immobilizer antitheft alarm
Power door locks
Power windows
Tilt/telescope steering wheel
15-inch steel wheels
Roof antenna
AM/FM stereo cassette
Heated power side mirrors
Cruise control

Options:
Four-speed automatic transmission
Electronic stability program
CD changer

Jetta GL TDI
Jetta GL TDI Wagon

1.9-liter four-cylinder diesel
Five-speed manual transmission
Dual front and side air bags
Side curtain air bags
Four-wheel disc brakes
Anti-lock brakes (ABS)
Air conditioning
Immobilizer antitheft alarm
Power door locks
Power windows
Tilt/telescope steering wheel
15-inch steel wheels
Roof antenna
AM/FM stereo cassette
Heated power side mirrors
Cruise control

Options:
Five-speed automatic transmission
CD changer
Electronic stability program

Jetta GLS
Jetta GLS Wagon

1.8-liter turbo four-cylinder
Six-speed manual transmission
Dual front and side air bags
Four-wheel disc brakes
Anti-lock brakes (ABS)
Side curtain air bags
Air conditioning
Immobilizer antitheft alarm
Power door locks
Power windows
Tilt/telescope steering wheel
Roof antenna
AM/FM stereo cassette
Cruise control
Heated power side mirrors
Front center armrest
Antislip regulation (ASR)
Electronic differential lock (EDL)
15-inch alloy wheels
Power sunroof

Options:
Electronic stability program
Five-speed automatic transmission
Monsoon stereo system
Heated seats
Leather upholstery package

Jetta GLS TDI
Jetta GLS TDI Wagon

1.9-liter four-cylinder diesel
Five-speed manual transmission
Dual front and side air bags
Four-wheel disc brakes
Anti-lock brakes (ABS)
Side curtain air bags
Air conditioning
Immobilizer antitheft alarm
Power door locks
Power windows
Power sunroof
Tilt/telescope steering wheel
15-inch alloy wheels
Roof antenna
AM/FM stereo cassette
Cruise control
Heated power side mirrors
Front center armrest

Options:
Electronic stability program
Four-speed automatic transmission
Monsoon stereo system
Heated seats
Leather upholstery package

Model	Standard Equipment	Options
Jetta Wolfsburg Edition	1.8-liter turbo four-cylinder Five-speed manual transmission Dual front and side air bags Four-wheel disc brakes Anti-lock brakes (ABS) Sport suspension Side curtain air bags Sport seats Air conditioning Immobilizer antitheft alarm Power door locks Power windows Tilt/telescope steering wheel Roof antenna AM/FM stereo cassette Cruise control Heated power side mirrors Front center armrest Anti-slip regulation (ASR) Electronic differential lock (EDL) 16-inch BBS alloy wheels Rear spoiler Dual exhaust pipes	Electronic stability program Five-speed automatic transmission Monsoon stereo system Heated seats Leather upholstery package Power sunroof
Jetta GLX **Jetta GLX Wagon**	2.8-liter VR6 24V Six-speed manual transmission Dual front and side air bags Four-wheel disc brakes Side curtain air bags Anti-lock brakes (ABS) Air conditioning Immobilizer antitheft alarm Power door locks Power windows Tilt/telescope steering wheel 16-inch alloy wheels Roof antenna Monsoon stereo system Cruise control Heated power side mirrors Front center armrest Leather upholstery Power sunroof Traction control Electronic Stability Program	CD changer Five-speed automatic transmission 17-inch alloy wheels Sport suspension

MODEL YEAR: 2004

Model	Standard Equipment	Options
Golf GL	2.0-liter four-cylinder Five-speed manual transmission Dual front and side air bags Side curtain air bags Four-wheel disc brakes Anti-lock brakes (ABS) Air conditioning Immobilizer antitheft alarm Power door locks Power windows Tilt/telescope steering wheel 15-inch steel wheels Roof antenna AM/FM stereo cassette Heated power side mirrors Cruise control	Four-speed automatic transmission CD changer
Golf GL TDI-PD	1.9-liter four-cylinder diesel Five-speed manual transmission Dual front and side air bags Side curtain air bags Four-wheel disc brakes Anti-lock brakes (ABS) Air conditioning Immobilizer antitheft alarm Power door locks Power windows Tilt/telescope steering wheel 15-inch steel wheels Roof antenna AM/FM stereo cassette Heated power side mirrors Cruise control	Four-speed automatic transmission CD changer

Model	Standard Equipment	Options
Golf GLS	1.8-liter turbo four-cylinder Five-speed manual transmission Dual front and side air bags Four-wheel disc brakes Anti-lock brakes (ABS) Side curtain air bags Air conditioning Immobilizer antitheft alarm Power door locks Power windows Tilt/telescope steering wheel 15-inch alloy wheels Roof antenna AM/FM stereo cassette Cruise control Heated power side mirrors Front center armrest Antislip regulation (ASR) Electronic differential lock (EDL) Power sunroof	Five-speed automatic transmission CD changer Monsoon stereo system Heated seats Leather upholstery package
Golf GLS TDI-PD	1.9-liter four-cylinder diesel Five-speed manual transmission Dual front and side air bags Four-wheel disc brakes Anti-lock brakes (ABS) Side curtain air bags Air conditioning Immobilizer antitheft alarm Power door locks Power windows Tilt/telescope steering wheel 15-inch alloy wheels Roof antenna AM/FM stereo cassette Cruise control Heated power side mirrors Front center armrest Power sunroof	Four-speed automatic transmission CD changer Monsoon stereo system Heated seats Leather upholstery package
Golf GTI 1.8T	1.8-liter turbo four-cylinder Five-speed manual transmission Dual front and side air bags Four-wheel disc brakes Anti-lock brakes (ABS) Air conditioning Side curtain air bags Immobilizer antitheft alarm Power door locks Power windows Tilt/telescope steering wheel 16-inch alloy wheels Roof antenna AM/FM stereo cassette Cruise control Front sport seats Heated power side mirrors Front center armrest Power sunroof Antislip regulation (ASR) Electronic differential lock (EDL) Dual exhaust system	Six-disc CD changer Five-speed automatic transmission Monsoon stereo system Partial Leather trim Sport suspension 17-inch alloy wheels Electronic Stability Program

Model	Standard Equipment	Options
Golf R32		
	3.2-liter VR6 24V	CD changer
	Six-speed manual transmission	
	4MOTION all-wheel drive	
	Dual front and side air bags	
	Side curtain air bags	
	Four-wheel disc brakes	
	Anti-lock brakes (ABS)	
	Blue Four-piston brake calipers	
	Multilink Sport suspension	
	Sport seats	
	Heated front seats	
	Air conditioning	
	Immobilizer antitheft alarm	
	Power door locks	
	Power windows	
	Tilt/telescope steering wheel	
	18-inch alloy wheels	
	Side skirts	
	Front spoiler	
	Rear spoiler	
	Power sunroof	
	Roof antenna	
	Monsoon stereo system	
	Cruise control	
	Heated power side mirrors	
	Windshield wiper rain sensor	
	Front center armrest	
	Dual exhaust	
	Projector fog lights	
	Automatic climate control	
	Trip computer	
	Anti-slip regulation (ASR)	
	Electronic differential lock (EDL)	
	Electronic Stability Program (ESP)	
Jetta GL 2.0		
Jetta GL 2.0 Wagon		
	2.0-liter four-cylinder	Four-speed automatic transmission
	Five-speed manual transmission	CD changer
	Dual front and side air bags	Electronic Stability Program
	Side curtain air bags	
	Four-wheel disc brakes	
	Anti-lock brakes (ABS)	
	Air conditioning	
	Immobilizer antitheft alarm	
	Power door locks	
	Power windows	
	Tilt/telescope steering wheel	
	15-inch steel wheels	
	Roof antenna	
	AM/FM stereo CD/cassette	
	Heated power side mirrors	
	Cruise control	
Jetta GL 1.8T		
Jetta GL 1.8T Wagon		
	1.8-liter turbo four-cylinder	Five-speed automatic transmission
	Five-speed manual transmission	Electronic stability program
	Dual front and side air bags	CD changer
	Side curtain air bags	
	Four-wheel disc brakes	
	Anti-lock brakes (ABS)	
	Air conditioning	
	Immobilizer antitheft alarm	
	Power door locks	
	Power windows	
	Tilt/telescope steering wheel	
	15-inch steel wheels	
	Roof antenna	
	AM/FM stereo CD/cassette	
	Heated power side mirrors	
	Cruise control	
	Anti-slip Regulation (ASR)	
	Electronic Differential Lock (EDL)	
Jetta GL TDI-PD		
Jetta GL TDI-PD Wagon		
	1.9-liter four-cylinder diesel	Five-speed automatic transmission
	Five-speed manual transmission	Electronic Stability Program
	Dual front and side air bags	CD changer
	Side curtain air bags	
	Four-wheel disc brakes	
	Anti-lock brakes (ABS)	
	Air conditioning	
	Immobilizer antitheft alarm	
	Power door locks	
	Power windows	
	Tilt/telescope steering wheel	
	15-inch steel wheels	
	Roof antenna	
	AM/FM stereo CD/cassette	
	Heated power side mirrors	
	Cruise control	

Model	Standard Equipment	Options
Jetta GLS 2.0		
Jetta GLS 2.0 Wagon		
	2.0-liter four-cylinder	Electronic Stability Program
	Five-speed manual transmission	Four-speed automatic transmission
	Dual front and side air bags	CD Changer
	Four-wheel disc brakes	Heated seats
	Anti-lock brakes (ABS)	Leather upholstery package
	Side curtain air bags	
	Air conditioning	
	Immobilizer antitheft alarm	
	Power door locks	
	Power windows	
	Tilt/telescope steering wheel	
	Roof antenna	
	Monsoon stereo system	
	Cruise control	
	Heated power side mirrors	
	Front center armrest	
	15-inch alloy wheels	
	Power sunroof	
Jetta GLS 1.8T		
Jetta GLS 1.8T Wagon		
	1.8-liter turbo four-cylinder	Electronic Stability Program
	Five-speed manual transmission	Five-speed automatic transmission
	Dual front and side air bags	CD Changer
	Four-wheel disc brakes	Heated seats
	Anti-lock brakes (ABS)	Leather upholstery package
	Side curtain air bags	
	Air conditioning	
	Immobilizer antitheft alarm	
	Power door locks	
	Power windows	
	Tilt/telescope steering wheel	
	Roof antenna	
	Monsoon stereo system	
	Cruise control	
	Heated power side mirrors	
	Front center armrest	
	15-inch alloy wheels	
	Power sunroof	
	Anti-slip Regulation (ASR)	
	Electronic Differential Lock (EDL)	
Jetta GLS TDI- PD		
Jetta GLS TDI-PD Wagon		
	1.9-liter four-cylinder diesel	Electronic Stability Program
	Five-speed manual transmission	Five-speed automatic transmission
	Dual front and side air bags	CD Changer
	Four-wheel disc brakes	Heated seats
	Anti-lock brakes (ABS)	Leather upholstery package
	Side curtain air bags	
	Air conditioning	
	Immobilizer antitheft alarm	
	Power door locks	
	Power windows	
	Power sunroof	
	Tilt/telescope steering wheel	
	15-inch alloy wheels	
	Roof antenna	
	Monsoon stereo system	
	Cruise control	
	Heated power side mirrors	
	Front center armrest	
Jetta GLI 1.8T		
	1.8-liter turbo four-cylinder (from 02/04) Six-speed manual transmission	Electronic Stability Program
	Dual front and side air bags	CD Changer
	Four-wheel disc brakes	
	Anti-lock brakes (ABS)	
	Red brake calipers	
	Lowered sport suspension	
	Side curtain air bags	
	Sport seats	
	Air conditioning	
	Immobilizer antitheft alarm	
	Power door locks	
	Power windows	
	Tilt/telescope steering wheel	
	Roof antenna	
	Monsoon stereo system	
	Cruise control	
	Heated power side mirrors	
	Power sunroof	
	Front center armrest	
	18-inch alloy wheels	
	Rear spoiler	
	Front spoiler	
	Side skirts	
	Fog lights	
	Dual exhaust pipes	
	Antislip Regulation (ASR)	
	Electronic Differential Lock (EDL)	

Model	Standard Equipment	Options
Jetta GLI 2.8	2.8-liter VR6 24V (before 02/04) Six-speed manual transmission Dual front and side air bags Four-wheel disc brakes Sport suspension Side curtain air bags Anti-lock brakes (ABS) Sport seats Air conditioning Immobilizer antitheft alarm Power door locks Power windows Tilt/telescope steering wheel 17-inch alloy wheels Roof antenna Monsoon stereo system Cruise control Heated power side mirrors Front center armrest Anti-slip Regulation (ASR) Electronic Differential Lock (EDL) Electronic Stability Program (ESP)	CD changer Leather upholstery Power sunroof

MODEL YEAR: 2005

Model	Standard Equipment	Options
Golf GL	2.0-liter four-cylinder Five-speed manual transmission Dual front and side air bags Side curtain air bags Four-wheel disc brakes Anti-lock brakes (ABS) Air conditioning Immobilizer antitheft alarm Power door locks Power windows Tilt/telescope steering wheel 15-inch steel wheels Roof antenna AM/FM stereo cassette Heated power side mirrors Cruise control	Four-speed automatic transmission CD changer
Golf GL TDI-PD	1.9-liter four-cylinder diesel Five-speed manual transmission Dual front and side air bags Side curtain air bags Four-wheel disc brakes Anti-lock brakes (ABS) Air conditioning Immobilizer antitheft alarm Power door locks Power windows Tilt/telescope steering wheel 15-inch steel wheels Roof antenna AM/FM stereo cassette Heated power side mirrors Cruise control	Four-speed automatic transmission CD changer
Golf GLS	1.8-liter turbo four-cylinder Five-speed manual transmission Dual front and side air bags Four-wheel disc brakes Anti-lock brakes (ABS) Side curtain air bags Air conditioning Immobilizer antitheft alarm Power door locks Power windows Tilt/telescope steering wheel 15-inch alloy wheels Roof antenna AM/FM stereo cassette Cruise control Heated power side mirrors Front center armrest Anti-slip regulation (ASR) Electronic differential lock (EDL) Power sunroof	Five-speed automatic transmission CD changer Monsoon stereo system heated seats Leather upholstery package
Golf GLS TDI-PD	1.9-liter four-cylinder diesel Five-speed manual transmission Dual front and side air bags Four-wheel disc brakes Anti-lock brakes (ABS) Side curtain air bags Air conditioning Immobilizer antitheft alarm Power door locks Power windows Tilt/telescope steering wheel 15-inch alloy wheels Roof antenna AM/FM stereo cassette Cruise control Heated power side mirrors Front center armrest Power sunroof	Four-speed automatic transmission CD changer Monsoon stereo system Heated seats Leather upholstery package
Golf GTI 1.8T	1.8-liter turbo four-cylinder Five-speed manual transmission Dual front and side air bags Four-wheel disc brakes Anti-lock brakes (ABS) Air conditioning Side curtain air bags Immobilizer antitheft alarm Power door locks Power windows Tilt/telescope steering wheel 16-inch alloy wheels Roof antenna AM/FM stereo cassette Cruise control Front sport seats Heated power side mirrors Front center armrest Power sunroof Anti-slip regulation (ASR) Electronic differential lock (EDL) Dual exhaust system	Six-disc CD changer Five-speed automatic transmission Monsoon stereo system Partial Leather trim Sport suspension 17-inch alloy wheels Electronic Stability Program
Golf R32	3.2-liter VR6 24V Six-speed manual transmission 4MOTION all-wheel drive Dual front and side air bags Side curtain air bags Four-wheel disc brakes Anti-lock brakes (ABS) Blue Four-piston brake calipers Multilink sport suspension Sport seats Heated front seats Air conditioning Immobilizer antitheft alarm Power door locks Power windows Tilt/telescope steering wheel 18-inch alloy wheels Side skirts Front spoiler Rear spoiler Power sunroof Roof antenna Monsoon stereo system Cruise control Heated power side mirrors Windshield wiper rain sensor Front center armrest Dual exhaust Projector fog lights Automatic climate control Trip computer Anti-slip regulation (ASR) Electronic differential lock (EDL) Electronic Stability Program (ESP)	CD changer

All Jetta—The fifth generation Jetta was introduced for model year 2005.

INDEX

The Best Tools for the Job.

 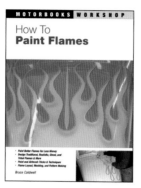  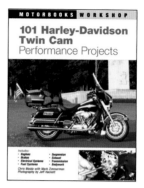 

Other Great Books in this Series

Performance Welding Handbook
2nd Edition
0-7603-2172-8 • 139436AP

How To Paint Flames
0-7603-1824-7 • 137414AP

How To Build
Vintage Hot Rod V-8 Engines
0-7603-2084-5 • 138703AP

Honda & Acura
Performance Handbook
2nd Edition
0-7603-1780-1 • 137410AP

Hot Rod
Horsepower Handbook
0-7603-1814-X • 137220AP

How To Build the Cars of
The Fast and the Furious
0-7603-2077-2 • 138696AP

How To Tune and Modify Engine
Management Systems
0-7603-1582-5 • 136272AP

Corvette Performance
Projects 1968–1982
0-7603-1754-2 • 137230AP

Custom Pickup Handbook
0-7603-2180-9 • 139348AP

Circle Track Chassis
& Suspension Handbook
0-7603-1859-X • 138626AP

How To Build A West Coast
Chopper Kit Bike
0-7603-1872-7 • 137253

101 Harley-Davidson Twin-Cam
Performance Projects
0-7603-1639-2 • 136265AP

101 Harley-Davidson
Performance Projects
0-7603-0370-3 • 127165AP

How To Custom Paint Your Motorcycle
0-7603-2033-0 • 138639AP

101 Sportbike Performance Projects
0-7603-1331-8 • 135742AP

Motorcycle Fuel Injection Handbook
0-7603-1635-X • 136172AP

ATV Projects: Get the Most Out
of Your All-Terrain Vehicle
0-7603-2058-6 • 138677AP

Four Wheeler
Chassis & Suspension Handbook
0-7603-1815-8 • 137235

Ultimate Boat
Maintenance Projects
0-7603-1696-1 • 137240AP

Motocross & Off-Road
Performance Handbook
3rd Edition
0-7603-1975-8 • 137408AP

How To Restore Your
Wooden Runabout
0-7603-1100-5 • 135107AP

Ultimate Garage Handbook
0-7603-1640-6 • 137389AP

How To Restore John Deere
Two-Cylinder Tractors
0-7603-0979-5 • 134861AP

How To Restore Your Farm Tractor
2nd Edition
0-7603-1782-8 • 137246AP

Mustang 5.0
Performance Projects
0-7603-1545-0 • 137245AP